P9-DHC-955

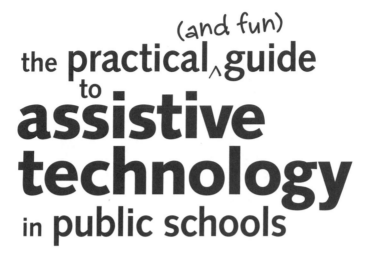

the practical (and fun) guide to
assistive technology
in public schools

Christopher R. Bugaj
Sally Norton-Darr

International Society for Technology in Education
EUGENE, OREGON • WASHINGTON, DC

the practical (and fun) guide
to assistive technology in public schools

Christopher R. Bugaj and Sally Norton-Darr

© 2010 International Society for Technology in Education
World rights reserved. No part of this book may be reproduced or transmitted in any form or by any means—electronic, mechanical, photocopying, recording, or by any information storage or retrieval system—without prior written permission from the publisher. Contact Permissions Editor: www.iste.org/permissions/; permissions@iste.org; fax: 1.541.302.3780.

Director of Book Publishing: *Courtney Burkholder*
Acquisitions Editor: *Jeff V. Bolkan*
Production Editors: *Lynda Gansel, Tina Wells*
Production Coordinator: *Rachel Williams*

Graphic Designer: *Signe Landin*
Copy Editor: *Kristin Landon*
Proofreader: *Nancy Olson*
Book/Cover Design: *Kim McGovern*

Library of Congress Cataloging-in-Publication Data

Bugaj, Christopher R.
  The practical (and fun) guide to assistive technology in public schools /
  Christopher R. Bugaj and Sally Norton-Darr. — 1st ed.
    p. cm.
  Includes bibliographical references.
  ISBN 978-1-56484-263-3 (pbk.)
  1. Children with disabilities—Education—United States. 2. Self-help
devices for people with disabilities—United States. 3. Special
education—Technological innovations—United States. I. Norton-Darr, Sally.
II. International Society for Technology in Education. III. Title.
LC4019.B84 2010
371.9'0433—dc22

2009052860

First Edition
ISBN: 978-1-56484-263-3

Printed in the United States of America

International Society for Technology in Education (ISTE)
Washington, DC, Office:
    1710 Rhode Island Ave. NW, Suite 900, Washington, DC 20036-3132
Eugene, Oregon, Office:
    180 West 8th Ave., Suite 300, Eugene, OR 97401-2916
Order Desk: 1.800.336.5191
Order Fax: 1.541.302.3778
Customer Service: orders@iste.org
Book Publishing: books@iste.org
Book Sales and Marketing: booksmarketing@iste.org
Web: www.iste.org

Images © istockphoto.com: *Cover*, Helle Bro Clemmensen; *pg. 55*, Mark Stay; *pg. 265*, Dandanian
ISTE® is a registered trademark of the International Society of Technology in Education

About ISTE

The International Society for Technology in Education (ISTE) is the trusted source for professional development, knowledge generation, advocacy, and leadership for innovation. ISTE is the premier membership association for educators and education leaders engaged in improving teaching and learning by advancing the effective use of technology in PK–12 and teacher education.

Home of the National Educational Technology Standards (NETS) and ISTE's annual conference and exposition (formerly known as NECC), ISTE represents more than 100,000 professionals worldwide. We support our members with information, networking opportunities, and guidance as they face the challenge of transforming education. To find out more about these and other ISTE initiatives, visit our website at **www.iste.org**.

As part of our mission, ISTE Book Publishing works with experienced educators to develop and produce practical resources for classroom teachers, teacher educators, and technology leaders. Every manuscript we select for publication is carefully peer-reviewed and professionally edited. We value your feedback on this book and other ISTE products. E-mail us at **books@iste.org**.

About the Authors

Christopher R. Bugaj, MA, CCC-SLP, earned his Bachelor of Science in Education at the State University of New York at Fredonia and earned his Master of Arts in Speech Pathology at Kent State University. Chris hosts and produces the award-winning *A.T.TIPScast*, a podcast on the implementation of assistive technology in public schools (www.attipscast.wordpress.com). He is a founding member of the Assistive Technology Team for Loudoun County Public Schools in Virginia and is an active member of the American Speech-Language-Hearing Association. Chris also works as an adjunct professor for George Mason University. Together with his wife, Melissa, Chris produces the podcast *Night Light Stories* featuring original stories for children (www.nightlightstories. blogspot.com). Chris lives on a mountain in Harpers Ferry, West Virginia, where he enjoys playing in the worlds created by his imaginative and tenacious children, Tucker and Margaret.

This book is dedicated to my children and my loving and supportive wife. Bud, Rooters, and Maggers—thanks for making every dream come true. And thanks to Sally, for not laughing in my face when I exclaimed, "I know what this book is missing … zombies!"

Sally Norton-Darr, MS, CCC-SLP, is an assistive technology trainer for Loudoun County Public Schools in Virginia as well as a nationally certified speech-language pathologist. Sally earned her degrees from The Pennsylvania State University in Speech Pathology and Audiology. She has been fortunate to work in a number of settings such as the public schools in Utah, as a director of speech therapies for the State of New Jersey, and in private practice for adolescents and adults in Virginia before returning to clinical practice in the public schools. She has presented nationally and regionally to diverse audiences on a wide range of low-, mid-, and high-tech strategies, interventions, and solutions and is published in the *Journal of Speech and Hearing Disorders*. Born and raised in Pittsburgh, she now calls the hills of Virginia home, where she shares her life and adventures with her intrepid and wonderful husband Dick, the best kids a mom could ever want, and a menagerie of furry creatures, some of whom are even welcome in the home.

This book is dedicated to my family, Dick, Molly, Alex, and my remarkable mom … and to Chris, for making this happen.

Acknowledgments

To the original team members, Barry, Mark, Rebecca, and Judith: Frederick Douglass once said, "If there is no struggle, there is no progress." Yep, Mr. Douglass, that about sums it up. The content presented within this book would not be possible without our hours of engaging debate. Each problem was like tackling a Rubik's Cube. We flipped it, turned it, twisted it, pulled it, passed it around (heck, we even took the stickers off it every once in awhile), and just when we'd get one side done we'd realize that it needed to be flipped, turned, twisted, and pulled again. Yeah, we struggled. There was conflict, disagreement, frustration, and turmoil, but in the end there was progress. We were designing. We were sculpting. We were shaping. Most importantly, we were building. And man, was it worth it! So, thank you, each one of you, for your dedication and inspiration. None of this would be possible without you.

To the administrators, Mary and Debbie: Thanks for your trust. Your faith in what we were trying to accomplish when building the team was really inspiring. Thank you for having the wisdom to leave things alone when things needed to be left alone, and thank you for offering guidance when we requested it. Thanks for believing in all of us.

To the current team members, Cindy and Karen: Thanks for lighting the fire that led to this book. You took out the lasso, threw it around our horns, and yanked. Thanks for pulling us into this grand adventure. If you hadn't said, "Hey, we should present on 'how to build an AT team' at a conference," this book would never have been written.

To our spouses: Awww, shucks. It takes time to write a book. Time we could have spent washing dishes, cleaning the house, grocery shopping, doing the bills, and every other chore it takes to make a household work day in and day out. You filled in those hours so we could write this book. Thanks for that and thanks for not holding it over our heads. That's just one of the many reasons we love you. Not to mention, you're the first editors of the book. Thanks for every constructive comment! That's just one of the many other reasons we love you.

To our editors and everyone at ISTE: Thank you for seeing the potential in what we had to offer. Thanks for giving us the opportunity to put our ideas down in print and thanks for helping us organize them in a fashion that will make the most sense to people.

Finally, a large thank you to all of the other people who mentored us along the way, including other teachers, parents, and students.

Contents

part 3
building an assistive technology team

chapter 4
finding the path

chapter 5
reasons for building an assistive technology team

chapter 6
choosing assistive technology teammates

chapter 7

defining responsibilities for an assistive technology team 83

chapter 8

building and promoting an assistive technology team 109

chapter 12

conducting the evaluation

chapter 13

the assistive technology evaluation report

introduction

What to Expect

Long ago in a galaxy far, far away, two lonely, overworked speech pathologists embarked on separate journeys—leading them, much to their surprise, to this book you hold in your hands.

We want to share our adventures with you to help you avoid obstacles as you build your assistive technology team. Whether you are beginning your journey alone or sharing your quest with others, we will provide insight and shortcuts to success. We have benefited from the wisdom of those who preceded us, and we intend to share the lessons we learned to provide a road map to a happy and productive assistive technology team. Oh, yeah—and we wrote it in a fun, engaging way so as not to bore the pants off you.

Assistive Technology

We figure you have heard the term "assistive technology," or can infer its meaning, but still may have some questions. We'll get into the legal definition of assistive technology in a bit, but when people at a party ask "What do you do for a living?" we usually tell them that we help other educators implement tools and strategies to assist students with special needs. In this book we try to minimize the legalese and maximize the informal dialogue to quickly and easily get you the information you need and want.

Assistive technology is a relatively new field, so we don't claim to have all the answers. Indeed, those who have been on this journey for a long time continue to revise and review their practices and service delivery. We invite you to join those pioneers and welcome you to our continuing adventure. To some, assistive technology may not sound exciting, but we know that you, our reader, share our spirit. We welcome your curiosity and know that you will enjoy the trip. We have been fortunate to have wonderfully supportive mentors and are excited to offer you the guidance and innovations that have worked for us. It wasn't until we stepped out of our offices and began to visit colleagues from other states and districts that we recognized the growing interest in our innovative approach to the field.

This book offers tips, tricks, and strategies to those providing assistive technology services in U.S. public schools to students in preschool through high school. It is intended for any educator interested in creating or expanding the practice of assistive technology in public schools. We have come to the realization that assistive technology can offer solutions to learners in general and hope that you will see its relevance in meeting the needs of all students.

Providing assistive technology services in schools happens in a lot of different ways. Some states have small school districts based on townships and municipalities. Some have giant mega-huge countywide districts. Typically it is the school district, as a public agency, that must ensure that both assistive technology devices and services are provided if they're required for the student to receive a free, appropriate public education. We recognize that each district or education agency is going to have its own little twist on the provision of assistive technology services. It doesn't matter if you are an official who works in the state capital putting miles and miles on your car to help students across the state use assistive technology, one lonely volunteer in a district of two schools, or anyone in between. There is something in this book for each of you!

If you are sitting with a pile of requests for assistive technology on your desk and your head in your hands, then this book is for you! We appreciate your diligence, dedication, and curiosity and thank you for joining us on this wild ride. We invite you to use this book as a tool to help get the job of providing assistive technology services to students done without pulling your hair out. The book will:

- Help you get started when you are the only person for an entire school district charged with the task of providing assistive technology services

- Provide a fresh perspective on the assistive technology process in school settings

- Recommend strategies for how to consider assistive technology for every student

- Propose methods for building and expanding your assistive technology team

- Offer advice on how to minimize paperwork while simultaneously maximizing the effect of assistive technology services

- Outline an easy-to-implement process, from consideration through implementation to follow-up, for every recommendation

- Suggest an easy approach to collecting data on the effectiveness of assistive technology devices and services

- Reaffirm that you are headed down the right path as you provide services to students

The Rules

As soon as you were born, the world started to impose rules on you. Do wear clothes in public, but don't wear clothes in the bath. Do eat your vegetables, but don't throw your food on the floor. Do play quietly in your room, but tell someone when you need to go potty. As you grew up, even more rules were imposed upon you. Do wear your seatbelt, but don't drive while distracted. Do make plans for the future, but don't put all your eggs in one basket. Do stop to smell the roses, but don't forget to wear sunscreen. Because you're so used to these rules, we thought we'd give you a few of our own. The following are the rules for this book.

Do ...

- understand that assistive technology = AT. Say it with us: A–T.

- skip around this book and read only one section at a time as needed. It's our hope that this book will address your particular area(s) of need. Just go ahead and jump to that section. As a rule, each part of this book will be "free-standing" and will not depend on information in other sections. We never read a nonfiction book from front to back. We don't expect you to read this book that way either.

- use this book to help you provide assistive technology services in school settings. This book references laws and practices found within the United States. International readers may find that some sections do not apply based on the educational system in their respective countries. However, many of the ideas and methodologies described in this book are universal enough to be useful to educators from other nations.

- use our suggestions in other settings. Our perspective is to serve students in a public school setting, *but* you will be able to use our philosophy in providing services in other settings. Yep, hospitals and residential facilities, too!

- take every opportunity to learn more and to share your knowledge. Not only are there new tools every day, thanks to the wonders of technology, but also there are new ways of using old tools.

- believe that with the right tool or strategy you can work magic! Arthur C. Clarke once said, "Any sufficiently advanced technology is indistinguishable from magic." Put on your robe and take out your wand, because you have the opportunity to say "Abracadabra."

- keep smilin'—assistive technology is fun stuff.

Don't …

- limit yourself to only the strategies and solutions offered in this book. What's cool about assistive technology is that it's infinite. There's always going to be more than one solution to a challenge.

- fall into the "But that's the way we have always done it" excuse. Bologna! If the only reason you're doing something a certain way is because it has always been done that way, then you're doing it for the wrong reason. Choices pertaining to assistive technology should be based on logic and reason, not tradition.

- think that we have all the answers. The ideas in this book have worked for us and will work for you, but we'd be foolish to think we know everything. Just like you, we're learners for life!

- constrain yourself to working with students in special education. Invariably, strategies and solutions put in place for one student will end up helping other classmates as well.

- be afraid. Go ahead and give it a try. You're a pioneer. Take chances.

Our Glossary: The Language We Speak

The following is a short guide to the terms and jargon we use in this book so that you know what we're talking about. You may use different initials or acronyms in your neck of the woods.

Accommodation. Any tool or strategy necessary for providing a student with free and appropriate access to their education. The implementation of accommodations is outlined within a student's Individualized Education Program (IEP).

Administrator. Any person at the various levels of administration throughout a school district including assistant principals, principals, coordinators, supervisors, directors, assistant superintendents, superintendents, and school board members.

Assistive technology team. In public schools, the group or individual who is responsible for assessing, recommending, procuring, modifying, and providing assistive technology supports to students with disabilities in order for them to receive a free and appropriate education. This team, which in many ways resembles the popular A-Team of the 1980s—daring and resourceful problem solvers—may, in reality, consist of only one person volunteering to try to provide mandated assistive technology services. In such instances this volunteer becomes an assistive technology team … of one. If this is your situation, we have some valuable information for you, even though we keep referring to the single, solitary you as a whole team (cue *The A-Team* theme music).

Assistive technology trainer. Also known as assistive technology consultant, assistive technology specialist, assistive technology practitioner, assistive technology facilitator, assistive technology person, or assistive technologist … the list goes on, so insert your title here. For the sake of consistency we use the term *assistive technology trainer* as the title for the person who helps brainstorm solutions for a struggling student but who also has the power to make recommendations for technology that might cost some extra cash.

Case manager. The person on the IEP team designated by the school district to draft the IEP. In many cases this person also provides special education services to the student.

Child study committee. Sometimes there are students who have not been identified as having a disability who begin to demonstrate some difficulties in school. A child study committee is made up of concerned staff and family members who meet to discuss a student who is demonstrating difficulty in school but who has not been evaluated and identified with a disability. Usually, this is a somewhat informal conversation, although interventions outlined by the committee may be drafted and documented.

Educator. Any person who has the responsibility of working to educate students. This could be a general education teacher, special education teacher, specialist, teaching assistant, or even a parent.

IEP. An Individualized Education Program (IEP) is a document or type of contract developed, by law, for any student who has been formally identified with a disability impacting educational progress. An IEP includes the following sections: the present level of functional and academic performance, a list of accommodations that are necessary for a student to receive a free and appropriate public education, a set of goals, and a description of services necessary to meet those goals. By law every IEP must consider the assistive technology needs of the student for whom it was created. The IEP is the most important document for a student receiving special education services because it outlines the expectations for everyone involved in that student's education.

IEP team. The purpose of the IEP team is to develop the IEP for a student. The team consists of administrators, educators, family members, other advocates, and, if appropriate, the actual student. Using evaluations, collected data, and experiential knowledge, it is the responsibility of the IEP team to establish what's necessary for the student to receive a free and appropriate public education. The team as a whole, rather than one individual, makes collaborative decisions about a student's IEP.

Present level of academic and functional performance. This is the part of the IEP where the student's current functional and academic abilities are described. This is also the section of the IEP where the results of the most recent evaluations are listed. This description guides the team in deciding the needs and, consequently, the goals the student should work toward for the duration of the IEP.

Review/Revision. The Review/Revision is a formal amendment noting changes to a student's established IEP. A Review/Revision is the official way of saying, "Hey, that plan needs a bit of tweaking; we're going to try this instead." It is a no-fault and thoughtful approach to refining the original program to best meet the student's needs.

Related service provider. Any person, other than the general education or special education teacher, who provides services to a student. Related service providers include, but are not limited to, speech-language pathologists, occupational therapists, physical therapists, teachers of the visually impaired, and teachers of the hearing impaired.

School district. Because the primary focus of this book is the delivery of assistive technology services in schools, we need to define what we mean by "schools." Let's define "school district" as any facility or organization providing services to school-aged students. These organizations are called all sorts of things in different parts of the country, such as public districts and area education agencies. For simplicity's sake we'll just call them all "schools."

part 1

defining
and understanding
assistive
technology

chapter 1

definitions, laws,
and
how to interpret them

Definitions of AT and Its Components

It should be noted that we refer only to federal legislation within the United States in this book and that individual states may have added additional clauses or definitions as part of state legislation. It should also be noted that individual countries might have their own unique legal definitions of assistive technology. When practicing assistive technology in a school district, it is important to become familiar with the laws surrounding assistive technology at all levels of government.

no-tech, low-tech, mid-tech, high-tech

I do not like this high-tech Sam.
I do not like it Sam-I-Am.

I will not plug it in the wall.
I will not try it if you call.

I will not insert the battery.
It's far too heavy for me to carry.

I do not want to hear it speak.
That's not the answer that I seek.

I do not care about the cost.
Take it back, all hope is lost.

I will not, cannot, turn it on.
I've said my piece so now be gone!

What is that you say?
You think there is another way?

Something without electricity?
Well, show me then, let me see!

It's simple, it's easy, it's cheap, it's free!
Show me now, what can it be?

That's it, that's all, this tiny thing?
It's ingenious, it's clever, it's amazing!

I can use this everywhere.
In every place, from here to there!

Thank you so much for bringing it by.
I'm so happy I could cry.

With this tool, this strategy,
I'll be a success, just wait and see!

In establishing the practice of assistive technology, we need to start with a foundation. A big part of the foundation is the law that ensures that students with disabilities will work to achieve goals while being provided a "free and appropriate education." Assistive technology has come into the public consciousness not only because of its practicality but also as a result of federal legislation. There is a whole history of laws associated with special education, but this isn't a history book. We are not lawyers and don't want to spend a lot of time on the legal stuff. However, we are grateful for those who have created and backed legislation supporting assistive technology.

Contemporary legislation guides current assistive technology practice. There may be lots of better places to look for information regarding the details of assistive technology legislation, but because so much of what we suggest is based on the most current federal legal definitions (SEC. 602. Definitions. 20 USC 1401. P.L. 108–446, Dec. 3, 2004.), we've included them here for reference.

Federal law divides the definition of assistive technology into two component parts: *Assistive Technology Device* and *Assistive Technology Service.*

Assistive Technology Device. The term *assistive technology device* means any item, piece of equipment, or product system, whether acquired commercially off the shelf, modified, or customized, that is used to increase, maintain, or improve functional capabilities of a child with a disability.

Assistive Technology Service. The term *assistive technology service* means any service that directly assists a child with a disability in the selection, acquisition, or use of an assistive technology device. Such term includes—

a. the evaluation of the needs of such child, including a functional evaluation of the child in the child's customary environment;

b. purchasing, leasing, or otherwise providing for the acquisition of assistive technology devices by such child;

c. selecting, designing, fitting, customizing, adapting, applying, maintaining, repairing, or replacing assistive technology devices;

d. coordinating and using other therapies, interventions, or services with assistive technology devices, such as those associated with existing education and rehabilitation plans and programs;

e. training or technical assistance for such child, or, where appropriate, the family of such child; and

f. training or technical assistance for professionals (including individuals providing education and rehabilitation services), employers, or other individuals who provide services to, employ, or are otherwise substantially involved in the major life functions of such child.

—SEC. 602. Definitions. 20 USC 1401. P.L. 108–446, Dec. 3, 2004.

These definitions provide the tent pole supporting assistive technology practices. But they aren't the only place where assistive technology is referenced in federal legislation. Assistive technology is mentioned in a few other parts of the law as well.

> Almost 30 years of research and experience has demonstrated that the education of children with disabilities can be made more effective by . . . supporting the development and use of technology, including assistive technology devices and assistive technology services, to maximize accessibility for children with disabilities.
>
> —*SEC. 601. Short Title; Table of Contents; Findings; Purposes.*
> *20 USC 1400. P.L. 108–446, Dec. 3, 2004.*

> [Federal funds may be used] to support the use of technology, including technology with universal design principles and assistive technology devices, to maximize accessibility to the general education curriculum for children with disabilities.
>
> —*SEC. 611. Authorization; Allotment; Use of Funds;*
> *Authorization of Appropriations. 20 USC 1411. P.L. 108–446, Dec. 3, 2004.*

Furthermore, the definition of assistive technology services is expanded upon in the Assistive Technology Act of 2004 (a law relating to employment, not education) to include the following: "a service consisting of expanding the availability of access to technology, including electronic and information technology, to individuals with disabilities" (SEC. 3. Definitions. 29 USC 3002. P.L. 108–364, Oct. 25, 2004).

The Meaning of "Any"

"Assistive technology device" has already been defined, but we want to point out the most important part in the whole darn definition: "any item." *Anything* can be called "assistive technology" if it is "used to increase, maintain, or improve functional capabilities of individuals with disabilities." So, if a bottle cap is used to increase the functional capabilities of a student with a disability, it is assistive technology. If a pinecone is used to maintain the functional capabilities of a student with a disability, it is assistive technology. If a large stone is used to improve the functional capabilities of a student with a disability, it is assistive technology. Anything you can think of, *anything*, can be assistive technology. Markers, blackboards, papers, rulers, protractors, Velcro, laminate, erasers, posters, or any other item that you might find in any typical classroom can be considered assistive technology if it is used to increase, maintain, or improve the functional capabilities of a student with a disability.

Figure 1.1 Anything can be assistive technology

The Meaning of "Accessible"

The Assistive Technology Act of 2004 includes two little words that are easy to miss: "access to." The Individuals with Disabilities Education Improvement Act of 2004 (P.L. 108–446) states that assistive technology services and devices are used to "maximize accessibility for children with disabilities." Considering "access to technology" and "maximizing accessibility" allows you to include alterations to an individual's situation in order for that individual to use technology.

For example, there is a student named Karen who is sitting in the back of the room. Karen has difficulty paying attention and is easily distracted as the teacher puts notes on the board in the front of the room. The teacher now decides to "preferentially seat" Karen (never seen that accommodation on an IEP before, have you?) by moving her to the front of the room. Karen then starts to pay more attention to the notes and is less distracted. The teacher, probably without realizing it, implemented a tenet of assistive technology practice. By moving Karen to the front of the room, she provided Karen with access to the screen. Providing a student with a disability access to technology is part of practicing assistive technology in a school setting. This means that anytime anyone makes an adjustment to a student's environment to provide access to technology, that is, in reality, implementing assistive technology principles. Remember this fact when making decisions regarding assistive technology in public schools—it has far-reaching implications, including how to collect data, how to consider assistive technology for every student on every IEP, and how to integrate recommendations into an IEP.

Examples of AT Devices

It is impossible to list every assistive technology device known to humankind. The list is not finite or static and would be longer than Santa's. Even if we could list everything, we wouldn't want to, because assistive technology needs are unique to each student. There is no script, template, or formula that can accurately give every possible solution based on behaviors presented by students. There are websites and other tools that can give ideas of what to try, but those are ultimately limited. They can't provide every single possible solution, and neither can we. However, in general, assistive technology devices can be divided into these categories:

Low-tech tools. Tools that fall into this category don't require electricity to function. Slant boards, chalk, highlighters, pencil grips, schedules, calendars, sticky notes, footrests, pictures, symbols, and index cards are all examples of low-tech tools. Some educators refer to this category as "no-tech/low-tech," but, technically speaking, if there isn't a physical item being used, then it isn't a device, it's a strategy.

Mid-tech tools. Tools in this category use batteries or have some basic circuitry involved. Lights, buzzers, vibrating switches, touch windows, basic environmental control units, portable word processors, and static display communication devices are examples of tools that fall within the mid-tech category.

High-tech tools. The tools in this category also may use batteries, but they also have some advanced circuitry involved. Computers, software, dynamic display communication devices, and electronic portable desktop assistants are examples of high-tech tools.

Examples of AT Services

The essence of the definition of an assistive technology service is that devices are just tools. Tools don't do you any good if you've got the wrong ones or if you can't use them. An assistive technology service is a wonderful concept that makes a whole lot of sense. Educators working in assistive technology look at students and say, "How can we help?" Assistive technology is more than a law … it's a way of looking at problems and offering solutions.

An assistive technology service can be as simple as conversing with an educator about the best way for a student to move from the carpet square to the snack table or as complex as orchestrating a long-term, multiphase, interdisciplinary concatenation of events to implement a robust communication system that will follow a student far into the future beyond the time spent in the educational setting. Every action an educator takes that involves a student using a device to improve functional capabilities is considered an assistive technology service. The legal definition of "assistive technology service" itself provides a list of examples, but the following noncomprehensive list includes more specific situations that represent assistive technology services:

- Providing a student with an opportunity to use a communication device

- Brainstorming with other educators about the best way to organize a desk

- Implementing a behavior management system

- Teaching students or other educators how to use a software program

- Explaining to a parent the differences between two different devices

- Attaching a mount for a switch near a computer workstation

- Adding Velcro to a visual schedule

- Creating a format template for a word processing document

- Meeting with school administration about training opportunities for their staff to better differentiate instruction

- Working with a vendor to acquire a device for a student

- Developing a plan for a student's use of a device when transitioning to a new environment

The AT Continuum

There is a continuum. No, not like the time-space continuum in science fiction shows. This continuum concerns the thought process for solutions for students. Basically, it runs from least restrictive to most restrictive solutions. Think about the solutions that will most easily fit into a student's routine. The less you mess with the routine, the better chance you have at successfully integrating that solution over a long period of time. Solutions that interfere least with a student's routine are, most often, the easiest to implement. The easiest solutions to implement are often the ones that require little or no intrusion or special equipment, for example, a pencil grip or visual schedule. The solutions with the fewest frills fall into the no-tech/low-tech category, the least restrictive end of the spectrum. The opposite end of the spectrum might include a dynamic screen communication device or environmental control unit to remotely access household appliances. It doesn't matter what category a solution falls into—no-tech/low-tech, mid-tech, or high-tech—what does matter is that it is the right tool for the job, offering the least restrictions while providing a solution that works over the long haul for that student.

so simple a monkey could do it

Once upon a time, there were three monkeys trapped in a pit, and they couldn't escape. They scratched at the walls of the pit, they clawed at the earth surrounding them, they called for help, and they jumped as high as they could—but nothing seemed to work. However, these were determined little monkeys, and they refused to give up.

The first monkey had an idea. "I'm going to build a rope from all of these roots." He set to work pulling roots from the sides of the pit and fashioning them together into knots. It took a long time, and pulling the roots made his arms very tired.

The second monkey had an idea. "I'm going to build a ladder from all of these stones." He set to work pulling stones from the sides of the pit and stacking them. It took a long time, and lifting the stones made his arms very tired.

The third monkey, after a few moments of watching the other two monkeys, had an idea. "I'm going to get us out of here, without using a rope or a ladder." The first and second monkeys looked quizzically at the third monkey, who was smiling a huge smile.

"How?" the first and second monkey asked together.

"Watch," said the third monkey, taking the first monkey and leading him to the wall of the pit. Next, he took the second monkey and hoisted him up on top of the first monkey. He then climbed on top of the second monkey, now standing on the shoulders of the first monkey, and leapt into the sky, landing squarely on his feet on the edge of the pit. "You see?" said the third monkey as he extended his hand down to grab the second monkey, who was already jumping to grasp it. The first monkey then leapt from the ground and grabbed the extended hand of the second monkey. With one pull, and a little "Umphf," all three monkeys left the pit forever.

"That was a good idea," said the first and second monkeys as they scampered away. The third monkey smiled again and said, "It would have been a better idea to have not fallen into the pit in the first place."

■ ■ ■ ■ ■

The Best Answer

This book is all about technology, but we're saying it, right here, right now: technology is not always the best answer. When considering assistive technology devices, it is prudent to first look for solutions and strategies that don't involve technology. These "no-tech" solutions are often the easiest to implement and have the best chance for generalizing across all environments. The moment technology is implemented to address a problem, you immediately take a step toward the land of "more complicated." That's not to say all technology is complicated or confounding. It's not. But implementing a tool, any tool, inherently means that you are creating other tasks. Consider the following questions that come up when you implement a hammer (the tool) to place a nail in the wall to hang that picture of your dear ol' mum.

- Where do I keep the hammer?

- Where do I keep the nail?

- Does someone else know where the hammer is?

- How big a hammer do I need?

- How big a nail should I use?

- What do I do if someone else is using the hammer?

- What do I do if I can't find the hammer?

- What do I do if I lose the hammer?

- How much does the hammer cost?

- What if I miss when I swing the hammer?

- What if I want to move the picture later?

- What if the wooden handle of my hammer is broken?

A simple tool. A simple task. Lots and lots of questions. We could have gone on and on, but we figure you've nailed it by now: start with no-tech strategies first, and move up from there. If you do so, you'll hit the nail on the head every time without a lot of monkey business.

chapter 2

this is not
assistive technology

So far we have given you some examples of what assistive technology *is*. Just to keep things legal, you need to know what is specifically defined as *not* assistive technology in the legislation. The term assistive technology device "does not include a medical device that is surgically implanted, or the replacement of such device" (SEC. 602. Definitions. 20 USC 1401. P.L. 108–446, Dec. 3, 2004). Therefore, cochlear implants, pacemakers, or any other medical devices that are surgically implanted are not considered assistive technology, so leave those types of recommended solutions to the experts. Now that's clear, let's address some other misconceptions about assistive technology.

Popular Misconceptions

Our moms still don't know what we do. We explain and explain, but our moms still end up telling their friends that what we do is "something in education helping students with computer stuff." Okay, those are our moms. We love them, and we'll have to live with that. But we refuse to live with that from other educators. As someone interested in assistive technology (and you must be if you're reading this book), you'll encounter some, if not all (if not more!), of these popular misconceptions.

Things That Aren't True

- The purpose of assistive technology is to help students become independent.

- Assistive technology is only computer stuff.

- Assistive technology makes a teacher's job easier.

- Assistive technology is just for students with severe disabilities.

- I'm not tech-savvy enough to implement assistive technology.

- Students with learning disabilities don't need assistive technology.

- An evaluation needs to be done to provide assistive technology services.

- Assistive technology is just for students with communication difficulties.

- Assistive technology always costs a lot of money.

- Data should be collected on every assistive technology device.

- A trial needs to be conducted for every assistive technology device before it is purchased.

- Only people with specialized training in assistive technology can provide assistive technology services.

- A separate implementation plan needs to be written for every assistive technology device.

- A formal evaluation for assistive technology can take place anywhere.

The Non-Declaration of Independence

Have another look at the definitions of assistive technology device and assistive technology service. Do you see the words independent or independence anywhere in those definitions? Nope. Assistive technology is often regarded as helping students become more independent, and this can be true because students often become more independent based on their technology use. However, providing a means for a student to become more independent is not part of either definition, nor is it the main purpose for considering assistive technology for a student. Increased independence is often a by-product of assistive technology and is considered when choosing a device, but it is typically not the reason to choose a device.

Consider the following goal: "Judie will make requests." (We know, we know—we didn't include all of the criteria, etc., in the goal. We're keeping it simple for the sake of this example.) Judie might have a communication device that helps her make requests. Judie needs some verbal or visual prompts to make the requests, which means she is not making requests independently. She's using the device, but she's not using it independently. Now let's step into our time machine and visit Judie sometime in the future. Judie has made progress and doesn't need as many (or any) verbal or visual prompts. Her goal might state, "Judie will independently make requests." Again, she's using the device, but the difference is that she doesn't need (or she's working toward not needing) any prompts. In this example, the device has *nothing* to do with her independence— it's just the vehicle for her to make the request.

one is the loneliest number

If you do any sort of research on assistive technology, even just brief searching on the Internet, you'll learn that anyone working in assistive technology wants to jam the thought down your throat that assistive technology does not necessarily mean computers. Heck, we've mentioned that point at least twice in this book already!

Computers and software are instructional tools just like pencils, erasers, paper, markers, scissors, crayons, chalk, overhead projectors, and the thousands of other objects you find in the classroom. There is an understandable temptation (dare we say tendency?) to think of computers as tools for independent work and independent work alone. There is one chair, with one monitor, with one keyboard, with one mouse; therefore it is easy to project that one student should be working alone at that workstation. However, when computers are grouped into the same category as other instructional tools and considered as equals in their educational properties and potential, the viewpoint shifts.

Instructional tools can be used independently, in group activities, or in activities with direct instruction provided by an educator. Computers, and the software within, are no different from other instructional tools. At times they are appropriate for independent work, but at other times students might need to access software in a guided forum. A teacher might need to sit at a computer next to a student to provide a guided learning experience, just like doing an activity using other instructional tools such as pencils and paper.

■ ■ ■ ■ ■

Productivity Tools To Make Teachers' Jobs Easier

Nowhere in the definition of either an assistive technology service or an assistive technology device does it specify that assistive technology should make a teacher's job easier. In many cases, teachers who are working with individuals using assistive technology services and devices are doing a lot more work than a teacher who is not using those strategies. However, there are tools that can make the task of successfully implementing assistive technology easier for a teacher. These tools aren't assistive technology tools themselves, but that doesn't mean they shouldn't be provided.

To use a practical example, a teacher might need to adapt a book for a student using picture symbols where each word in the story is represented by a symbol. The teacher could cut pictures out of magazines or use clip art, placing pictures above each word of the newly generated story. That would work, but it would take an eternity. Instead, teachers could use symbol-generating word processing software or a word processor with word-for-word symbol-generating features (Fig. 2.1). In this scenario, the student wouldn't necessarily need access to the software, but it sure would make the teacher's life easier. These types of teacher productivity tools should be considered general instructional technology rather than assistive technology. The device and service are being provided to the teacher, not the student, and therefore are not technically assistive technology. However, it's assistive technology personnel who will typically provide some of these specialized tools if they aren't available to every teacher in the district.

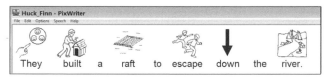

Figure 2.1 Symbol-generating word processing sample

Restricting Students Is the Path to the Dark Side

Assistive technology has absolutely nothing to do with restricting students. Nothing. Zip. Nada. It has everything to do with access, the complete opposite of restriction. You might be thinking, "Um, no kidding, you've only written that, like, 100 times already." Yeah, we know—but sometimes situations get muddy and it is hard to keep "maximizing accessibility" in mind. There may come a time when someone might ask you to restrict a student's access to technology. You may be tempted to trek down this path, but trust us when we say it leads only to the dark side. You will not find the light you seek at the end of *that* tunnel.

It's time for an example. Tyler is a clicker. Tyler sits at the computer and just clicks away like crazy—clicking and clicking and clicking. Click-click-click. Clickety-click-click. Tyler doesn't have any navigational purpose for his clicking, but he's clicking, clicking, clicking, and that's good enough for him. Tyler's teacher asks you for assistance and says, "Tyler is clicking. He won't stop. Is there a way we can take the mouse away or make it harder for him to click so he will stop clicking?" Hmmm? Is there? Probably. There are lots of ways to prevent Tyler from clicking. Limiting his use of the computer, putting foam under the mouse button, or providing a touch screen are all ways to immediately eliminate the clicking. But when we do, we've taken our first step toward the slippery slope that leads to the dark side. Tyler was exhibiting a behavior that was inappropriate. By taking away Tyler's opportunity to perform that inappropriate behavior, we've eliminated the behavior, right? Wrong. Tyler will move onto another inappropriate activity, sure as sugar. If he isn't clickety-click-clicking the mouse, he will be tappety-tap-tapping his feet or pickety-pick-picking his nose. We haven't taught Tyler a darn thing. So, what should we do? We should return to the assistive technology principle of "maximizing accessibility" by providing Tyler and his teachers with strategies that could be used to make the computer more accessible. How can we provide access for Tyler to use the computer appropriately without clickety-click-clicking? Consider the following possibilities:

- Create a lesson (or multiple lessons) on how to appropriately use the mouse.

- Read stories (either commercial or homemade) to/with Tyler about how to use the mouse appropriately.

- Model appropriate mouse behavior by taking turns with Tyler as he works through an activity involving the computer.

- Watch a short video with Tyler (possibly over and over again) on how to use the mouse properly.

- Analyze why he is clicking. Is he clicking to meet some sort of sensory need? If so, could a different sensory activity take the place of clicking?

- Any combination of the above.

These strategies may not instantaneously resolve Tyler's clicking. It may take time for Tyler to break his habit of over-clicking the mouse, and that is okay. Taking time to reach a goal is okay. Once he's over the clicking, he's over it for life! Taking time to reach a goal is a way better solution than not trying to reach the goal at all.

part 2

assistive technology
and
the IEP

chapter 3

how to consider
assistive technology in the IEP

Public schools differ to a large degree in the way they
address assistive technology. In some urban and
suburban areas, school districts have huge populations
jammed into a relatively small geographic area. In other,
more rural, areas, the population of students may be
small in a large geographic area. What every public
school district has in common, however, is the responsibility of serving students with disabilities. If a student
has a disability, assistive technology needs to be considered, at a minimum, once a year during the annual IEP
meeting.

Access to Any Item for Any Student for Any Goal

Goals are written by the IEP team and provide the focus for what the student is working to achieve throughout the course of that year. Students can have communication goals, math goals, goals for written expression, whatever. This book isn't about how to write IEP goals. It is about how to incorporate assistive technology devices and services to help students meet those goals. Assistive technology devices can be *any* item that assists a student to achieve any goal. Assistive technology services can be *any* action that assists a student to use any item to achieve any goal. That bears repeating. *Any* goal. Here's a simple way to remember it. Assistive technology devices and services focus on providing access to any item for any student for any goal. Remember that phrase and you'll know what it means to consider an assistive technology device.

A "Thoughtful" Consideration

We checked a variety of dictionaries, and the definitions are very clear in describing that when something is *considered* it is given "careful and deliberative thought." Therefore, when considering assistive technology at an annual IEP meeting, the IEP team should be giving the devices and services that will be used by the student careful and deliberative thought.

consider this

Oh rats! It's dear ol' Mum's birthday tomorrow, and you forgot to get her a card! Quick, throw on the bathrobe, slip on the slippers, gas up the car, and run out to the local corner store! Now decide. Funny, but not offensive. Clever, but not sarcastic. Touching, but not sappy. Ugh! None of these cards seem to match exactly what you want to say and you *know*—you just know—that your sister has found the perfect card for her. She's always doing stuff like that just to show you up! How can you show your mom that you care when the writers of the cards are so boring? Couldn't just one of those writers look into your soul and know what you wanted to say? If there were just a way to … wait … there is a way! Make your own card! You know, you've got the glue, the glitter, the construction paper—heck, you even have a computer! Yeah, that's the ticket! This way you can express exactly what you want to say, without relying on some hack who can't get his novel published. Create it from scratch and Mum will post that card on the fridge for all her friends to see. And where will Sis's fantabulous card end up? In the trash with the rest of the store-bought junk! Happy Birthday, Mum! Happy Birthday!

■ ■ ■ ■ ■

The same principle for selecting a birthday card can be applied to considering assistive technology during an IEP meeting. Premade lists of possible technologies written by someone else may work, but they aren't as meaningful or comprehensive as coming up with this list on your own.

Assistive technology is considered in many different ways at annual IEP meetings; some of these methods are better than others. Some systems might use a check box beside text that reads, "Has assistive technology been considered?" Technically, if the IEP team checks the box, this documents that assistive technology has been considered, but it lacks the "careful and deliberative thought" component of the definition. Also, when using the check-box system, not checking the box is not an option. The check in the box might as well be part of the template, because no IEP team would ever leave it unchecked.

Another method used by some systems is the checklist approach. The checklist approach provides a list of technologies, perhaps even included in the IEP template itself in check-box fashion, or in a separate document. The list might be several pages containing possible assistive devices covering all domains from self-advocacy skills to writing abilities. Although this approach creeps a bit more toward decisions made using "careful and deliberative thought," it continues to have inherent limitations. No form can possibly list every single assistive technology device. A list could be used as a guide or frame of reference, but by using the list the IEP team runs the risk of falling into one of two traps: they might find themselves limiting options to only those items on the list, or they might start shopping, eventually choosing items that aren't really necessary.

Assistive Technology Devices Are Accommodations

An accommodation is whatever the student needs to ensure a free and appropriate public education, and it is a required part of any IEP. The question the IEP team asks itself when developing the accommodations is, "What does this student need to ensure a free and appropriate public education?" To answer that question, the IEP team is forced to carefully and deliberately think about the needs of the student.

Accommodations vary based on the needs of individual students, but some common examples of accommodations might be preferentially seating a student, providing directions or questions in auditory format, extending the time a student has to complete an assignment, limiting the number of questions a student has on a test, and instructing a student individually rather than in a group setting. Because the IEP team is already in the mode of considering what the student needs when developing the accommodations, this is also the perfect time to consider assistive technology.

If the concept of an assistive technology device includes "any item" and providing "access to any item," consider the implications. Almost every accommodation becomes assistive technology. In fact, we challenge you to think of an accommodation that isn't providing either "an item" or "access to an item." To examine this, let's take a look at some common accommodations and see if they provide "an item" or "access to an item."

Preferential seating. Difficulties with vision, hearing, attention, or behavior are just some of the reasons why an IEP team might determine that moving a student to a different part of the room is a necessary accommodation. If the student needs to be moved closer to the blackboard, the "item" the student is being provided access to is the blackboard. If the student is being moved to increase attention, then the "items" the student is being provided access to are whatever tools he is working with at the time (pens, paper, etc.).

Providing directions and tests in an auditory format. An IEP team may determine that a student needs to be able to hear directions and questions on tests in order to have a free and appropriate public education. In this case the student is being provided access to the test itself. The test is the item to which the student is being given access.

Extended time to complete an assignment. Allowing a student to take additional time to complete a task provides that student with access to whatever is involved in the activity. If the student requires more time to complete a finger-painting project, then the items the student is being given access to are the paints, paper, and smock. If the student needs additional time to complete a Styrofoam model of a complex carbohydrate, then the student is being given access to the toothpicks and Styrofoam balls. Without the accommodation for additional time, the student would be denied access to the necessary items to complete the activity.

Limiting the number of questions on a test. In this accommodation the student is required to complete only 25 questions on a test instead of 50. Alternatively, a student may be given a modified test that has only 25 questions on it. Depending on the nature of the student's needs, either accommodation might be implemented. In this scenario the item the student is being given access to is, again, the test itself. Without the accommodation the student is provided 50 questions and, for whatever reason, cannot complete the test. Maybe the student becomes too overwhelmed and shuts down after 25 questions. Maybe the student, even given extended time, would spend an exorbitant amount of time to complete 50 questions. Whatever the reason, without the accommodation, the test is not accessible to the student.

Instructing a student individually rather than in a group. The student with this accommodation needs information presented without other students in the immediate vicinity. When instruction is provided in a group setting, the student is not processing the information in the same way as when the instruction is provided individually. In this scenario, the items to which the student is being provided access are the materials contained in the lesson. That might be a book, a worksheet, a journal, software, or any instructional material. By providing the instruction in a group setting when the student can only use those materials when being instructed individually, the student is being denied access to those tools. By the same token, when instruction is provided in an individual setting, the student is provided with access to those tools.

We recognize that the principle that *assistive technology devices are accommodations* may be a hard pill to swallow at first. So swish it around your mouth for awhile with a big gulp of water. If you have access to some IEPs or when you're involved in the creation of the next one take a look at the accommodations the IEP team has decided upon. Are there any accommodations listed that absolutely, positively, (no way, no sir, no how) could not be considered an item or providing access to an item? Accepting that every accommodation is assistive technology and that every assistive technology device is an accommodation makes the entire process of considering assistive technology (and understanding assistive technology) easier for the members of the IEP team. As an IEP team, when you are considering accommodations, you are considering assistive technology. Therefore, in order for an IEP team to provide "careful and deliberative thought" to assistive technology, it must also give careful and deliberative thought to accommodations. Just like taking an aspirin—once that pill is in your belly, you'll start feeling a whole lot better.

The Hidden Benefit of AT as an Accommodation

One of the great struggles in implementing any assistive technology device for a student's educational plan is getting that device to become part of the student's routine. Students may be introduced to devices, state that they like the devices, and even use the devices effectively in isolated situations. However, for students to really be successful with assistive technology devices, these devices need to be integrated into the necessary aspects of the students' education throughout the school day. If a device is viewed as something extra or additional, it inevitably ends up on a shelf, unused. An approach to ensure that a device is integrated into a student's routine is to consider the device no differently than any other accommodation. Most teachers are familiar with accommodations and making provisions for students requiring them. In fact, teachers should have access to and knowledge of the accommodations for every student with whom they interact. If an assistive technology device is outlined as an accommodation, it stands a better chance of being noticed, and therefore integrated, by all teachers than if it is listed somewhere separately in the IEP.

Proving Assistive Technology Was Considered

You might find this hard to believe, but there will be people who attend IEP meetings who haven't read this book. Gasp! Gufah! The horror! We know, it's shocking! Because they haven't read this book, they might not realize that by outlining the accommodations needed by the student, they were also considering assistive technology. Therefore, it might be wise to add some sort of statement in the IEP that addresses the fact that the IEP team did, indeed, consider assistive technology. This statement could also point out where it was addressed, to direct the reader of the IEP. The following is a suggestion as to how you might write the statement documenting that assistive technology was considered:

> The assistive technology needs of this student are included as accommodations on the IEP.

The other thing you could do is buy copies of this book for everyone at the IEP meeting and ask them to read this section ahead of time. That works, too!

Students without Accommodations

Assistive technology needs to be considered for every student with an IEP. Assistive technology can be considered by outlining the accommodations a student will be receiving. However, some students don't need accommodations, and therefore, by extension, they don't need assistive technology. That's not to say that the student won't be using technology. The student will be using technology. Every student uses technology. This just means that the student doesn't need technology to guarantee a free and appropriate public education. Even if a student will not need any accommodations or assistive technology, the IEP team still needs to document that the members considered assistive technology during the IEP meeting. The following is a suggestion as to how you might write this statement:

> The assistive technology needs of this student were considered and no assistive technology is needed at this time to guarantee a free and appropriate public education.

Use versus Need: The Battle Rages On

Every student uses technology every day. However, students simply *using* technology is different from students *needing* technology. It is the task of the IEP team to delineate which technology is which. A tricky task, to be sure, but luckily the IEP team has a guide to help answer the "use versus need" question: Free and Appropriate Public Education (FAPE). When trying to decide if a student needs an accommodation, the IEP team asks the pertinent question, "Does the student need this for a free and appropriate public education?" If the answer is "yes," then it is included as an accommodation. If the answer is "no," then it is not an accommodation but can, and probably should, be included in the Present Level of Academic Achievement and Functional Performance. We know this is a bit confusing, so here's a practical example.

Andre uses a document holder when transferring handwritten work into the computer. He places his handwritten paper into the slot of the document holder and easily turns his head, keeping his eyes and head on the same horizontal plane as he types. The holder allows him to easily transfer handwritten information into a word processing document without having to look down repeatedly and without any neck muscle pain or fatigue. He is also more efficient in the process because he doesn't lose his place in the transcription as often. When it is time for the IEP team to address accommodations while formulating the IEP, the team will ask the question, "What does Andre need to ensure a free and appropriate public education?" Although Andre uses a document holder, likes to use it, and has shown success with its use, he probably doesn't need the paper holder to ensure that he is getting a free and appropriate public education. The document holder (in Andre's case) is being used and it is helpful, but it is not absolutely necessary. Therefore it is not included as an accommodation on the IEP. If the IEP team really wanted to document the use of the holder without saying that it is necessary in order for Andre to receive a free and appropriate public education, then a sentence could be included in the Present Level of Academic Achievement and Functional Performance. The statement might read, "Andre uses a paper holder when typing documents and has reported that this improves the ease of transcription while preventing neck muscle fatigue."

AT Written into Goals Is a Big No-No

There are many things in life that you just shouldn't do. You shouldn't run with scissors. You shouldn't tease a crocodile with bits of meat. You shouldn't root for the Dallas Cowboys. And no matter how great the temptation, you definitely shouldn't write technology into a student's goals.

If you did include technology, a goal might be written that states, "Using graphic organizing software, Ellen will write a five-sentence paragraph" or "Using his communication device, David will answer who and what questions." This might not sound so strange, but what if you included the non-electric equivalent technology? For example, "Using paper and a pencil, Ellen will write a five-sentence paragraph" or "Using his mouth, David will answer who and what questions." Now you can see that it is superfluous to add this information as part of the goal.

Also, what inevitably happens when technology is placed in the goals is that an inconsistent model erupts from student to student. It is better just to state the goal without any mention of the tools and list the tools as accommodations. Therefore, the way to write these goals would be "Ellen will write a five-sentence paragraph" and "David will answer who and what questions." The accommodations could be written for Ellen as "Access to graphic organizing software during writing assignments" and, for David, "Use of a communication device during communication exchanges." Having the assistive technology written in a consistent manner for every IEP helps to ensure that these tools are considered for every student, not just the students with severe disabilities. A consistent approach to giving "careful thought" to the assistive technology needs during IEP meetings helps ensure that no student ever slips through the cracks.

AT at a Minimum

The IEP team can reconvene at any time to give additional consideration to assistive technology. Minimally, the IEP team must consider assistive technology once a year at the annual IEP meeting, but it can be, and usually is, considered much more frequently. Consideration of assistive technology is a dynamically layered process. Unofficially, teachers are making decisions about assistive technology on a daily basis. Where to position a student to maximize attention, which writing implement and surface to use, which lessons will be hands-on and which will be strictly auditory-visual, and which sorts of visuals are needed for a student to understand the concepts being presented are all decisions related to assistive technology. In many cases, these decisions are made solely by the teacher and not by an IEP team. Assistive technology can also be considered by having discussions with other teachers and service professionals about strategies to try to address a learning difficulty. More officially, the IEP team can reconvene at anytime to reconsider any portion of the IEP, including assistive technology.

You Know It, Whether You Know You Know It or Not

Every member of every IEP team has the ability to brainstorm solutions for problems and come up with strategies to address concerns. Therefore every IEP team member has some working knowledge of assistive technology. It's true!

Some team members might have more experience working with certain types of devices, while others might have more generalized skills to provide practical solutions. Depending on the goals delineated for a student, some team members might have more expertise, but that should not negate or overshadow the contributions of others. For example, if a student has a communication goal, it is prudent to seek the advice and counsel of a speech-language pathologist, but the contributions of the general education teacher, based on her knowledge of communication, are also valuable.

Because everyone on the team has some knowledge of assistive technology, it is not necessary to have someone with "assistive technology" in his or her job title present at every IEP meeting. Heck, it isn't necessary to have someone with an assistive technology background or job title present at *any* IEP meeting. The team members themselves are the individuals who are knowledgeable in assistive technology, and informal meetings can take place with an assistive technology trainer prior to IEP meetings to increase awareness and knowledge of how to integrate assistive technology into a student's IEP.

The One, the Only: Recommending an AT Evaluation

There is only one assistive technology service that needs to be listed in an IEP: an assistive technology evaluation. Assistive technology isn't the same as other related services in that the service is not working on remediation. If you go back and scope out the definition of "assistive technology service," you'll see that of all the verbs listed, "remediate" isn't included. One of the verbs you do see in the definition is "evaluate," and therefore, the request to conduct an assistive technology evaluation should be documented in the IEP.

It is easy to confuse assistive technology services with other related services in an IEP. Conceptually, there are similarities between assistive technology services and other related services such as speech therapy, occupational therapy, and physical therapy. For instance, in both types of services, there are individuals who conduct evaluations to determine recommendations provided to an IEP team. The difference is that those related services are working to remediate. Therapy services are working to develop a skill or behavior of a student. For example, speech therapy is geared to increasing the communication abilities of a student. Through periodic intervention with the speech-language pathologist, the student is learning skills and techniques to remediate a communication disorder. Therefore, therapy services are provided on a schedule using a specified, ongoing time frame. For example, a student might receive speech-language therapy 60 minutes per week to work on specifically targeted goals to remediate the communication disorder. Assistive technology services are not provided in this same fashion. Once an evaluation is complete, the assistive technology trainer is providing tools and methods for using those tools not for the purpose of remediation, but for the purpose of accessing the student's education.

A Healthy DIAT: Differentiating Instruction with AT

Every teacher is potentially a teacher of students in special education, regardless of endorsement or certification held. That is, every teacher has the responsibility of teaching every student in the class, including any student with a disability. As teachers develop lesson plans, they ask themselves, "How am I going to get this concept across to every student?" and "How can I adjust the lesson to meet the needs of each student?" This practice is known as *differentiating instruction*. Differentiating instruction is not an easy task, but teachers have a number of resources they can turn to for guidance. For example, teachers can brainstorm with other teachers in their building or district, or use free social networking applications such as Classroom 2.0 (www.classroom20.com) to collaborate with anyone in the world.

Using various technologies to aid in the differentiation of lessons is applying the principles of assistive technology. We like to refer to this as having a healthy DIAT (Differentiating Instruction with Assistive Technology). Teachers use available technology to allow all students in their classes to participate and have access to the curriculum.

The Good, the BAT, and the UDLy: The Universal Design for Learning

Technically, teachers differentiate instruction for all students, not just students receiving special education services. Some purists might argue that if a piece of technology is being used to help a student who does not have a disability, then that technology is not, by definition, assistive technology—it is just instructional technology. Yeah, and those purists would be right (lousy purists!). Therefore, careful consideration needs to take place when choosing instructional technologies in order to provide for the needs of all students. The principle of Universal Design for Learning (UDL) comes into play here.

According to the Center for Applied Special Technology (CAST; www.cast.org/research/faq/), Universal Design for Learning is a "framework for designing curricula ... that enable all individuals to gain knowledge, skills, and enthusiasm for learning. UDL provides rich supports for learning and reduces barriers to the curriculum while maintaining high achievement standards for all students." In case it didn't fly off the page and slap you in the face as you were reading it, the key word in that definition is "all." This means that technology using the UDL framework would be available to all students in the educational environment. Not special education only, not non–special education only—*all*.

We know already that the best all-around assistive technology is the technology that is already available to the student in the educational environment. This assistive technology is the least restrictive, and it will be more readily accepted by students. It will also be more easily implemented and will provide the best chance for successful integration into a student's life. Therefore, schools and classrooms that are outfitted with technology using the UDL framework are providing the best assistive technology.

udl trainer/udl team

What if the job title wasn't assistive technology trainer but Universal Design for Learning (UDL) trainer? The definition of Universal Design is outlined in the Individuals with Disabilities in Education Improvement Act of 2004:

> Universal Design means a concept or philosophy for designing and delivering products and services that are usable by people with the widest possible range of functional capabilities, which include products and services that are directly usable (without requiring assistive technologies) and products and services that are made usable with assistive technologies.

> —SEC. 3. Definitions. 20 USC 1401. P.L. 108–446.
> Note: P.L. 108–446 states that Universal Design is defined in SEC. 3.
> Definitions. 29 USC 3002. P.L. 108–364. The excerpt above is taken from
> the definition as stated in P.L. 108–364.

From this definition it could be proposed that a person (or team) employed by the school district could have the responsibility to design and deliver products and services, including assistive technology, that are usable by people with the widest range of capabilities. The scope of a UDL trainer or a whole UDL team could include the provision of tools and strategies to all students, not just students with disabilities.

Although Universal Design is not mentioned in the No Child Left Behind Act of 2001, which states that school districts need to demonstrate achievement for all students, the educational principle of UDL certainly lines up nicely with the intent of the law. As an assistive technology team works to integrate tools and strategies for individuals with disabilities, they can advertise and spread the principles of UDL throughout the school district. In this way, the assistive technology team serves the same function as a theoretical UDL team. However, the assistive technology team always runs the risk of having someone say, "Hey, aren't you supposed to be just for students with disabilities?" By calling the same team a different name and broadening the responsibilities to include the provision of services to all students, the school district makes a statement that the resources of the team are to be used to meet the needs of anyone, not just students with disabilities.

Oh, and we could even move some letters around to make the job title have a catchy acronym like "TURDLE," for Trainer of Universal Resources Designed for Learning in Education. TURDLE Team? TURDLE power! The team could have catchy slogans like "Tools in a half shell!"

■ ■ ■ ■ ■

Use Whatchya Got

"Piece of cake," "No sweat," "Easy-peasy," "A walk in the park," said the teacher whose classroom is universally designed for learning and who differentiates instruction for each and every lesson.

Is this the reality for most teachers? No, probably not. "Easier said than done" might be more apt. If you consider the number of students in a class and the number of lessons that occur throughout the course of the school year, it doesn't take long to realize that the task of teaching all students isn't easy. How do teachers begin to look at the classroom and individual lessons to incorporate the concepts of Universal Design for Learning and differentiated instruction? Well, there is a systematic approach to considering assistive technology devices, and it starts with *using whatchya got.*

Here's how it works. First, the teacher outlines the lesson and content he or she is trying to convey to the students. Then the teacher analyzes the students' abilities, asking questions such as, "Will Laura be able to read this, or will I have to modify the text in some way?" and "Will Luke need this lesson chunked into small segments over several lessons to understand it?" The teacher isolates how each student in the class will need to have the lessons modified. At this stage, identification of student needs is most important; the teacher isn't trying to figure out what technology is going to be used to modify the lesson. Once those needs are identified, then the teacher begins to decide which technology might be needed for successful student learning. When deciding what technology to use, teachers should start with what is available to the student in the classroom environment. Teachers who use this approach increase the chances for every student to successfully acquire the content while being actively engaged in the lesson. As Figure 3.1 suggests, the further one moves away from the student, the more difficult (and more restrictive) the technology becomes.

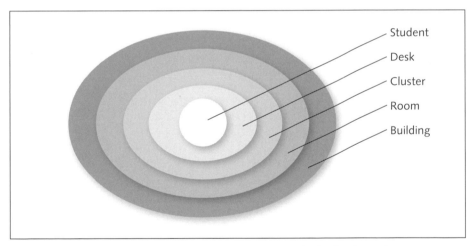

Figure 3.1 Technology becomes more difficult and restrictive the further the tools are from the student

part 3

building
an
assistive
technology
team

chapter 4

finding the path

Who You Gonna Call?

Picture yourself as the special education teacher for a student named Cindy. Cindy begins to experience some difficulties meeting her goals as outlined in her IEP. As a responsible teacher, you try some different strategies and tools for a while, but nothing seems to be working. You've gone to your fellow teachers for advice. You've tried some of the great suggestions they offered, but unfortunately, Cindy is still having difficulty meeting goals, and time is marching on for her. Where else can you turn? Consulting teachers? Tried them. Related service providers? Been there, done that! Administrators? Tried those as well. Geesh, you even tried rubbing your magic lamp, but the genie is too busy doing business in Arabia to help out. But there is one last person you haven't tried. One last ace in the hole who just might be able to come up with a tool or strategy that will assist Cindy in meeting her goals. Who is this suave, debonair, ingenious individual with a trick or two up the sleeve? Why, it's an assistive technology trainer, of course!

A Question of Money: Accommodations That Cost

Imagine you are the special education teacher for a student named Faissal. For Faissal, you are pretty sure you know the exact combination of tools and strategies that will allow him to make progress on his goals. You're all ready to list those suckers as the accommodations needed to guarantee Faissal a free and appropriate public education. There is just one tiny, eentsy little problem. Your tools and strategies include a piece of software that costs money, and not just $50 that you might be able to pull out of the petty cash drawer hidden in the secretary's desk, but significant money.

What are the rules in your district for accommodations that cost money? Will an administrator with more clout than the school principal need to be present at the IEP meeting as the authority who can apportion funds? If so, how do you decide upon the dollar amount imposed as the spending limit before an administrator need be present? Do you reconvene a meeting in order to invite that administrator if a parent recommends an accommodation of additional expense? What would you do if you were forced to justify the reasoning for the accommodation? Heck, do you as the teacher even feel comfortable writing in accommodations for technology that costs money? Whoa, take a look at that hornet's nest of questions you've stirred up because some dollar signs got involved! Luckily, though, you don't have to worry about any of that—because you've got an assistive technology trainer there with a can of bug spray.

New Tools of the Trade: Teachers Need Assistance

Imagine you are the special education teacher for a student named Richard who just moved to your school from a different county. There you sit, reviewing his former IEP, head in hands. He's got technowizzers, jibberjabbers, pollywhippets, and goobonutters in his IEP and you don't know how to use any of them! How are you going to find the time to learn all this technology? With any luck, this student will have some clue how to use them, but he's going to be looking to you, his teacher, for support. Quick, is it too late to transfer? But then the door opens, and a ray of sunshine slowly spreads forth, filling your room and illuminating your spirit—because you know, without even looking, that the person opening your door is your salvation! Lucky for you—you don't have to go it alone. You've got an assistive technology trainer to help you learn the new machinery and master its potential.

Zoom–Zoom–Zoom: Keeping Teachers Up to Speed

Imagine you are the special education teacher for any student in any modern-day classroom. Technology, even educational technology, is accelerating at an ever-increasing pace. Your students are living it. They're using technology in their lives, and you're trying to find engaging ways to use that technology to support their education. But it seems like every day there is some new website or gadget that everyone else seems to know about but you. Then, by the time you learn that, everyone else is onto the next newest techno-craze. The over-whelming rate of new technology development sometimes just makes you want to give up and call it quits. But who is that leaping out to grab the towel just before it hits the floor? It's your assistive technology trainer encouraging you to learn one new thing at a time and reminding you that each new technology piece might be the one that completes the puzzle for a student. It's your assistive technology trainer telling you that you're not alone and that you can take steps together to ensure that every student gets what is necessary.

Is Help on the Way?

Imagine you are the special education teacher working for a district that doesn't have an assistive technology trainer or that has a trainer whose job responsibilities also include maintaining a full-time speech therapy, occupational therapy, or physical therapy caseload. Where would you go for help? Who would you turn to when you need help making decisions about assistive technology? How could you keep up with all of the latest technology available to help students?

Without the assistive technology trainer, the world of special education would indeed be a scary, lonely, intimidating place. Lucky for you, you've got a dedicated assistive technology trainer in your district … Don't you?

chapter 5

reasons for building an assistive technology team

Resistance Is Futile: It's the Law

It's the law that assistive technology be considered. There's no getting around it. School districts may be able to avoid it for a while, but eventually the fact will need to be faced. However, there's no law that mandates the creation of an assistive technology team to help people make those considerations.

"A job worth doing, is worth doing right!"

But maybe there should be. To quote our moms, "A job worth doing is worth doing right." An assistive technology team helps to provide guidance and wisdom to the IEP team in order to get the job done correctly. An assistive technology team can construct the policies and procedures that the IEP team can then use to consider the assistive technology needs for every student. After all, if you've got to comply with the law, you might as well do it in a way that maximizes the benefit to the district as a whole—by creating an assistive technology team.

The Ripple Effect: One Tool Helps Many

Pick up a stone and toss it into a pond. Hear it splash with a loud kerplunk as it breaks the surface of the water. See the ripples spread out in all directions moving onward and outward. Tossing that one rock caused a chain reaction that brought about changes to the entire pond.

Pick up a ball and throw it at a stack of bottles. Hear it shatter the bottom bottle with an ear-piercing crash. See the bottles fall downward, clattering on the floor as they drop. Throwing that one ball caused a chain reaction that brought about changes to the entire pyramid.

Pick up the phone and call the assistive technology team to brainstorm strategies about one student. Discuss strategies and tools to help that student meet educational goals. See how those strategies and tools apply to more than just that one individual. Making that one phone call caused a chain reaction that brought about changes to the entire classroom.

What One Person Can Do, Another Can Do

Individualized Education Programs (IEPs) are unique for every student. That is a completely true statement. However, if you were to compare the IEPS for 100 different students in the same age range with the same identified disability, you'd find that there are many, many similarities.

Special educators have two full-time job responsibilities. Their primary responsibility is to educate students (duh, that's why we call them "educators"). Their secondary responsibility is to collaboratively write the IEPs for those students. How can they find the time for both jobs? Luckily there are many useful methods to streamline the IEP drafting process. For instance, perhaps they use a template for each student when writing the Present Level of Academic and Functional Performance page of the IEP—just plugging in numbers for test scores rather than rewriting the similar test summary sentences for each student. Special educators might have familiar lines that they use repeatedly across every IEP they draft as a way to keep things consistent for themselves. Writing goals that are generally the same for students who demonstrate similar needs can generate consistent activities.

These streamlining techniques also apply to the drafting of accommodations for students. If a student needs a tool or strategy for a free and appropriate public education, then that is included as an accommodation—and remember, accommodations are assistive technology. As soon as a special educator drafts an accommodation in an IEP, it immediately becomes a deposit in the mental bank so that it can be pulled up and used for other students. The mental bank of accommodations can never be too robust, and it is never, ever filled. The assistive technology team provides a never-ending well of resources that can be tapped into repeatedly. In this way, accommodations can be repeated across many IEPs to address the needs of various students. If a special educator (or other member of the IEP team) doesn't know about a tool or strategy, then it will never be written as an accommodation. Once brainstorming with the assistive technology team occurs, the resource bank has grown forever for every subsequent student.

Bad to Good to Great to Elite: AT Can Help You Get There

There are four types of educators: bad ones, good ones, great ones, and the educational elite. Let's start off by being honest about the reality that there are just some among us who aren't very good at being educators. By using euphemisms like "pedagogically uninspired" or "instructionally struggling," we only sugarcoat the fact that, just as in any profession, there are those who have trouble cutting the mustard. You know it. We know it. Heck, they probably know it. As you read this, the image of someone you know is probably popping into your head.

Next, there are a group of educators who are good at what they do. Educators in this group typically enjoy what they do, making it even easier to do it well. Students thrive in their classrooms, and everything runs smoothly. These educators usually go out of their way to make sure all students are learning to the best of their abilities. Good educators are not afraid of change, adapt when necessary, and collaborate for the benefit of the students.

Great educators are the mentors in the school. They maintain all of the qualities of a good educator, but also become the leaders in the school. Great educators are the people the good educators go to when they are stuck on a problem or need advice.

The final group of educators is the educational elite. These are the educators who win all of the awards, go on tours sharing their educational strategies, get television stations to do news reports about their teaching methodologies, and write books on their educational practices. (Hee hee hee, we just called ourselves elite. Seriously, you wouldn't want to read a book from two individuals who didn't believe themselves among the elite in their profession, would you?)

The trick in education, as in any profession, is to continually strive to move up to the next step. We don't mean working to be an administrator, but to advance to the next tier of educator. If you feel you're "pedagogically uninspired" or "instructionally struggling," for the sake of your students you've got to try to be better. If you're good, then you've got to work toward being great, and if you're great, you've got to work to become elite. You can spot great and elite educators a mile away. They are the ones who think that even though a lesson went perfectly, there is always room for improvement.

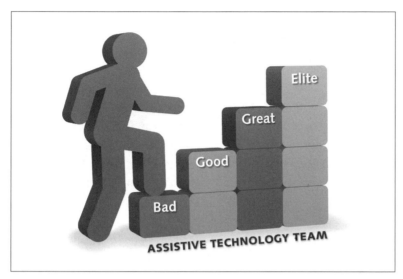

Figure 5.1 An assistive technology team helps lift educators to the next step.

An assistive technology team can be considered the steps each educator is climbing. As each educator attempts to improve by learning new teaching practices, the assistive technology team will be there to provide tools and to help with the metamorphosis. If educators are willing to learn, they can consult with the assistive technology team to learn strategies to make themselves better. Educators who want to achieve greatness can also consult with the assistive technology team to learn how to implement technology to meet the needs of their students. Great educators will be doing a lot already, but, because they're great, they will be craving more knowledge about what they can use for every student in the classroom. Finally, the educational elite will have learned a long time ago that there is no limit to the knowledge that can be gained. The educational elite will challenge the assistive technology team to improve upon itself, forcing each member to learn new tools and strategies.

share the wonder

The teachers gathered round the storytelling stool for story time, their favorite part of the monthly staff meetings. They laid out their carpet squares in concentric semicircles and sat, crisscross applesauce, waiting patiently and quietly for their favorite guest storyteller to arrive.

Usually their ears were filled with the dulcet tones of their principal or assistant principal telling them about this policy or that procedure. Some stories were filled with evil budgeteers who attacked budgets, cutting and hacking them to pieces. Other stories featured gargoyles that flew down from their perches on the administration building, snatching up teachers who didn't eat all their state standards. But what would today's story bring? Anticipation was building and the teachers began to whisper. "What do you think he'll tell us this year?" "Something scary, I hope!" "No, not scary, I'm hoping for a tale of daring and cunning!" Even more teachers murmured, "I'm sure it will be a tale of suspense and intrigue." "Yeah, and cool gadgets used to get out of tight spots!" "Don't forget the quips. I love the quips."

Finally, the principal walked into the room and gestured to the teachers to calm down. "I know you have been looking forward to this, so I won't keep you waiting." Sweeping his arms back toward the door, the principal announced, "Here's our very own assistive technology trainer!" Gasps of excitement filled the room as a ruggedly handsome man strode through the door. He jogged the last few steps, swung his leg over the stool and grabbed the front of the seat with both hands as he sat down. "Are you teachers ready for a story?" he asked, flashing a dazzling smile while cocking his head. The crowd before him nodded in silent awe and a few found the courage to mumble, "Uh huh."

"Today's story is called 'The Schoolhouse Thief.' Once upon a time, a long time ago, there lived a little schoolhouse, not unlike the school we are sitting in today. It had hallways like this school, it had students like this school, and it had teachers, like all of you. One day, just like any other day—in fact, I think it was a Thursday, just like today—the school was robbed...."

■ ■ ■

the schoolhouse thief

The thief inched around the corner of Nichols Elementary School like a living shadow. If you were looking at the school, you would have seen only the blackness of the night, not the figure dressed like a ninja sliding along the outside walls of the building. You might have thought it was a raccoon or possum that scaled the drainpipe to gain access to the roof. It might have sounded like a bat flapping its wings when the thief entered the school through the air-conditioning vent. It was dark when the thief entered the building—and it was dark again, the next night, when the thief left with something very, very valuable in hand.

The thief used the air ducts as his own personal highway around the building, avoiding security cameras and remaining undetected. He carried only one tool in his gloved hands: his digital camera. He wiggled his way through the ducts toward the first classroom. Once he was in place the thief stopped and rechecked his camera to make sure it was operational and ready for surveillance. From his vantage point, perched in the ducts above the room, he could see every corner—the perfect spot to observe what he needed to see.

Throughout the day the thief slipped through the ducts like an eel, silently moving from room to room snapping photos. The photos were not of students, but rather of the technology the students used in their lessons. The thief diligently took shots of computer programs, portable word processors, editing checklists, color-coded notebooks, an assortment of colors of highlighter tape, Popsicle sticks, and much, much more. The amount of technology this school used was, to put it mildly, amazing. The thief silently switched his camera into movie mode and took short snippets of technology use in action. The vast amount of knowledge he was gaining, along with the collections of pictures and videos he was gathering, would serve him well later when he returned from whence he came.

As the day wound its way to a close, the thief looked at the number of artifacts he had collected. He had taken more than 400 photos and 30 videos of all different tools or strategies that would be useful to other educators. This was a brilliant haul, a virtual gold mine of intervention techniques and implementation methodologies that made all the time spent skulking around in the dark feel worthwhile. He couldn't wait to burn his newly acquired collection of work onto a single DVD.

As the thief waited by the duct in the cafeteria for the janitor to lock up for the day, he stopped to ponder the many schools he had infiltrated in his time. Every school was different, and every school had its own unique ways to implement technology. His collection of strategies, tools, and techniques grew larger and more robust with every school he visited.

At last all was quiet. The thief lifted himself out of the ducts that had been his home for the last 24 hours. He lowered himself down the drainpipe, landing on his feet like a cat, and dashed off into the cover of the woods. "Another school successfully harvested," he thought while his teeth glimmered in the moonlight. And then he was gone.

■ ■ ■

"So, did you enjoy the story?" asked the storyteller, surveying his still-rapt audience.

Some teachers looked around, blinking, as if coming out of a daze. Others looked up at the drop ceiling, wondering if they were being watched right now.

"Is that a true story?" asked one teacher in a beguiled tone.

The assistive technology trainer, smiling a knowing smile, reached behind his back to pull out a DVD, which he held up for all to behold. "You be the judge," he said. "One of the best parts of my job as an assistive technology trainer is that I get to travel from school to school, room to room, teacher to teacher, and share the wonders I see occurring in every classroom. Sure, I have a few ideas of my own, but a lot of what I do is to act more like the conduit that brings the energy from the power plant to the house rather than actually being the light bulb itself."

He tossed the DVD into the crowd and a teacher quickly snatched it out of the air and clutched it possessively. Her neighbors jealously looked at her, badly wanting the prize for themselves. But the handsome man raised his hands to address the restless crowd.

"You can't keep this knowledge for yourself. You must share the knowledge contained within," the man said, pointing to the DVD. "Don't let these strategies remain a secret. Share the knowledge. Share it with everyone."

With that, he left them, ending his march to the door with a little jog. The teachers erupted in applause just as the door swung shut. The principal ended story time by reminding everyone that the next story time would include educational movies and a slide show, and by inviting the teachers to place their carpet squares back in their cubbies.

■ ■ ■ ■ ■

The Digital Rapids: Fear Not Technology

Like the mirage shimmering before your eyes in the middle of a desert, there is an illusion that contemporary students have a working knowledge of every little piece of technology out there because they have grown up with it. They don't, but every generation does have a youth–adult technology gap, with the stream of technology running right through the middle. With today's digital technology, that stream is flowing so fast it's actually more like a river with multiple sets of class 5 rapids. This speed of change can be intimidating. New technologies, especially new websites, seem to be springing up daily and, in turn, are absorbed by the mass public before educators even ask the question, "How can we use this?"

Some educators may fear these turbulent digital waters and feel that they are not "tech savvy" enough to integrate these tools into their daily lessons. But the assistive technology team rides those rapids every day for a living—let them be the crazy river rafting guide who doles out the life jackets and paddles along while saying, "Hold on, this might get a little choppy, but we'll make it through okay." An assistive technology team guides educators who might feel overwhelmed by the amount of technology available to them and provides a methodology for implementing technology in a way that is manageable. Step by step, little by little, day by day, each educator can become more confident with navigating the rapids, thanks to the guidance of the assistive technology team.

I Scream, You Scream, We All Scream for NCLB

The No Child Left Behind Act of 2001 (P.L. 107–110), commonly known as NCLB, states that each state will develop a plan to demonstrate adequate yearly progress (or AYP) for all students. NCLB further establishes four subcategories of students for whom adequate yearly progress must be measured separately, requiring that "continuous and substantial improvements" be made. These four subcategories of students are economically disadvantaged students, students from major racial and ethnic groups, students with disabilities, and students with limited English proficiency.

Many schools and educators may view these groups as separate entities and think that the AT team works only with students with disabilities. However, it may help to think of each of these groups as a different flavor scoop of ice cream in a sundae. Sure, each flavor could be eaten separately—but when they melt together into a flavorful soupy substance that isn't just strawberry, chocolate, mint, or vanilla but a combination of all four, the result is even more delectable. Then think of the assistive technology team as the spoon you use to eat the whole sundae (unless you lick the bowl, which we encourage you to do—go ahead, no one is looking). The spoon is used for all four scoops, not just one.

An assistive technology team may help to come up with tools and strategies that can help meet adequate yearly progress, not just for students with disabilities, but for all four subgroups. The best tools are the ones that serve more than just one person. Although it might not be the original purpose or even the responsibility of a team, it can take the tools recommended for students with disabilities and apply them to any student in need.

For instance, an assistive technology team may have implemented a symbol-generating program, such as Mayer-Johnson's Boardmaker, for creating picture symbols to be used with students with receptive and expressive language difficulties as outlined in their Individualized Education Programs. However, as the other educators begin to observe how these picture symbols are used, they could begin to use the picture symbols in their own classrooms to enhance communication and understanding for students with limited English proficiency, students from major racial or ethnic groups, and students who are economically disadvantaged. In this way, the assistive technology team has, in effect, added a productivity tool to the entire school to benefit all of the subcategories outlined in No Child Left Behind and helped the school achieve adequately yearly progress.

Sprinkles, Whipped Cream, and a Cherry on Top: Every Student Benefits

What's a sundae without some toppings? Add some whipped cream, toss on some sprinkles, and then plop down a big ol' red cherry right on top of your dessert delicacy! Yum, yum, yum. Now that's good eatin'!

The sprinkles in our educational sundae represent the students who don't quite fit into any of the four subcategories as outlined in No Child Left Behind, but who certainly could use some help. Every educator has a story of the student who struggled in class, was evaluated to determine the existence of a disability but found not to have one, and therefore did not receive an Individualized Education Program. Every educator has a story of a student who doesn't fit into one of those four subcategories, yet could really benefit from additional supports. There isn't always an abundance of these students, but they are "sprinkled" throughout every school. These students still require tools and strategies to help them be successful in school.

The whipped cream represents all of the other students in the school who might generally do well but have rough patches from time to time. All students need to learn strategies and how to use tools to help them in their education. At times, for any number of variables, students might struggle for a while. Maybe they are struggling with one specific concept, maybe they are in a temporary slump, or maybe they have more significant issues in their personal lives. For whatever reason, at times even the students who typically might not need special assistance require tools and strategies to help them meet their own educational goals.

No sundae would be complete without adding the cherry as the final tasty morsel. The cherry in our delicious educational sundae represents the students who are the educationally enlightened. These are the A+++ students who consistently do well and who are looking to be challenged in unique ways. In public education there is no doctrine decreeing that all students need to be challenged to the limits of their abilities; however, many teachers (rightly) attempt to do this regardless of the lack of necessity. Like the sprinkles and the whipped cream, these students aren't defined as separate categories under No Child Left Behind, but they exist nonetheless. These students take the technology provided and use it to create solutions no one else discovered. The technology used by these students allows them to unlock hidden talents they might not have otherwise known existed.

Like the ice cream, the tool used to eat each of these scrumptious morsels is still the spoon, and the spoon is still the assistive technology team. Although the focus of the team is to provide tools, strategies, and solutions to meet the needs of students with IEPs, these tools, strategies and solutions have the potential to benefit any student who needs them.

Live Long and Prosper: Life Skills

"When are we ever going to use this stuff?" Every high school students thinks it in one class or another. Actually, there might be an expletive in that sentence somewhere; after all, we're talking high school. Why do I need to know what happened in the Civil War? Why do I need to know how to read the periodic table? Calculus? Are you serious? What practical application does that possibly serve? Of course, there are practical applications for all of these concepts, but that may not be immediately apparent to the high school student who is too busy thinking about Friday night and the girl two rows up on the left with shockingly red hair and the brilliant smile. The value of some skills, however, registers loud and clear. Here are just a few skills students need to be able to use in order to survive and thrive independently or semi-independently:

Communication

- Text messaging
- Keyboarding
- Using cell phone etiquette
- E-mailing
- Carrying on a conversation

Researching

- Navigating the Internet
- Asking for assistance

Personal skills

- Maintaining hygiene
- Driving
- Keeping a calendar
- Doing laundry
- Shopping for food
- Shopping for clothing
- Preparing food
- Contacting emergency rescue services

Money management

- Banking online
- Using a credit card
- Maintaining good credit
- Writing a check
- Budgeting money

Occupation maintenance

- Dressing appropriately for different situations
- Finding a job
- Interviewing
- Managing time
- Maintaining a job
- Getting along with others

These skills are important for students to learn, whether they have a disability or not. Learning these skills and putting them into practice creates functional members of society. When all is said and done, the goal of education in society as a whole is to create functional members of society.

Real-life skills are made available to students through the use of technology. An assistive technology team leads the students and their teachers to discover technology that is useful in developing these life skills. An assistive technology team is charged with the task of finding technology solutions that can be integrated as seamlessly as possible into the student's life to help the student accomplish all necessary life skills. Teachers have the potential to make a difference in a student's life, and this ability is what makes the profession of teaching so rewarding. Providing a tool or strategy to a student that is used to access a life skill might be the most meaningful of all the educator's job responsibilities—and it's all made possible by an assistive technology team.

Pennies in the Piggy Bank: Spend Technology Money Wisely

Money makes the world go round, and money is the root of all evil. Therefore, the world is moved by evil forces. Cheery thought, isn't it? Cheery or not, the fact remains that schools operate on budgets. As a result, many people have money on their minds when it comes to making decisions about assistive technology. It's not a stretch to think that creating an assistive technology team is going to cost some money. Even if your team consists of only one full-time person, that's one full-time position that needs to be added to the budget. Once in place, however, an assistive technology team instantly begins to save the district money.

The assistive technology team can eliminate erroneous spending on technology by individual teachers. Teachers may see a piece of equipment or software in a catalogue, decide "I think this will be good," and place an order with allocated classroom funds. This process tends to be a bit willy-nilly and can lead to wasted funds. But if technology purchases are filtered through an assistive technology team, the technology can be evaluated for its effectiveness before multiple purchases of something not so useful occur. It also provides an opportunity for the assistive technology team to suggest tools that are most flexible for meeting the needs of students. Having this standardized approach to technology acquisition for every IEP team saves the district money by eliminating the purchase of any untested, unproven tools. This is not to say that individual teachers shouldn't play a role in determining what technology is used within the classroom—they definitely should play an integral part in technology decisions. However, the best decisions on how to spend funds are made by collaborative groups rather than individuals.

The best assistive technology is that which is least restrictive or minimally invasive for the student. The best solution for an individual student is technology that can be used universally in every environment. Strategies that use no technology or are low-tech solutions should be considered and tried before mid-tech or high-tech solutions are attempted. An assistive technology team considers this premise when making decisions about technology and parades these concepts whenever decisions about technology acquisition are being made. Much of the time, the most universal and least restrictive solution is also the free solution. For example, a school district could certainly spend funds to buy document holders for every computer in every school, or they could flip a CD case inside out and use a clothespin to serve the same purpose (Fig. 5.2). It's the role of an assistive technology team to seek cost-effective technologies that can be used in place of a more expensive alternative. An assistive technology team can help make decisions about spending at the student, school, and district levels to help put the money that has already been apportioned to good use while proposing how to use funds that will be necessary for the future.

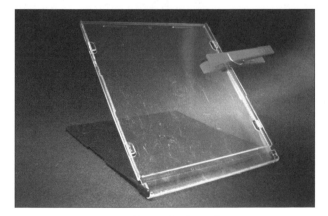

Figure 5.2 Document holders—the free solution

eating in saves more money than eating out

Everyone loves to go out to eat. Sit down, sip on a drink, and relax while someone else does all the work. No juggling ingredients. No criticism of your cooking skills (or lack thereof). You get appetizers! You don't have to clean up when you're all done. You didn't have to do a thing … except pay for it. You paid for transportation to the restaurant. You paid for that spinach artichoke dip appetizer that you just had to have. You really paid for the overpriced drinks. The flirtatious server who dropped compliments on you like they were snowflakes in Buffalo in January is now expecting a tip for all that hard work. You knew that eating out was going to cost more than eating in, and now you've got to decide: on your budget, was it worth it?

Some school districts may be under the impression that assistive technology services, especially evaluations, should be contracted out to agencies that have "assistive technology experts." You know, where someone has decided that an "expert" will have all the answers that will solve students' problems. There might be a frame of mind that an assistive technology team (even a team of one) isn't necessary, in an effort to save money or because of the relatively small number of evaluations.

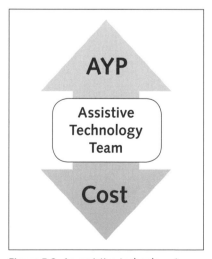

Figure 5.3 An assistive technology team boosts AYP and saves money

Private evaluations from outside agencies can yield one of four outcomes: (1) their recommendations are strategies or tools that the IEP team has already considered or has already tried; (2) they recommend products or tools that have an additional cost associated with them without first considering the tools already available within the student's environment, or the agency has partnered with a vendor and their recommendations are biased toward particular products (regardless of student need); both situations that add to the complexity of the decision; (3) their recommendations are completely appropriate and exactly what the student needs to have access to a free and appropriate public education; (4) the evaluation contains recommendations that are some combination of 1, 2, and 3.

Given these possible outcomes, in most cases the bang just isn't worth the buck for evaluations conducted by outside agencies. That is, a school district has paid a fee (probably a hefty one) to have a student's assistive technology needs evaluated, but the evaluation may have more potential to raise questions than to provide solutions. A functioning AT team in a school district virtually eliminates the spending on private evaluations conducted by outside agencies.

■ ■ ■ ■ ■

Time in a Bottle: Streamline Strategy Shopping

You can't buy it, bottle it, bank it, or save it for later. It is the biggest enemy of every educator. Time. You've probably said to yourself. "I wish I had the time to …" or "If only I had more time I'd …" or "I really need to take the time to …" or "There just isn't enough time to …" and so on, ad infinitum. It could be argued that time is far more valuable to education than money. The amount of time a student has in the public education system is finite. When that student enters the first year in the public school, the clock starts ticking—and every second counts.

When a student is struggling, educators implement interventions. Sometimes these interventions work on the first attempt, providing the student with a wonderful solution to a problem. Other times, multiple attempts are necessary to find the tool or strategy that works for a student. An assistive technology team can save precious time by providing feedback to an educator regarding what has worked well in the past with other students. Not only can an assistive technology team streamline the tool and strategy selection process, it can also provide proven implementation strategies that allow the tools to be used with the highest probability of success. An assistive technology team helps educators eliminate strategies that don't work—which, in effect, saves valuable time that would otherwise be wasted.

chapter 6

choosing
assistive technology
teammates

It's Not What You Know,
It's What You're Willing to Learn

So you've decided to create an assistive technology team, and you've got the backing of your administration! Congratulations! Now it's time to find the right people for the team. Finding the right people to be on the team is like picking your own apples right off the tree. There are plenty of apples to choose from, but only a few you'd want to put in your bushel, and even fewer you'd want to pick if you were making a pie to enter into the county's pie-baking contest. You need to inspect each apple carefully, looking for bruises, rots, and yucky worms.

Choosing the right apples might make all the difference between the pie you'd feed your in-laws and the pie that could win the blue ribbon at the county fair.

Your first instinct when building a team might be to find people who have some knowledge of assistive technology devices. Maybe someone with experience with augmentative communication devices would be appropriate? Maybe someone who has some computer experience? Maybe someone who has actually touched an environmental control unit before? Nah … none of those are actual priorities when it comes to selecting the members of an assistive technology team.

The following is a list of qualities, in order of importance, to consider when deciding who should be on the team:

1. Feels the job they have done is never quite good enough

2. Works hard

3. Is motivated

4. Problem-solves

5. Possesses a willingness to learn

6. Respects others (especially educators) by demonstrating the attitude that other educators are peers

7. Excels at written and verbal communication

8. Works as a team player

9. Is flexible

10. Fears nothing

11. Multitasks

12. Is creative

13. Is knowledgeable in assistive technology (Eek!)

The majority of these qualities are those any recruiter would desire in any employee for any job. It isn't any surprise that "Works hard" is near the top of the list. However, notice where "Is knowledgeable in assistive technology" comes on the list. In truth, we debated whether this should be on the list at all. It should *not* be a prerequisite that someone have working knowledge of assistive technology to be on the assistive technology team. It is entirely possible for someone to have some experience with assistive technology and be a total slacker. Who would you rather have on your team: the person who knows how to program a device but sits with feet up all day playing solitaire, or the person who busts their hump while still being willing to learn how to program a device? We'll choose the latter every time to be our teammate. The person who is willing to work hard, learn more, and take initiative will quickly gain the knowledge it takes to provide effective assistive technology services. This individual will surely surpass those who already have some knowledge about assistive technology but are resting on their laurels. The person who has even some of the qualities listed above "Is knowledgeable in assistive technology" is far better suited to be on the team than the person who already "knows it all." The truth is, you'll probably know who fits this description and who doesn't, because the star that shines the brightest is the easiest to see.

Slim Pickins: Hard-Working Folks Are in Demand

The first people considered for the assistive technology team are usually related service providers, especially speech-language pathologists (SLPs) and occupational therapists (OTs). And in fact, they might be the perfect choice for team members. Related service providers have proved themselves capable of learning new things, managing large amounts of work, working successfully on teams, and integrating services. As an additional bonus, these individuals have some experience using tools and strategies to help students meet their educational goals. However, a problem exists with using these individuals as team members—they are hard to come by. The shortage of SLPs and OTs makes it hard to reassign them to the assistive technology team. But although the SLP or OT position vacancy might be difficult to fill, the benefits outweigh the costs. The right therapist in the role of an assistive technology team member can decrease the demands placed on all of the other therapists in the school district by providing insights about supports that can be put in place to help that discipline.

Multidisciplined, Schmultidisciplined

There is only one way an assistive technology team should look: attractive. That's right—no ugly people on the team. That is the one and only rule that you should have. Of course beauty is in the eye of the beholder, so you get to decide who's dazzling enough to be on your team.

There is no formula that says each person on the team should have a different educational background. There is no rule that says there should be at least one speech pathologist, one occupational therapist, and one physical therapist. But if you're one of those people who needs a guideline, here it is: Disciplines don't matter … much. It is acceptable to have two SLPs on your team and no OTs, or the reverse. In fact, it would be better to have two people with the same educational background who are hard workers than to have one person from a different background who lacks the qualities of a good team member. Quality of work overrides educational background every time.

Another reason the assistive technology team doesn't need members from every discipline is because those disciplines are already represented in the student's IEP team. And as the assistive technology person, you will collaborate with *all* of the members of the student's IEP team, including the related service providers, to make decisions.

The Dangers of a Multidisciplinary Approach

Moviegoers know how a bad sci-fi monster movie would put together a team to investigate the strange alien creature that crash-landed in the Mojave Desert. You get one of each specialist to describe the attributes of the monster: the biologist with Coke-bottle glasses to tell you how interesting it is, the sharp-as-a-tack medic with more curves than a roller coaster to remind you that it's a living being, the exoteric psychic to tell you what the creature thinks, the tough as nails, ripped to the max ex-marine to tell you how dangerous it is, and the wily veteran to assure you that there is no earthly way the creature could escape.

Building an assistive technology team is nothing like that. There is no requirement that an assistive technology team have one of each discipline on the team. In fact, there is a very real danger when a team is multidisciplinary that people will get pigeonholed into their specialty areas. When a request for help determining tools for a student is received, there might be a natural tendency to make assignments based on the area in which the student is struggling. For example, if a student is experiencing communication difficulties, it could be assumed that the SLP should be the one on the team addressing those concerns. If a student is experiencing writing difficulties, it might be assumed that the OT should be the one on the team making recommendations. This is a trap—not just an ordinary trap, either. It is one of those Indiana Jones type traps that lops your head off if you aren't careful! What is the likelihood that the number of requests that arrive will be equally distributed among all domains? Will the number of requests to address writing difficulties match, even remotely, the number of requests where communication is the biggest concern? Even if the requests are initially equally balanced, they will not continue in that fashion. That is a promise. These inequalities can tear the team apart because nothing gets under people's skin more than watching someone else sit around doing nothing while they're working their tail feathers off.

The other trap is that responding to requests based solely on the discipline of individual team members is ultimately restricting. If the OT on the team provides all the strategies with regard to writing, how will the other assistive technology trainers learn strategies to address writing challenges? Furthermore, if the IEP team is looking for strategies to help with writing, it is likely that they have already asked the onsite OT for advice. The educator contacting the assistive technology team may be looking for strategies from a team member with a different background or perspective. Keep in mind that an assistive technology team consists of teammates who can each offer different insights and perspectives. When the AT member with an SLP background is asked to address a situation focusing on writing difficulties, that person has teammates to turn to for support. If a particular discipline is not represented in the assistive technology team, the assistive technology trainer still has the related service providers on the IEP team for collaboration. By staying away from pigeonholes and experiencing a multitude of difficulties, each member of the team becomes a better, more well-rounded, and more versatile assistive technology trainer.

Avoiding the Phantom Menace through Equality

If you've been lured to the dark side and decide to distribute requests for assistance based on discipline, then you will have to face the following question: "What do we do when we get a request that does not pertain to a discipline we have on the team?" What if requests come to the team to address concerns related to vision, yet there is no teacher of the visually impaired on the team? How do you decide who responds to that request? Not easy questions to answer, are they? But if you decide to split things up without considering the professional discipline of the trainer, then you no longer have that concern, do you? Adopting the policy that each team member is an equal "assistive technology trainer" capable of handling any request for assistance lets you avoid the problem entirely.

Another strategy to use to keep from falling into the "distribute cases based on discipline" trap is to apply a spin to the concept of person-first language. Rather than saying, "I'm a speech-language pathologist on the team," say, "I'm an assistive technology trainer with a speech background." Even better, just say, "I'm an assistive technology trainer" and leave it at that. Every recommendation is given more validity. The recommendations are coming from an assistive technology trainer rather than from a specific discipline. There should be a general understanding that once people become part of the assistive technology team, they stop seeing themselves solely as experts in their previous discipline and start to see themselves as assistive technology trainers. As Obi-Wan Kenobi said to Luke Skywalker when he first felt the Force flow through him, "That's good. You've taken your first step into a larger world." In this case it is the world of assistive technology!

It's Okay to Say That You Don't Know

You are not the smartest person in the world. You can't know everything. In fact, if you did know everything, I'm pretty sure people would just get jealous and resent you for that fact. Nobody likes a know-it-all (except our spouses—they love know-it-alls), and no one even expects you to know everything. There you go. We just gave you permission to not know things. It is totally, 100% fine to not know the answer. Here's all you have to say when someone asks you something that you don't know: "I'm not sure, but I'll find out!" Say it out loud right now to practice. Say it often. Parents, teachers, heck, everyone will love you for it. By saying you're "not sure," you're letting them know that it is okay for them not to know it either. By saying "I'll find out," you're letting them know that they have someone willing to go an extra step for them. Then make sure you follow through on your promise, or the phrase will mean nothing.

Stating that you don't know but that you're willing to find out is also the key to eliminating any insecurity you might be having about making recommendations that might be outside of your specialty area. You might be thinking, "I'm not an occupational therapist, so how can I make recommendations about writing?" or "I'm not a speech-language pathologist, so how can I make recommendations about communication?" By admitting you don't know and by being willing to learn, you make yourself a better overall assistive technology trainer.

a robot's story

Robot number PL 94-142 zipped down the ship's hallway on her way to an important job interview, weaving around the other machines that speckled the corridor. Suddenly she hit a major backup along the main thoroughfare of the ship. She couldn't be late. Late was unacceptable. She linked to the ship's network and found out the backup was caused by a containment leak in pod 7. She quickly scanned her vast database of every piece of technology known to machine or biological entity and came up with just the right tool to reroute traffic. PL 94-142 loved solving problems with technology, and in fact that was why she was applying for the new job. One of her subroutines had just discovered that some small organic life forms were having problems learning. PL 94-142 knew she could find just the right technologies to help them, a whole database full, if only she were hired.

But even with traffic cleared, PL 94-142 was running late. She engaged her hyper-core turbo thrust to increase her speed by 17%. The data processed immediately through her circuitry-lined head shell. If no other obstacles impeded her movement she would make it to the interview on time, if, of course, her circuits didn't melt first. "Thirty seconds until lateness" warned a silent digital signal that passed directly through the central processor of PL 94-142's motherboard. She couldn't be late because then they wouldn't hire her and she wouldn't be able to fix anything. Rounding the final turn PL 94-142's OSA (optical sensor array) locked onto the target destination. Instantaneously PL 94-142 calculated the distance, rate of speed, and time of arrival. Racing toward the door PL 94-142 increased acceleration by another 4%. The friction in PL 94-142's motors caused a low screeching noise to erupt from the chest plate covering PL 94-142's navigation system.

PL 94-142 closed in on the door. Fifty feet. Forty feet. A thunderous clanking noise. Thirty feet. Twenty feet. A pop and a repeated clang. Ten feet! Five feet! The groaning inside the chest plate grew louder, sounding like a wounded animal screaming for mercy. Mercy came swiftly as PL 94-142 screeched to a halt arriving at the door with 11 seconds to spare.

An infrared beam blinked on and scanned PL 94-142's identification engraving located just below her OLFSA (olfactory sensor array). The holographic door disappeared and the force containment unit dissipated. A green light blinked once above the door while simultaneously sending the message "Enter" to PL 94-142's OSA. PL 94-142 rolled into the room slowly.

The room was white, like every other part of the ship. A white kidney-shaped table sat near the far wall. Seated around the table were the representatives from the Council of Health and Educational Well-Being, Assistive Technology division, or C.H.E.W.A.T., as it was known around the ship. PL 94-142 rolled into the empty space in the center of the U and extended her pincer grasper. After complete extension, PL 94-142 rotated the gesticulatory unit right and left to simulate a waving motion while pivoting on her center axis. Each creature nodded acceptingly in succession as PL 94-142 momentarily rested the wave in front of each creature.

"PL 94-142—please engage verbal processing unit: Mary," said Scarlax, the purple creature in the center. PL 94-142 replied, in a synthesized female voice "Affirmative. VPU initiated. Voice: Mary."

"Excellent!" said Zibug, the chubby furry being on the left. "Let's get started, PL 94-142. I received a data stream earlier this week from our personnel office stating that you were seeking employment as an assistive technology trainer? Is that correct?"

"Affirmative," replied PL 94-142.

"This is a big change from your current position. Do you have the necessary qualifications to provide such a service to all of the varied species of creatures residing on this ship?" Scarlax asked, his purple flesh jiggling with concern.

"Assistive technology trainers are supposed to be organic," interrupted Morcor, the slime-covered officer on the right, gurgling with irritation. "No robot is qualified for this position."

"PL 94-142 is familiar with the functions of every piece of equipment in the known universe," responded the robot. "PL 94-142 maintains the ability to analyze student data at 128 million computations per second while simultaneously cross referencing the equipment database to generate equipment recommendations organized by probability of success based on known factors."

"Ha! Is it that easy, PL 94-142? Simply analyze the data collected on a student and poof!, you've got yourself proven recommendations?" gurgled Morcor as slime passed over the lips of her gigantic maw while forming the word "recommendations."

"Affirmative," nodded PL 94-142, circuits blazing in anticipation of being hired for the job.

"PL 94-142, what about brainstorming solutions together with the teachers? Is their data not valuable as well? What about solutions that do not require equipment? Would every solution need a piece of equipment?" inquired Zibug, her orange fur ruffling.

"Affirmative," confirmed PL 94-142. "Equipment will provide solutions to every problem. Brainstorming is not necessary. Teachers will use what PL 94-142 tells them to use because of the expected probability of success."

"Ah, probability of success may be high, PL 94-142," agreed Scarlax. "But providing equipment when it is not needed is not very cost effective, not to mention that it restricts the student to using that device."

"And teachers will want a say in what tools and strategies are implemented with a student. Teachers have shown again and again that 'potential' solutions become 'used' solutions when the teacher takes part in the decision-making process," added Morcor.

PL 94-142 widened her ocular lens. Solutions that don't require technology? Restrictions on students? Cooperation with the teacher? These were unfamiliar new concepts. She initiated an analyzing subroutine immediately, sensing the job slipping from her pincer-graspers.

"PL 94-142 will help many small organic life forms by providing equipment that will work," she pleaded, core temperature rising by one degree.

"There is no doubt that you want to help," encouraged Zibug, "but PL 94-142, can your programming handle the complex interactions that occur between the assistive technology trainer and the teacher? We believe it takes a, pardon the expression, 'natural touch' to work with a teacher along with the many life forms in an instructional unit. We're sorry, but analyzing data is not good enough. The teachers need to trust their assistive technology trainer and, most importantly, form a bond with their assistive technology trainer."

PL 94-142's metal dome crinkled in disappointment, but only for a moment, as the results from the subroutine lighted her CPU. New circuits formed allowing her to calculate a response.

"PL 94-142 has learned many things during this interview and wishes to make a new request. PL 94-142 requests to join your mentor program and work with an organic-based assistive technology trainer to increase knowledge of forming relationships with teachers while simultaneously building a database of no-cost solutions."

The C.H.E.W.A.T. committee members were surprised. Maybe this wasn't an impossibility after all. Leaning in to discuss privately, the three creatures interfaced about the ramifications of letting a robot participate in the mentor program. Morcor's slimy head-shakes slowly turned into nods. PL 94-142 waited silently for a reply.

"Congratulations, Robot PL 94-142," stated Scarlax. "Because of your desire to help and proven ability to learn, we have decided to allow you to take part in the C.H.E.W.A.T mentor program. This is a first, PL 94-142, an experiment.

We believe that you can prove that working together, robot and life form, or computer and being if you'd rather, can lead to greater results for students than just the life form or just the robot working individually. You start tomorrow."

"Thank you. Thank you," PL 94-142 squeaked as she zoomed out of the room, motors whizzing and turbines humming. Tomorrow was going to be the first day of a new beginning.

■ ■ ■ ■ ■

Take Me to Your Leader: The Assistive Technology Team Leader

When the aliens attack, and you know they will, threatening to fry your brain with their death ray unless you take them to your leader, you need to be able to confidently march them down the hall, point to a room and say, "The person you're looking for is in there!" To prevent your disintegration, because these aliens will turn you into dust without even thinking about it, this person needs to be a strong leader. Someone who can talk to the aliens, try some diplomacy on their little green behinds, and, if need be, blast them back to their home world!

We aren't going to try to define every talent a team leader needs to have to keep you from ending up hauling rocks on some orange planet in a distant solar system. However, we will take a shot at defining the roles and responsibilities of the Assistive Technology Team Leader. We've broken the roles and responsibilities into three categories: Shoulds, Coulds, and Should Nots.

The Assistive Technology Team Leader should ...

- Be the single point of contact for higher-level administration

- Be the go-to person for team members when they have grievances

- Organize and run team meetings

- Consult with each team member individually at least once a year, but as much as necessary, on any topic

- Attend administrative meetings in the district pertaining to technology and policy

- Foster an environment and culture of innovation and determination

- Advocate for the assistive technology team and students with disabilities

- Be vested in the success of the assistive technology team

- Encourage and promote professional development within the team

The Assistive Technology Team Leader could ...

- Maintain the inventory

- Coordinate purchasing so that vendors have one point of contact

- Maintain a full or partial caseload

- Have no caseload

- Collect data on team initiatives

- Collect and analyze caseload data

- Collect data on internal staff development (what the team members are learning)

- Collect data on staff development workshops (what the team is providing)

- Develop the budget

- Coordinate with local, state, national, and international officials

The Assistive Technology Team Leader should not ...

- Develop overarching goals of the team

- Construct the team's initiatives

These bullets are items the team should develop collaboratively to shape a unified vision.

Oh Captain, My Captain: Team Leader Inclusion

The leader of the team might have a separate position within the district, or "leader" might just be a title within the team that does not correspond to any monetary or administrative distinction. Either way, the team leader shouldn't be a separate administrator who only sporadically attends meetings or checks in every once in a while. The leader needs to be a part of the team, not a distant figurehead with other responsibilities beyond assistive technology. This person, however selected or appointed, is the face of the team—the one who needs to be able to be diplomatic when the situation calls for diplomacy, humorous when the situation calls for humor, and tough when the situation calls for toughness. The leader should be gregarious enough to win over friends who will support team initiatives.

your social quotient

Your assistive technology team always needs a lot of help from a lot of people. People all over the school district will be assisting the team in making progress and accomplishing its goals. Most people are eager to lend a helping hand the first time you ask—but if you forget to thank them or fail to express your appreciation, the team could rapidly find itself becoming very lonely. As a rule, each year the team should assign at least one person to be the social coordinator for the team. The social coordinator's responsibility is to remember to thank everyone who has gone out of their way to help the team. They can plan birthday parties, organize gifts, buy cards and candy, and send out letters of thanks to anyone who the team deems as needing a big ol' pat on the back for helping out the cause. The social coordinator can also plan special event celebrations, such as baby showers, wedding showers, and birthdays, for individual team members. The team might want to ask everyone to contribute to a "social fund" to cover the costs of these events. Make no mistake: the social coordinator fulfills one of the most important functions of the team. It may seem like a small thing, but honoring someone's birthday can promote team bonding while also greasing the gears for future favors.

■ ■ ■ ■ ■

chapter 7

defining
responsibilities
for an
assistive technology team

With Great Power Comes Great Responsibility: Defining the Plan

Maybe it was from gamma radiation. Maybe you were born with a genetic mutation that altered your DNA. Maybe you were bitten by a genetically altered or radio-active insect. Or maybe your parents sent you on a rocket to Earth just as your home planet was about to be destroyed. Maybe you read this book. Somehow, anyway, you got your AT powers and knowledge. But with great power comes great responsibility. Whether you're the sole assistive technology trainer or just one of the members of your district's team of superheroes, you have a job to do.

Actually, you have many jobs to do—and the first one is to define everything you need to accomplish to establish the assistive technology team.

Your Granddaddy Master To-Do List

The First–Then board is a great behavioral support to introduce a student to a visual schedule. Picture symbols of the current and next activity are placed in the appropriate areas then adjusted for each subsequent activity. It can also be used as an intervention to reward a student for completing a task. For example: First: Complete worksheet—Then: Computer time. Simple and very effective. Try this same strategy with the team's master to-do list (Fig. 7.1).

Break out the interactive whiteboard if you have one, but a big ol' pad of paper will work nicely, too. As a team, sit down and make a list of all the things you need to accomplish as you move forward. This is your "Granddaddy Master To-Do List." Lucky for you, we made a start on all this work for you. Not only did we develop a list for you, but we also think we have answers to all of these questions here in this book. Be sure to discuss these as a team so that our solutions will lead to *your* solutions. If they work for us, they might just work for you.

Here are some things that should/could go on the Granddaddy in question format. Once you have created a list, prioritize the items on the list. Then, once you answer these questions, cross them off and give yourself a pat on the back. To make it easier for you to wrap your brain around, we've split the Granddaddy into two main categories—Internal Procedures and External Procedures. Internal procedures are the tasks that need to be completed by the team, for the team. External procedures are the tasks that need to be completed by the team, for other educators.

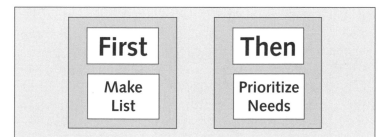

Figure 7.1 First–Then board for your Granddaddy Master To-Do List

granddaddy master to-do list

internal procedures

How will caseloads be distributed equally among all trainers?

Will each trainer have a set number of schools based on the number of special education programs in each school?

How will individual and classroom evaluations be conducted?

What data needs to be collected on assistive technology services and how will the data be collected?

How will inventory be tracked? Who will be in charge of inventory and purchasing?

How will caseloads/workloads be tracked?

How does the team learn what it needs to learn? How does the team conduct internal staff development?

When and how often will the team have team meetings?

What forms are needed and what will they look like?

What are the procedures for summer assistive technology services?

What other responsibilities does each trainer have? Who sits on committees? Who is the social coordinator? Who tracks external staff development? Who builds the website?

external procedures

How will an IEP team request an assistive technology evaluation?

How will an educator know when to request an evaluation?

How does an IEP team integrate recommendations from an assistive technology trainer into the IEP?

How can administrative support be fostered?

How will educators learn about assistive technology services?

How will trainers follow up with educators and students?

How many staff development workshops will be offered to educators?

How can the team promote awareness of its own existence to other entities in the school district?

It's Ours! We Own It: Team Power

One thing to note before the genesis of the Granddaddy Master To-Do List is that this list should be created and owned by the team. The assistive technology team leader should participate, and other higher-level administrators can be invited to participate; but ultimately, if the list is externally generated for the team, the team runs the risk of not having complete buy-in.

Let's try an analogy here to make this point crystal clear. Two similar students need assistive technology devices. One student—let's call him Jerry—doesn't have the opportunity to choose his preferred solution; he is just handed a device and told to use it. A second student—let's call her Maggie—works in conjunction with her teachers (and assistive technology trainer) to pick out a device she wants to use. If all other variables are equal, which of these two students will more effectively integrate the device? We'll place our money on Maggie, because she was given ownership in the decision. This same concept applies to the creation of the Granddaddy Master To-Do list. If the team members are given the opportunity and responsibility to develop their own policies, these individuals are more likely to value and practice those policies.

The Scenario Test Strategy:
Try It On and See If It Fits

As the assistive technology team makes decisions on all of the items on the Granddaddy Master To-Do List, it is a good idea to run those decisions through a series of scenarios. We call this strategy "scenario testing." This strategy is basically just reviewing each procedure, from start to finish, using all sorts of different scenarios. Will our procedure work for teachers of the visually impaired? For administrators? For preschool students? For students transitioning from one school to another? Will our procedure work for someone who is using low-tech strategies? For a student who needs word prediction software? For a student who needs an augmentative communication device? For a student who needs to use a pencil grip? Will this procedure work if we are working with twins when the 63 moons of Jupiter align while Orion is in the southern hemisphere during high tide? If your procedure works in every scenario, then you know you have a good solution.

how to distribute caseloads

When an assistive technology team consists of more than one person, you need to decide how to distribute the caseloads equitably. In truth, there is no way to make the caseloads absolutely equal, because there are too many variables. Every single situation is unique and presents its own challenges. So, here is our suggestion. Get a list of all of the special education positions in the district per school, not including the related service staff. Add up the number of special education teacher positions in each school and score each school with that number. Then assign each school to a specific assistive technology trainer geographically, in a way that keeps the combined school scores as equal as possible. Each time a new team member is added (or subtracted), the scores can be used to reassign schools/cases. This model provides a way of keeping the caseloads as equal as possible by keeping one parameter constant: assistive technology trainers serve all special education teachers. Furthermore, this model makes it easy for teachers to get to know their assistive technology trainer because they won't be getting a different trainer for each request. Assistive technology trainers will feel more like a part of the school, and teachers will ultimately feel more comfortable going to that single person to brainstorm strategies.

■ ■ ■ ■ ■

Team Meetings

In order for a fledgling assistive technology team to crack out of its shell, the collective minds that make up the team need to discuss exactly how they will develop into something that is going to spread its wings and soar through the sky. For the first few years the assistive technology team meetings will need to be held frequently. Initially, in fact, these meetings could be held as often as once a week. At team inception there are many policies that need to be established, both internally and externally, in order to establish a synergistic vision of purpose. Without these policies, individual trainers will be confused as to their respective roles and be left wondering what protocols are in place to help guide them through their job responsibilities. Even established assistive technology teams that have been in existence for a number of years need to meet periodically to keep everyone on the same page, solidify a collective mission, and update members on current practices. The following are a list of strategies to help you stay on track during team meetings:

Agendas. One team member should be chosen to be the agenda creator. Everyone on the team submits items to discuss at the meeting to the agenda creator. This person collects all of these ideas in the agenda for the next meeting. If it makes things easier, using an online discussion board or other online tools (such as wikis) could serve as a strategy for creating an agenda. Using an open-ended, unfiltered agenda provides everyone with the opportunity to contribute to the creation of what will be discussed at each team meeting.

Time frames. When the team is discussing a topic of great importance, it might take some time to hammer out all of the points and reach a decision that everyone can accept. Extended debate on a whopper of an agenda item might lead to fatigue with the discussion, and people will start thinking, "I don't care. I give in, because I'm tired of talking about it." This is a bad situation. Decisions based on people relenting because they're tired of the discussion will breed resentment faster than a jackrabbit on a bullet train moving at the speed of light. Everyone needs to feel like the decision that has been made is based on logic and reason, even if they don't agree with the decision.

In order to prevent this fatigue, set time frames for how long a discussion will last. If time is growing short and a decision has not been reached, then take the last 15 minutes to list everyone's ideas so you have a starting point when it is time to resume the discussion. This will provide everyone the time to consciously process what's been explored as well as allow everyone's subconscious a crack at absorbing the discussion. When it is time to revisit the discussion, everyone on the team will feel rested and the team as a whole can be assured that the decisions will be made thoughtfully and with fresh perspectives.

Minutes. Using a rotation model, everyone on the team should get to experience the joy of being the person to record the minutes of the meetings. The meeting minutes, or summary of items discussed, will serve as documentation of the decisions made. As time marches on and as decisions begin to pile up, some decisions might become cloudy and vague or be forgotten entirely by individual team members. By archiving the minutes, the team has a running record of every decision, which can be used as a source of reference. The minutes can also serve as a mini to-do list for each trainer. Using various colors to highlight portions of the minutes is a way to delineate collective decisions, stressing tasks that need to be accomplished, and to emphasize responsibilities. A final copy of the minutes can be saved in a shared location readily accessible to all team members. In the distant future, the minutes will also provide a historical perspective to reflect on team growth and accomplishments.

Divide, conquer, and share. No one person, or even an entire team, knows everything there is to know about assistive technology. The field of assistive technology is dynamic and growing. People around the globe are perpetually coming up with new tools and new ways of implementing existing tools. The best you can do is learn as much as possible whenever you can.

It's easy to get caught up in the hustle and bustle of meeting the daily needs of students and teachers. There never seems to be enough time to learn new tools and strategies. However, one way to ensure that new tools and strategies are being explored is to schedule an internal staff development time for each meeting. The team could generate a list of tools and strategies of interest to everyone on the team. This list should include an exploration of the tools already available within the school district, as these are the tools that will be most readily accessible to students and most frequently recommended by trainers. Each trainer could research an item from the list and give a short presentation about it during the meeting. Vendors or other presenters also could be invited to come and demonstrate their innovations. These short introductory trainings will give the team a working knowledge of the tool or strategy while minimizing the time it takes to prepare the presentation.

You are not alone. Most days you're out there doing your job on your own—evaluating students, providing consultations, and conducting trainings. When your team meets again, take time to share success stories during meetings. Find time to brainstorm tools and strategies that could be used for more difficult scenarios encountered in the schools. Brainstorming can create a positive energy that will inspire and encourage those in need. Always remember, especially during rough patches, that you're a team working together to provide for students who need your services. As a team member, one trainer is never alone and has built-in supports to lean on.

The team that plays together stays together. In order for a team to jell, there needs to be trust. Earning the trust of another person and learning to trust other people takes time. As in any relationship, the more quality time that can be spent fostering and caring for the relationship, the more likely it is that the parties in the relationship will begin to trust each other. If you need ideas for activities that team members could do together, watch any sports-centric movie. Any sporting movie worth its salt will have a scene where the star athlete bonds with the rest of the team during an enjoyable activity. In most cases, the scene involves the team heading to an establishment to partake of some nourishment followed by a few frosty beverages. If that sort of thing works for the team in the movies, why wouldn't it work for your assistive technology team?

Other activities that bring a team together could include golf competitions (miniature golf works if not everyone on the team can swing a five-iron), go-cart racing, movie nights, dining out at a restaurant, video game competitions, trivia contests, food drives, charity walks, orienteering, geocacheing, apple picking, hiking, rock climbing, spelunking, attending sporting events, poker nights, skydiving, synchronized snake charming, grizzly wrestling, scorpion juggling, and tornado chasing. Any activity you can think of that might be fun to do with more than one person can be organized and done together as a team. If the event is planned far enough in advance, arrangements can be made so that everyone on the team can be present to participate in the fun. Teammates who trust each other will work better together and be more willing to share thoughts, experiences, and concerns—ultimately leading to a more productive team.

ATlantis Online. Assistive technology teams produce stuff, loads and loads of stuff. Handouts for workshops, tutorials on computer applications, and assistive technology evaluations are just three examples of this stuff. Teams collect all sorts of resources, too, loads and loads of resources. Documents, spreadsheets, multimedia presentations, and websites are just some of the thousands of different resources that will be collected. Assistive technology teams generate ideas, too, loads and loads of ideas. Ideas about new workshops to offer, tutorials to create, and ways to better serve educators and students are three examples from an array of ideas generated by the team. To make sense of all of these materials and ideas, the team should develop a shared online filing cabinet to warehouse all of these informative goodies.

There are a number of different options the team can consider when creating an online warehouse. The team could establish a shared hard drive over a computer network. Folders could be created to house and organize the information. Online course delivery services, such as Blackboard or Moodle, are other resources that could be tapped. A course could be set up where everyone on the team is an instructor and able to use the tools of the course to share materials and hold discussions. Furthermore, a wiki could be an alternate online tool used to share ideas as well as materials. Whichever tool is chosen, the team should make sure that the information stored within the system is secure and backed up. With each item that is added to this information warehouse, the importance of backing up the data and keeping it secure grows. In time, this area could become a river from which the entire team drinks, and an ocean where everyone swims, and a dock where everyone can securely moor their data. Securing and backing up the information eliminates the risk of the data being swallowed by the sea and lost forever to digital undertow.

No matter what you choose, remember to give it a wickedly awesome-sounding name—something catchy and flashy that summarizes its function. You know, something like "The Drive for Cool AT People" or the "ATomic Information Zone" or even the ever-popular "ATLas Hugged." If you don't come up with a cool-sounding name you'll end up with something boring like "AT Drive." We ask you, who's gonna want to use something with a name like "AT Drive" when you could have something edgy and memorable like, "The ATackle Box" or "Stargate ATlantis"?

Advisory Committees

Somehow in every school district, decisions are being made regarding technology. Depending on the nature of these decision-making processes, there may or may not be someone speaking up to ensure that students with special needs are being considered. Members of the assistive technology team can serve as advisors to counsel those responsible for making district-wide technology decisions. If a school district uses committees to make technology decisions, then members of the team should serve as representatives on these committees, to guide them to decisions that address the needs of the widest range of students. Because an assistive technology trainer spends much of the workweek in schools, as a committee member or advisor this trainer can bring perspectives to light that might not otherwise be considered. For example, when a committee or administrator is making decisions about furniture to buy, the assistive technology trainer can suggest adjustable tables or shelves so that they are equally accessible to all. The presence of an assistive technology trainer on committees or in the role of advisor not only gives the practice of assistive technology a voice but also increases the recognition of the team as a whole. Networking with other educators from other departments allows the assistive technology team to learn about the challenges and accomplishments of others. Participation on committees provides an opportunity for every member of that committee to learn from one another.

Staff Development Workshops

One initiative worthy of consideration is developing an armada of staff development workshops. These workshops would provide educators with an opportunity to increase their knowledge about the assistive technology tools and strategies available to them, and to learn how to implement them in their classrooms. The assistive technology team can use staff development workshops to increase awareness of best-practice techniques used in special education. Furthermore, the assistive technology team can use the workshops as a conduit for advertising services to educators who were previously unaware of what the team has to offer. Even if only two or three educators attend a workshop, that is two or three more educators who now have additional tools in their work shed that will be used to reach multiple students.

When developing content for a staff development workshop, consider the goals and needs of the school, the special education department, and even the entire school district. If a school has established a goal of improving the reading abilities of every student as part of a school-wide initiative, then a workshop on available tools can be developed and strategies can be implemented to assist and enhance reading development. If "increasing the use of communication strategies" is currently a hot topic in the special education department, then consider offering a workshop on strategies to facilitate communication. If the school district has decided that positive behavior support is going to be a district-wide initiative, then offer a workshop on tools and strategies that support this initiative. Conducting staff development at a convenient time and location on topics relevant to the educators' particular situation will help to ensure high levels of attendance. Providing hands-on workshops that offer tips that can be implemented immediately into a classroom can empower educators to use additional tools and strategies. Workshops can provide an educator with the needed spark that will ignite a bonfire that will burn for years to come.

assistive technology trainer tool kit

Holy broken device, Batman! How are we ever going to help this teacher and student? Just like Batman, an assistive technology trainer needs a utility belt to carry the many gadgets needed to be ready for any situation.

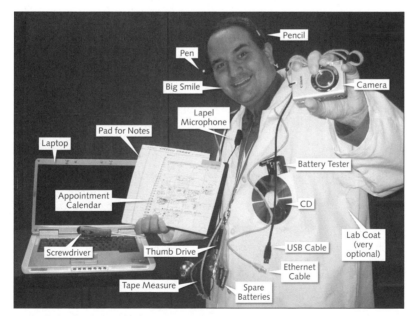

Figure 7.2 The essential assistive technology trainer tool kit

Now, the likelihood that the Joker will appear while you're out doing a visit at a school is pretty slim, so maybe you can skip the belt, but you should keep the following items with you or in your Batmobile (by which we mean your car). If you don't have these items, well, your birthday is less than a year away.

Time to hit up Commissioner Gordon (by which we mean your administrator) for some goodies:

- Screwdriver—oh heck, a whole set of screwdrivers

- Tape measure—you'd be surprised how often you need to measure a desk, door, keyboard, or room

- Calendar/planner—for scheduling hundreds of appointments

- Pad of paper—for taking notes and drawing pictures; this is a low-tech tool that allows you to do both

- Pens and pencils—well, if you're gonna have paper in your tool kit, you need to have something to write with

- Batteries, lots and lots of batteries—you always seem to need the size that you don't have

- Battery tester—time and money saver

- Battery charger—rechargeable batteries are awesome

- USB cable—portable word processors, computers, and printers all use this cable to transfer information, so it is always good to have a spare

- Ethernet cable—not every place is wireless, so this cable can help you plug into the Internet wherever you can find a spare jack

- Blank CDs—burn, baby, burn

- Digital camera—it doesn't have to be fancy; cheap will work, but you want your own because you'll be taking lots of pictures for lots of reasons

- USB thumb drive (maybe two or three)—an easier way to transfer and keep files; also useful for backing up files

- Laptop—you need one because of the amount of time you're going to spend out in the field; the greater distance you have to travel, the more imperative it is for you to use a laptop

- *The Practical (and Fun) Guide to Assistive Technology in Public Schools*— because this book is your best friend, you're going to want to keep it with you at all times. We know the authors. They're pretty nice people (well, one of them is anyway). If you meet them someday, they might even sign the book for you. There is no better way to "Oooh" and "Aaah" your friends than by showing them that you have a signed copy of a book about assistive technology!

■ ■ ■ ■ ■

Clones and Conferences: Learn, Baby, Learn

Many school districts have staff development days built into their calendars. During those days, educators participate in workshops designed to improve productivity, communication, and classroom strategies. These staff development days offer an opportunity for the assistive technology team to provide valuable information to educators. But if the team members are conducting workshops, they are prevented from attending presentations that would be valuable for their own professional development. The answer—cloning! Making duplicates of yourself is the only way to be in more that one place at a time. Just imagine: an assistive technology trainer could be presenting great tools and strategies in one room while simultaneously attending a presentation on pertinent information in the room next door.

Unfortunately, human cloning has not been perfected—at least, not to our knowledge. This means we must find our professional development elsewhere. To put it simply (and to stop cloning around), the assistive technology trainers should have an external mechanism in place for learning about new practices, products, and theories in the world of education. Attending local, regional, state, national, and international conferences is an essential way to gather such knowledge. By participating in external meetings and conferences, trainers will become acquainted with new tools as well as successful implementation strategies for those tools. When traveling to a conference, be sure to bring a few clones with you so that you don't miss any exhibits, any sessions, or any opportunities to meet new educators. When planning the initiatives for the team, funding for attendance at conferences should be a high-priority item. The wealth of knowledge that you and your clones bring back to share with the rest of the team could create a cyclone of ideas with widespread implications for future planning.

feed your brain

When zombies scrape their way out of their crypts and walk the earth they are looking for some nourishment. Oh, sure, they'll settle for any meat they can get—but if George Romero taught us anything, it is that zombies crave brains. Why is that? Is it that brains taste better than other parts of the body? No, probably not. It's probably because zombies think that if they swallow a brain, they will also absorb the knowledge packed within it. Zombie logic is simple. Eat brain, get smarter.

If you were a starving zombie working in assistive technology your natural inclination would be to eat the brains of those who know a thing or two about assistive technology. And where would a zombie think to find people with knowledge of assistive technology? Why, a college or university, of course. Unfortunately for you, only a few universities offer degrees in assistive technology so you'll need to take the initiative to seek out the knowledge in other ways. Luckily information pertaining to assistive technology is virtually everywhere you look. There is a wealth of information available if you look in the right places:

- Websites—such as Special Education Technology BC (www.setbc.org)

- Podcasts—such as the *A.T.TIPScast* (www.attipscast.wordpress.com)

- Online videos—such as the ones at Teacher Tube (www.teachertube.com)

- Webinars—such as the ones you can find at the Center for Implementing Technology in Education (www.cited.org)

- Groups in virtual environments—such as Second Life (www.secondlife.com)

- Social networking groups—such as the ones on Facebook (www.facebook.com) or Twitter (www.twitter.com)

- Conferences—such as the one hosted by the Assistive Technology Industry Association

- Listservs—such as the one hosted by the Quality Indicators for Assistive Technology Services Consortium

- Professional journals—such as the *Journal for Special Education Technology*

- Magazines—such as *Closing the Gap Solutions*

- Books—such as this one!

Assistive technology folks are also very generous with their knowledge, resources, and brains. With minimal effort you'll be able to find some excellent and helpful resources free of charge. Embrace your inner zombie and feast on the knowledge of others.

■ ■ ■ ■ ■

Know the Code: Inventory Tracking

Every item purchased or created by the school district via the assistive technology team should be labeled with a unique identifier so that it can be tracked in an inventory system. Then items can be recorded as "checked out" when distributed by assistive technology trainers to educators for implementation with a student or with a group of students. When a device is no longer needed, the educator returns the item to the assistive technology trainer, who in turn documents its return to the general inventory, allowing other trainers to perpetuate the process.

When choosing an inventory system, it's important to find one that is user-friendly and reliable. An inventory system that crashes frequently and loses data or a system that is cumbersome and awkward for people to navigate will cause more problems than it solves. The same principle that applies when selecting a tool for a student applies when selecting an inventory mechanism for the team: simplicity of use increases the likelihood of successful use. With that in mind, choose a system that everyone on the team feels comfy enough to snuggle up on the couch with, and implement it wholeheartedly.

The system could be something as simple as maintaining an Excel spreadsheet that is housed in a shared location (Fig. 7.3). Each trainer records the name of the device, the code on the device, the date it was checked out, to whom it was checked out, and, upon return, the date it is checked back in. If everyone on the team is comfortable using a database program such as FileMaker Pro or Microsoft Access, or an online spreadsheet such as in Google Docs, then a more sophisticated system can be implemented. If someone on the team or in the school district can develop a web-based database with fancy, spinning, three-dimensional visuals of each device accompanied with a sexy robotic voice that tells you how good you look when you're about to check out a device—well, then, all the better. Whether you are using an antiquated system from the Stone Age or a cybernetic tool from the future, the choice of tool doesn't really matter as long as it is reliable and easy for everyone to use.

	Code	Device Name	Student Name	Teacher	School	Date Checked Out	Date Checked In	Traine Name
1								
2	AAC4CWSL2	4 Comp. Comm. With Speech	Student 1	Teacher A	Great HS	8/30	5/5	Larry
3	EERP1	Reading Pen	Student 2	Teacher B	Awesome MS	8/30		Bar
4	CAAS12	Alphasmart 3000	Student 2	Teacher B	Awesome MS	8/30		Bar
5	VIQLOOK2	QuickLook	Student 3	Teacher C	Superb ES	9/1	5/15	Cur
6	AAC6L19	Cheap Talk 6	Student 4	Teacher D	Superb ES	9/1	5/15	Cur
7	AAC7L17	7 Level Communicator	Comments can be inserted into cells to make notes on equipment.		Stupendous MS	10/10		Mo
8	AACCT84	Cheap Talk 8 Direct			Stupendous MS	10/10		Mo
9	EECOIN11	Coinulator	Student 6	Teacher F	Terrific ES	11/18		Lisa
10	AAC6L5	6 Level Communicator	Student 6	Teacher F	Terrific ES	11/18		Lisa
11	AACOS7	One Step Communicator	Student 6	Teacher F	Terrific ES	11/18		Lisa
12	COMPOPT192	OptiQuest 19" Monitor	Student 7	Teacher G	Magnificent HS	12/15		Marg
13	COMPUSBD1	Thumbdrive	Student 7	Teacher G	Magnificent HS	12/15		Marg
14	COMPATO7	Laptop	Student 7	Teacher G	Magnificent HS	12/15		Marg
15	MSASCC9	Alphasmart Carrying Case	Student 8	Teacher H	Great HS	1/15	5/30	Larry
16	CADANA6	Dana	Student 8	Teacher H	Great HS	1/15	5/30	Larry
17	CAAS15	Alphasmart 3000	Student 9	Teacher I	Superb ES	2/22		Cur
18	MSASCC6	Alphasmart Carrying Case	Student 9	Teacher I	Superb ES	2/22		Cur
19	CAAS16	Alphasmart 3000 w Co:writer	Student 10	Teacher J	Stupendous MS	3/24		Mo
20	MSASCC11	Alphasmart Carrying Case	Student 10	Teacher J	Stupendous MS	3/24		M
	VIVPW1	Victor Vibe	Student 11	Teacher K	Great HS	4/17		

Figure 7.3 Sample equipment inventory tracking system

When choosing an inventory tracking system, consider one that's capable of aggregating important data that will provide answers to questions the team might have in the future. As the team grows and develops, it may be important to determine financial and inventory trends (Fig. 7.4). Much like determining whether a student has made progress by collecting data on the student's goals, the assistive technology team can determine its own progress by analyzing data that has been collected over a period of time. It is important to realize, however, that the primary function of the inventory system should be to maintain the current status of equipment and not for data analysis. If an inventory system has the ability to collect and sort data, those features should be considered a bonus within the system. Ease of use and reliability should never be sacrificed for data compilation.

Financial Trends	Inventory Trends
How much was spent on devices?	How many devices were broken?
How much was spent on certain types of devices?	How many devices of a certain type were broken?
How much was spent to support each school in the district?	How many devices were lost?
How much was spent per student?	How many devices were checked out per quarter?
How much was spent per disability?	How many devices were checked out based on individual evaluations?
How much was spent per assistive technology trainer?	How many devices were checked out based on classroom evaluations?

Figure 7.4 Examples of potential questions pertaining to financial and inventory trends

molly's tattoo parlor

"Yeah Windy, nice tat, dude!" said Vod, the single hit voice output device, to the touch window strolling out of Molly's Tattoo Parlor.

"Thanks, Vod. Doesn't it look sweet? Right here on my side. I'm pretty happy with it," agreed Windy as he surveyed the long line of devices waiting to enter.

"Yo! Check it!" hollered the portable word processor. "What's it say there, Windy? Whatchya get? Let's see it!"

"I can see it," declared the portable magnifier. "It says C-A-T-W-0-3. Looking good, my man!"

"Yo, Windy? You think they'll be able to get this goop off my face?" asked Vod as he shuffled

Voice Output Device

Touch Window

forward in line. "Someone slapped a sticker on me once. Then, when it got ripped off, all this gunk was left behind. They've just gotta get it off, ya know?"

Portable Word Processor

"You won't believe the stuff they have in there, Vod. Molly will clean you up so good you'll think you've got a dynamic screen on you. Trust me. I know. I just went through it and I feel just like I did when I got pulled out of my box," said Windy with a reassuring nod.

Portable Magnifier

"What about me?" shook the vibrating switch in a hopeful tone. "Did you see anything in there that can help me?"

"What's wrong with you, Vib? You look fine to me. What are you even doing in this line? You don't need a tattoo," said the enormous XY table standing behind Vib.

Vibrating Switch

"Oh, no?" said Vib, as he leaned all the way over to expose his base. "Take a look at this!"

"What? I can't see anything! What are you trying to show us?" said the XY table, sliding his tray back and forth in a shrugging motion.

"Yeah, Vib," agreed the portable magnifier. "I can't see anything—and if there were something to see, I'd be able to see it!"

"That's just it," explained Vib with a slight tremor in his voice. "There used to be a code on my rump in black marker. But I've been used so much it..., it..., it just wore away. What if I get lost? No one will know who I belong to. I could get thrown

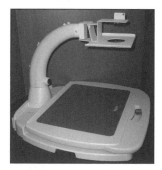

XY Table

away. Shoved in a closet. I don't want that to happen to me! Not to me!"

"Calm down, dude. Don't wig out," Windy said with a brief pat on the side. "That's not going to happen. Molly's gonna fix you right up with a tattoo just like mine. You'll be all set. Just chill out and relax, man."

Environmental Control Unit

"Yeah … yeah … yeah. I will," nodded Vib, still trembling slightly.

"Hey, Windy. Did it hurt when she gave you the tat?" asked the XY table.

"Nah, not a bit. Then again, I'm pretty used to getting poked and prodded all day, so for someone like you who just sits around hour after hour, my pretty lady, it might sting a bit," Windy chuckled.

Jelly Bean Switch

"Ha ha, very funny," chortled the XY table., "But if I were a girl I'd be called an XX table, now wouldn't I, smarty pants? Geesh. I was just asking if it hurt. Looks like sweet Molly gave you a bad attitude along with that tattoo. Sometimes you can be such a pane."

"Knock it off, you two," interrupted the environmental control unit in an authoritative voice. "It's JB's turn to go in. Good luck, JB!"

"Thanks! This is so exciting! I feel electric!" said the jelly bean switch as the parlor door swung shut behind him.

■ ■ ■ ■ ■

There are many different methods you can use to place codes on equipment. Placing a sticker on a device is one way to quickly label every device in inventory; however, over time stickers can be torn off, curl, or collect filth that is impossible to remove. Writing an inventory code on devices with permanent magic marker results in an identification system that is neither permanent nor magical. With everyday wear and tear, the ink will begin to wear off, making the codes difficult to read. There is only one sure way to prevent the code from disappearing from a device and that is to give it a permanent tattoo. Etching the code right into the device using an engraver will provide a permanent solution that will endure for the life of the device (Fig. 7.5). Of course, be careful to assess the device for tolerance to vibration before engraving. You might want to think twice before using the tattoo parlor if you have some delicate circuitry.

Figure 7.5 Code etched on device using engraver

License Detector: Software Tracking

Physical devices and hardware make up only one portion of the inventory maintained by the assistive technology team. The other major component is software. When software is purchased, what is really being purchased is a license to use that software. Every software publisher maintains rules and stipulations in their licensing structure, and it is the responsibility of the assistive technology team to ensure that these licensing restrictions are observed by the school district. Whether using a separate tracking system or incorporating software tracking into the hardware inventory process, the team should keep track of the number of licenses owned and how many are in use for every software title. One team member, possibly the team leader, could be responsible for maintaining this licensing information. This person would also be responsible for ordering more licenses as necessary.

Contact Lenses: Keep Track of Your Hard Work

It is crucial to have some collection method for recording consultations, evaluations, and trainings conducted by the assistive technology team. Tracking every contact every team member has with a student or educator will provide a way of analyzing how many people have been influenced by assistive technology. When attempting to promote the expansion of the team (or promote the very idea of creating a team), you can be ready with data about how many educators and students benefited from the services provided by the assistive technology team.

A caseload tracking system, just like an inventory system, must be both user-friendly and reliable. It is also essential that it be accessible to every trainer on a daily basis. The system might be something as simple as a color-coded Excel spreadsheet (Fig. 7.6) or as sophisticated as a web-based interface with back-end database with multitiered user roles. Assistive technology trainers should be able to enter basic data about a student as well as information about what transpired during the contact. If a teacher stops an assistive technology trainer in the hall and inquires about a student, the system should have a place to note this. The system should be able to document evaluations and differentiate them from consultations. Dates of every contact should be collected and catalogued within the system. Furthermore, the system should have a way of differentiating contacts the team has recently served from contacts that have not received services in a long time. Any system can be used as long as data can be sorted and extracted in an efficient manner.

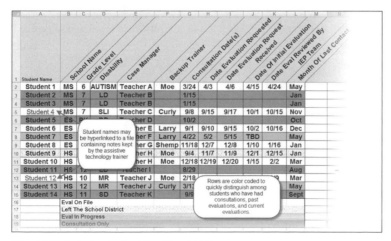

Figure 7.6 Sample caseload tracking system

Go Big or Go Home

We're not advocating fudging numbers. We're not saying you should lie if ever asked for some numbers from administrators. No, no, no. Never, never, never. We'd never advocate something like that. What we *do* advocate is keeping track of *every* contact the assistive technology team members have with teachers and students. Archives of all e-mails relevant to a service provided by the team to an educator or student should be maintained, and yearly personal calendars should be housed in a safe location in case dates of past events need to be retrieved. Every conversation and question, no matter how small or seemingly insignificant, should be tracked. You never know how one comment to a teacher might turn into a windfall of ideas or how one off-the-cuff suggestion to a teaching assistant might result in a flurry of activity. Therefore, every contact should be treated as significant and should be counted. In this way, when someone does come poking around for data, the assistive technology team will be confident that the numbers they have are as high as they can possibly be while reflecting the true nature of the job.

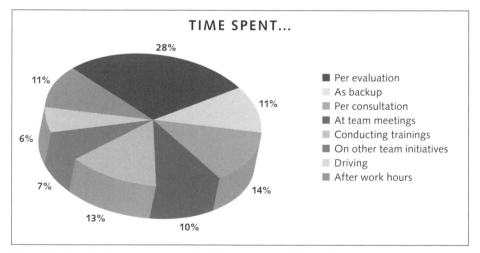

Figure 7.7 Sample pie graph showing the "time spent" breakdown for a trainer

The data collected can be used to make better decisions. If the data hasn't been collected, the team runs the risk of making choices based on intuition alone. Unless you're a cop on a television show, no one is going to listen to your gut feelings. Allocate 10 minutes at the end of each day to collect and compile the necessary data that can be analyzed later at the discretion of the team (Fig 7.7). This data could be important to building a case for the creation of an assistive technology team, promoting the growth of your team, or simply keeping the team members you have when budget cuts loom (Fig 7.8).

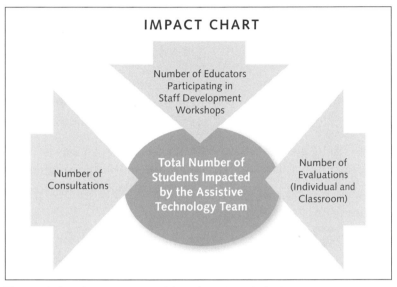

Figure 7.8 Data is necessary to evidence impact on students

Your Wish Is Granted: Funding Sources

You have to keep your eyes wide open. You can't even blink. If you blink or look away for just a split second, the tricky leprechaun will disappear forever. But now that you've caught that clever little troublemaker in your unwavering gaze, he has to lead you to his treasure. A common misconception is that leprechauns keep their gold at the end of the rainbow. This is hogwash. The "treasure at the end of the rainbow" story is nothing but leprechaun propaganda spread to lead the general public away from the real hiding spot: the special education department of a public school.

The majority of funding for assistive technology devices should come from the special education department. The budget for the special education department should include appropriations for assistive technology services and devices.

extra! extra!
read all about it!

Caseload analysis may be necessary to justify future positions, to validate position retention, to substantiate funding allocation, or even to advocate for the very creation of a team. Administrators making these decisions may associate assistive technology with other related services and therefore ask only about the number of evaluations completed by the team. If this occurs, don't provide the number of evaluations in isolation, but rather as part of a volley of information pertaining to every contact made by the assistive technology team. The number of evaluations could be a small percentage in relation to the number of consultations completed.

In this way, positions are funded through this department, devices are funded through this department, and, depending on resources available, innovative initiatives are funded through this department. And lucky for you, the wily man in green doesn't keep all his gold in one pot. All of the following are examples of where money can come from to help support the team:

Companies. Many businesses (local, national, and even international) are eager to partner with or sponsor public school initiatives. Larger companies even have programs in place through which money or technology can be acquired.

Universities. Partnerships with universities can be established to develop cohort programs that provide tuition reductions for groups of individuals who enroll in the program. Some universities may even provide equipment to school districts if student teachers are working within that school district. Universities may also provide equipment to a classroom or school district as part of a research study.

Organizations. Nonprofit organizations may have funding available that can be supplied to specific advocacy projects in public schools. Additionally, parent organizations can be invited to sponsor initiatives supporting students.

States. The department of education for the state may provide additional money to school districts for any number of reasons, such as increasing equity throughout the school districts in the state.

Individual families. Donations of equipment from families can also be a useful way of acquiring devices. For instance, if families upgrades their computers, they might choose to donate their old computers to the school district.

Grants. Companies, universities, states, or private organizations may provide money or equipment based on application and approval of a grant.

The special education department and the assistive technology team should understand that the funds appropriated in the budget for assistive technology should be sufficient to provide for the potential needs of the student population. The special education department and the assistive technology team should not rely on grants to provide the money necessary to support the needs of the student population. Grants can't always be counted on. They may fluctuate greatly over time, and like our friend the leprechaun, those funds could disappear in the blink of an eye. Money acquired from grants should be used for funding special initiatives and not relied upon to fund entire assistive technology teams. Examples of special initiatives could include the provision of interactive symbol-generating software in autism classrooms, implementation of a portable word processing cart within classrooms for students with emotional disturbance, or the integration of a personal desktop assistant (PDA) program for special educators to help with data collection. If your assistive technology team is awarded a grant, then it's not only pretty good, but also, it's pretty lucky (just like the Irish!).

ask and you shall receive

There is an old joke about a priest who prays to God every day asking to win the lottery. The priest explains all of the good things he could do with the money: bring warmth to the cold, food to the hungry, and remedies to the sick. The priest promises that he will use the money to spread hope and good tidings throughout the parish. As the months roll on with no lottery win, the priest gets more and more frustrated. Finally, the priest begs God to tell him why he hasn't won the lottery when God knows full well all the good the money can bring. Just then, a divine light shines down from a skylight window and a booming voice echoes through the halls of the church, "Buy a ticket!"

The simplest way to raise money is to simply ask for it. Raffles, bake sales, and car washes are all great fundraising ideas, but they take some planning and effort to pull off effectively. Asking for money directly is much simpler and, sometimes, even more effective. In the end, the worst that can happen is that the person or entity you are asking for money will say "no." The same goes for grants. Not all grant applications are big hairy monsters too huge to tame. In some cases the grant application is just a quick fill-in-the-blank form asking what you want and why you want it.

chapter 8

building and **promoting** an assistive technology team

Energize: Kitchen Confidential

Understandably, we glamorize gourmet chefs who start their own restaurants. These chefs bring together their passion for food, their boundless creativity, and their dedication to customer service in order to delight their patrons. It's a lot of hard work. They must present their business plan to the bank for financing, work with vendors to find the freshest ingredients, build their kitchen staff, and entice customers to dine there. But once it's established, the restaurant can become more than just a place to grab a bite to eat—it can become part of people's lives.

We urge you to keep the image of this intrepid entrepreneur in mind as you collect data, participate in committees, write proposals, and look for support in your endeavor to build the assistive technology team in your school district. There is no better feeling than being a part of the creative process. This is the reason people become educators: to impact students' lives with solutions that resonate beyond the classroom. Being on the assistive technology team will provide the opportunity to build an enduring legacy, something that will last long after you're gone. This creative spirit can be refreshing and ultimately rewarding. Energize!

Mobilize: Endurance Pays Off

There's nothing more frustrating in this world than knowing the right course of action and feeling powerless to take that course of action. You wish you had the authority or administrative support to take charge and solve the problem. Consider poor little gourmet rat Remy (à la *Ratatouille*). He had pored over cookbooks, watched all the cooking shows, and learned all the secrets of the kitchen and gourmet cooking. He knew …, he just knew … exactly how to make the perfect entrees and soups. But who wants a rat in the kitchen? A rat is persona non grata in a fine dining establishment. He couldn't make the changes to save the soup though he knew precisely how. Our intrepid rodent didn't give up though. He secreted himself into the toque of his new friend, Linguini, the novice chef, to share his knowledge and exhibit his craft and expertise. His perseverance paid off with acceptance and accolades.

You may be a part-time speech language pathologist, part-time occupational therapist, brand new special educator, 20-year veteran special educator, or even a volunteer assistive technology trainer—it doesn't matter. If you have a furry fellow hiding in your chef's hat whispering in your ear, telling you that an assistive technology team needs to be created, your course of action is clear. Even if it is a team of one, even if takes some effort, your district needs someone who is dedicated to the task of aiding other educators in making decisions about assistive technology.

You know it, maybe even a few others know it—but for some reason, even though you have told them, the people with the power to make that a reality haven't done so. This may seem like an obstacle, a hurdle, a roadblock, a 400-pound linebacker between you and what you know is needed. But it's none of those things. It's an opportunity. You know that for every door that closes, a window opens. It may take some time to collect enough of the right evidence to construct the right case to present to the right people who can make the team a reality. However, putting in the time, showing a little patience, and demonstrating all of the enduring benefits that an assistive technology team can offer will pay off in the end. Not just for you but for the students.

Persevere and look upon challenges as opportunities to triumph and add the secret seasoning needed for success. Treat your district with tasty morsels of assistive technology solutions. Cook up some delicacies to serve the hungry masses, be they rodent or not. Mobilize!

Conceptualize and Mesmerize: Strategies and Promotions

Everyone wants to be able to create like a gourmet chef. It could be something about the way the words *gourmet chef* roll off the tongue that just sounds cool and alluring, familiar yet exotic… You want to be that person who looks at an empty plate and says, "Let's put something there that fills a need, looks beautiful, smells good, and tastes great." A kitchen magician can create fantastic things with simple ingredients and simple things with fantastic ingredients. It's not just the ingredients that are important; it's the combination of science and art necessary to achieve the desired result. Chefs apply their knowledge and talents to create unique entrees that are fresh and nourishing, sustenance for the body and spirit.

In the endeavor to build and promote an assistive technology team, you get to be the chef, a position that is exciting and exhilarating. You get to be the one who combines form and function to generate something both practical and beautiful. An assistive technology team sustains and supports students and educators in unique ways, all while making people happy, too! Conceptualize and mesmerize!

Strategize and Evangelize: Assemble the Troops

Gourmet chefs create recipes and menus that meet their creative needs as well as the desires of the public. They may pretend the recipe popped out of their heads fully cooked, but just like most things, the recipe probably took a lot of trial and error and grinding away at little details to make the vision come to life. All of those preliminary details are necessary to create descriptive recipes and lovely, nourishing meals.

Detailed recipes allow anyone to pick them up, read them over, and then prepare the dish. The first step in building an assistive technology team is creating the recipe, which in this case is a plan of action stating what needs to be accomplished. The plan needs to be detailed enough that teachers, administrators, and parents can immediately recognize the benefits of having an assistive technology team. The plan needs to capture the entire vision of what you're trying to accomplish while inspiring others to "join you in the kitchen." Unlike a traditional recipe, your plan doesn't have to be on paper only. Think of it as a campaign platform or media blitz that you can use to deliver your message to others—an advertisement of your new restaurant and what it will offer. The plan should involve the initial stages of what you hope the team will accomplish during the first few years of its existence.

Before any cooking can begin, you need to select the right appliances, utensils, and ingredients for your kitchen. The second step in building an assistive technology team is finding partners in your cause. Who do you need to enlist to make the team a reality? Who needs to see the plan? Who needs to know about the advantages of a home-cooked meal? Who will stand behind you, who will stand beside you, and who will stand in your way? Strategize and evangelize!

Customize: Cater to Their Tastes

Just because you run a gourmet restaurant doesn't mean you can't learn something from the ice cream parlor down the street. It offers something that people want—a chance to sample those new exotic flavors without having to risk buying a whole scoop of something you don't like. Providing "free sample" workshops can demonstrate the impact the team can make on the school district, revealing the necessity of having a "full scoop" assistive technology team.

Always agree to provide assistance, and never say no to those who want to know more about assistive technology. Never say, "We can't do that." By offering assistance at every turn, the team will quickly build the reputation of being the "helpful assistive technology folks." Whenever there is an opportunity for the assistive technology team to do something to help the school district, seize it! Each time the team gets to showcase their abilities, they show their necessity and increase their visibility. Even if the assistance requested is not technically "your job," lending a helping hand will foster good tidings that will pay off down the road. In these instances, tactfully and subtly offering that this goes beyond your normal duties lets people know that you are cheerfully going the extra mile to help while piquing curiosity as to what your duties typically are. Examples of ways to assist others above and beyond typical responsibilities could include making visual symbols to help the school bus drivers interact with students more effectively, making data-collection forms and evaluation forms for other related services, and working with different groups of educators to establish an online information-sharing area.

Remember, the customer is always right. If someone wants it, whatever the request, deliver. If your customer wants snails with ketchup, then give 'em snails with ketchup. If a teacher wants a workshop on using graphic organizers, then present a workshop on implementation of graphic organizers. Of course, you can add your own twist (a little lemon juice, perhaps?) by suggesting strategies that will complement the workshop. "If you like graphic organizers, well, then, you've just got to try the voice record feature built right into the graphic organizing software…." Enticing folks to dine on your recipes takes time, energy, and a few free samples, but pays off in the end. Customize!

logo à go-go

We recognize cars by the emblem on the trunk. We may never have seen that particular model, but the trademark is recognizable. That's because the manufacturer has made a deliberate effort to embed that logo into your subconscious. Every company creates an emblem, symbol, or logo used to promote strength and uniqueness. Your assistive technology team can use this same method of creating an instantly recognizable symbol to make people aware of the good work being done by the team.

Developing a logo requires careful consideration, because it will be the mental image people will conjure when thinking about the team. The logo will be plastered on every form, tutorial, business card, poster, video, and any other type of visual media that is produced by the team. The logo needs to showcase the principles of the team. Consider the colors of the logo. Traditional and subdued, or edgy and eye-popping? Do the colors stand out on a document? Consider the style of the logo. Techno or organic? Does the design represent the team's unique qualities?

Now consider the slogan, motto, or catch phrase that the team will use to promote its underlying purpose. Every team of heroes has some sort of catchy slogan that is used to unite the team, inspire confidence, and sound wicked cool. The slogan should encapsulate the vision, goals, and ideals of the team. The slogan will be the team's rallying cry. Combining the slogan with the logo will solidify the meaning to anyone who sees the new oriflamme.

Once the logo and slogan are created, it's time to propagate. People love gifts and giveaways. With little cost the logo and slogan could be slapped on T-shirts, baseball hats, and coffee mugs, which could be used to promote the team (or the idea of a team). This new gear could be given away as door prizes during workshops or trainings, used to schmooze administration, or just be worn by the team on "spirit gear" Fridays. This will not only build team spirit but also serve as an advertisement of your solidarity and presence in the district. Go, team, go!

■ ■ ■ ■ ■

Centralize: The Assistive Technology Team Website

Your own assistive technology website can offer educators within your school district, as well as people around the world, information about assistive technology. Creating a dynamic website that serves as a centerpiece of the services the team offers will give anyone an easy way to learn more about the team. A website also provides a consistent way for individuals to make contact with the team. Making an effort to keep the website looking sharp is vital, because you never know when company's coming! The website is the welcome mat to the team, so it's worth spending the time to make it your pride and joy. The site can include the following:

- The team logo, slogan, and mission statement

- Definition of assistive technology

- Advertisements for upcoming workshops including descriptions and locations

- Staff school assignments

- Answers to frequently asked questions (FAQ)

- Contact information

- Curricular resources

- Spotlights on teachers who integrate assistive technology

- Podcasts

- Video tutorials

A website is a great place to store information for educators to have at their fingertips. Because there is an ever-growing number of resources available on the web, your site can offer team favorites, saving educators valuable time by giving them the resources that have already proved to be useful. Providing lists of website resources will minimize teacher surfing time while maximizing the usefulness of the site.

When you get the website looking just the way you like, and you are ready to launch the site, invite the school district to the inauguration! Entice educators to explore the site by providing an online survey that asks for opinions on each section of the site. Completed surveys could be entered into a drawing for fantastic prizes, such as a T-shirt sporting the assistive technology team logo. Centralize!

projection collection

In the process of creating the assistive technology team, you may need to spend some time collecting the data necessary to prove that the services being proposed are worthwhile (see figures below). No matter your position within the district (volunteer, part-time, full-time, part of an existing assistive technology team, or other), the process remains the same. Start by demonstrating what is currently being done, and then extrapolate from that data to show what adding team members could accomplish. Take advantage of any opportunity to demonstrate the impact the assistive technology team is having on all students, including the students in the subcategories outlined in No Child Left Behind.

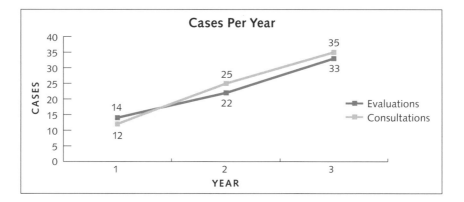

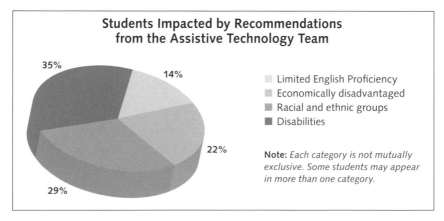

Recognize: The Competition

Every restaurant checks out its competition. What's their chef's special? How clean is their silverware? How many piercings do they allow their waitstaff to wear? What secret ingredient makes their crème brûlée so darn good? In the world of assistive technology, the same concept can be applied. Find out how neighboring school districts are managing the need for assistive technology. Whether a neighboring school district is doing much more or much less than your school district, that status can be used to your advantage. Showcasing the accomplishments (or lack of accomplishments) of another school district can provide insight as to which direction to take with your own school district.

If a neighboring school district has an established assistive technology team, ask them to share their experiences. Meet with them to "talk up" their results. The solutions they have found might be the solutions that will work for your school district. Every district is pretty new at this assistive technology stuff. By sharing with neighbors, far and wide, you will undoubtedly find a comrade with whom you can share stories, strategies, and solutions. Invite them over to your place and give them some morsels on the house! Drawing attention to what neighboring school districts are accomplishing can breed excitement in your own school district. Recognize and collaborate!

Organize and Economize: Take Stock Before You Shop

Just as the chef needs to check the fridge and cupboards for what is on hand before a meal, an assistive technology team needs an accurate list of any equipment that has already been acquired and distributed. If there has not been an assistive technology team in the past, this list might have to be compiled from scratch. When a device purchased by the school district is located, it should be coded and catalogued in an inventory system along with the other devices. Educators may have been acquiring devices from any number of sources. Past purchase orders will help provide key information about what has already been acquired around the district.

Collecting information about what assistive technology has already been purchased is valuable for several reasons. This information can be used to demonstrate what has already been spent on assistive technology so that trends for future spending can be estimated. This information also provides a baseline that can serve as a comparison point to the no-cost and low-cost services and solutions the newly anticipated assistive technology team can supply. Organize and economize!

Advertise: Seize Every Opportunity

The term "assistive technology team" has the word "technology" built right into it. Technology is a buzzword that triggers images of progress and change. People tend to support initiatives involving technology because of the perception that technology itself fosters progress and achievement. But many people might not really understand what assistive technology is all about or the impact it can have on students. These are the people you need to reach to spread the word.

Telling everyone about the tremendous impact assistive technology can have on the lives of students creates excitement about the possibilities. Joining committees that confer about student achievement, offering in-services to educators in the district, and having casual conversations in the hallways of schools will provide opportunities to bring the potential of assistive technology into view. Speaking with energy and passion about the field you love can inspire others to become energized and passionate as well. Remaining optimistic and enthusiastic is the way to make progress. Building a reputation for being helpful, resourceful, and innovative will help your team leave a lasting impression in the minds of everyone with whom they come in contact. Or, to put it simply: do good work with a smile on your face, and people will want to help you.

Once the vision is clear and all the key players in the district are known, it is time to call everyone in to dine. Shout it from the rooftops and ring that dinner bell. Come one, come all! The word will spread about how good the food is, and you will attract more customers who will return and bring friends. The yummy goodness that is the ease of applying assistive technology to students on a daily basis will begin to spread by word of mouth, which is the best kind of publicity. This will lead to more educators coming to enjoy the services of the assistive technology team. As the assistive technology team reaches more educators, more problems will get solved without becoming a burden to administration. When administrators begin to feel the load lighten, they will know they made the right choice in supporting the initiative to create an assistive technology team. Before long, everyone in the district will be spreading the news that the assistive technology team provides solutions to problems. Advertise!

overviews and orientations

One way to promote the team (or the notion of a team) and the services the team can offer is to conduct overviews on the topic of assistive technology services. An overview could be as easy as a 10-minute, informal discussion at a staff meeting. It doesn't need to be a big fancy production with glitz and glamor. A simple "let's chat" may do just the trick for letting people know what the team has to offer. The overview should be repeated each year at each school to as many educators as possible, because staff changes in a school from year to year. Each year new updates and initiatives can be shared with the staff as a way to let them know that the team exists to work for them and their students. In addition to holding these overviews at each school, the team can make guest appearances at related service staff meetings, parent resource centers, and administrative meetings. In fact, the team can offer to do an overview for any group of educators in the district, such as librarians, consulting teachers, or teachers of students with limited English proficiency.

Offering orientations on the topic of assistive technology is another way to promote the team and the services the team can provide. Orientations should include a brief review of the history of assistive technology and the legislation driving it. Engage the audience by including activities that demonstrate the purpose of different devices, from no-tech to high-tech. Don't be afraid to make the orientation entertaining. The more entertaining the show, the longer the messages embedded in the show will reside in the consciousness of the audience. Go ahead and give your audience a souped-up, slam-bam, hyper-charged presentation that includes special effects, fancy multimedia, and audience participation.

Fraternize: Enlist Student Support

Restaurants design their ambience and menus to attract a certain type of patron. You've been successful attracting educators. When promoting the team, it is easy to recognize that getting the support of other educators is necessary for the growth of the team. Mobilizing adults can bring forth change. But you must also bring students, the other group served by the assistive technology team, to your table. Motivating students to support assistive technology can provide an entirely separate energetic force to help promote team initiatives. By demonstrating devices and adaptations on Career Day, the assistive technology trainer might invigorate some students to get involved in assistive technology. An Assistive Technology Club can be created at any school level and sponsored (or co-sponsored) by an assistive technology trainer. The following is a list of activities students in an assistive technology club can support:

- Adapt classroom and curriculum materials for different learners

- Offer trainings on software to their educators

- Participate in interscholastic competitions centered on ways to use technology to assist others

- Produce podcasts and videocasts on topics that help differentiate instruction

- Visit special education classrooms to help peers with special needs use technology

- Build interactive activities that engage other students

Students can use their creativity and ingenuity for the benefit of the entire school district. Challenging students to develop innovative strategies and activities to assist others helps to build a better, stronger society. Furthermore, students who participate in an assistive technology club can add their active participation in the club when applying for admission or scholarships for higher education or jobs in the workforce. Through the guidance of the assistive technology team, student energy can be harnessed and redirected to the benefit of all. Fraternize!

poison

Some chefs are true alchemists, turning simple ingredients into a tasty treasure. But being alchemists, they might be tempted to lure customers back to the restaurant by adding a little something from their potions cabinet to the food. What should they choose? Truth serum? A healing elixir? A love potion? Perhaps a bitter poison?

Here's a hint—stay away from the poison! There's nothing that drives people away faster than toxins in their food. Focusing on the negatives rather than the positives will spoil everyone's appetite. The following is a list of phrases that might all be true but should never be spoken because they act like poison to both the speaker and the listener:

"I'm busting my hump volunteering here, something's gotta give!"

"I can't continue at this pace."

"I think I'm gonna quit."

"I can't keep up with the demand."

"You're just going to have to wait."

"I feel burned out."

"I don't care."

Sure, the squeaky wheel gets the grease, and generating pity can sometimes be a useful strategy to get people to take action—but there is a better way. When someone sees achievement against incredible odds, they feel compelled to contribute to the effort. If you can demonstrate that successes are happening with little or no support, people will want to become part of the great work being done to build upon those successes. Choose the love potion instead. Nothing brings people back to a restaurant faster than knowing the food will make them feel good.

■ ■ ■ ■ ■

Utilize: Enlist Parent Support

Restaurants may employ an individual, or several individuals, to pose as happy customers enjoying themselves in the establishment. These individuals might laugh heartily, pat their bellies in contentment, and moan loudly in pleasure as they take each bite. Servers might make a circuitous route around the floor of the restaurant passing table after table holding a tantalizing dessert at eye level before letting it rest strategically in front of a wide-eyed plant acting like a customer. Some might call these psychological tricks underhanded or dastardly. Others might call them clever and ingenious. Whichever the case, the fact that these techniques work to achieve the desired outcome cannot be argued. Similar promotional techniques can be used when attempting to develop or promote an assistive technology team. Parents who have witnessed changes in their child's achievement due to assistive technology can be incredible allies in the effort to promote the assistive technology team. These parents could be encouraged to address administrators privately and publicly about the advantages of having or expanding the assistive technology team. No group rallies to a cause quite as fast as parents advocating for services for their children. Utilize!

Fantasize, Visualize, and Actualize: Future Visions

Now that your restaurant is off and running, well on its way to becoming the most popular eatery around, almost bringing in more customers than it can handle, it's time to start thinking about expansion. Let your imagination take hold and shoot for the moon! Onward and upward!

When visualizing the future, where do you see the assistive technology team? Not just in a year or two years, but what about ten or fifteen? Could there be a dedicated assistive technology trainer in each school in the district? Could a techno-wizard be included on the team to manage hardware and software maintenance? Could an entire lab be constructed where the team could test software and conduct workshops? Be ready with possibilities and potential initiatives when budget time rolls around. Draft the ideas and plant the seeds now so that they have a chance to grow. Know where you want to go with your team and chart a course to get there. With your data and your stellar reputation, the sky is the limit! Fantasize, visualize, and actualize!

chapter 9

working with
instructional technology

The AT Zipper:
Pulling AT and IT Together

For many years the world of education was split into two entities known as Special Education and General Education. In the past, these entities acted like two positively charged magnets—repelling each other whenever they tried to come together. In the present, these two entities are woven together to create a tapestry that is not only brilliantly colorful but warm was well. Concepts such as integration, team teaching, universal design for learning, and differentiating instruction have claimed a foothold

the times, they are a-changin'

Come gather 'round teachers
Get in the zone
And admit that the students
Around you have grown
And believe when we tell you
You can't do it alone
If your time to you is worth spendin'
Then you better start learnin'
To text on your phone
For the times, they are a-changin'

Come computers and printers
Turn them on and begin
Flip up the screen and plug it on in
Every student can use them
wasting potential's a sin
And use them both now
Don't waste ink that's within
Introduce it now so later they win
For the times, they are a-changin'

Come network technicians
Please heed the call
We need your help
To get things installed
There is the computer
Over by the back wall
It's not just for one
But will be used by all
The students will need it
Starting early this fall
For the times they are a-changin'

(continued)

in classrooms. The line separating what makes up a "general education teacher" and a "special education teacher" is beginning to blur. Mottoes such as "We're all special education teachers" or "We're all educators and we're all special" are resounding messages of solidarity behind the cause of "Education for All."

The "Education for All" concept spreads from the top down as an administrative philosophy as well as from the bottom up with teachers working together within classrooms to ensure that every student is successful. These two directions present challenges for a school district's instructional technology department when they must implement computer hardware and software models that meet the needs of all learners. The task of ensuring that the computers and computer peripherals placed within a classroom will meet the needs of all the students while still adhering to budgetary constraints is daunting when you consider the variety of learners that make up a school district.

The assistive technology team can assist the instructional technology department with the task of selecting technology that meets the needs of all learners. By establishing a partnership, the assistive technology team can work with instructional technology to ensure that the implemented software titles are accessible to as many students as possible. Assistive technology can collaborate with teachers to provide solutions to the students who may require additional technology in order to access software. Working together, assistive technology and instructional technology can provide a well-rounded matrix of software with features that maximize the number of modalities a student has available to acquire information. In this way, the assistive technology team acts like a zipper between special education and general education to ensure that the tools being implemented by instructional technology meet the needs of as many students as possible.

the times, they are a-changin'
(continued)

Come principals and admin
Please lend a hand
Lead us on now
To technology land
The teachers and students
Heed your command
The equipment is rapidly agein'
Please support them now
As best as you can
For the times, they are a-changin'

The objective it is clear
The goal it is cast
Treat everyone equal
No one is last
Teach them all now
We've been given that task
There's no benefit to waitin'
And every student grows
The question's how fast
For the times, they are a-changin'

partying it up

In order to foster a relationship with the instructional technology staff, the assistive technology staff could invite them to social functions such as ice cream socials, pizza parties, and potluck luncheons. Invitations to after-work events such as golf tournaments, happy hours, and holiday parties let the instructional technology department know that the assistive technology team is extending a hand to build a cooperative relationship. During the events, the assistive technology team could make sure to mingle and talk to as many folks from instructional technology as possible. Face-to-face social networking, within the arena of appreciating the work being done, will strengthen relationships, resulting in improved overall service for students.

This Is a Test, and Only a Test: Software Evaluation

The instructional technology department works to build a network of computers in the school district that is reliable, efficient, and secure. Considering the amount of time and energy that go into constructing such an environment, coupled with the amount of people relying on the stability of that environment, instructional technology cannot afford to risk installing a rogue piece of software that may cripple the network. Therefore, software needs to be thoroughly tested before being installed on computers that are connected to the network in order to guarantee that it functions properly on the network and that, when installed, it performs as promised without interference from, or interfering with, other software titles.

During the testing phase of software deployment, the assistive technology team can assist the instructional technology department by explaining the functions of the software titles and the reasons for their use. If they understand how students will use the software, the instructional technology professionals will be better able to test the software in a practical way. For example, if the instructional technology department is testing a screen-reading software title, such as JAWS, it might not be immediately apparent that the software is used for individuals with visual impairments and, as such, might require a keyboard shortcut for activation. This information will be useful to the instructional technology department's testing process and help guarantee the creation of an appropriately functioning keyboard shortcut.

If software passes inspection by the instructional technology department, it can then be slated for installation. If the software does not pass inspection, two choices exist. One option would be to work toward altering the software in such a way that it does not harm the network. In some cases, instructional technology can make alterations during installations that allow the software to play nicely with the network. In other cases, the assistive technology team can facilitate conversations between instructional technology and the software manufacturer to provide solutions for the mutual benefit of all. The second option would be to look for different software, ideally a software title that serves the same function and does not have network compatibility issues.

temptation in the garden of installation

The snake slithered along the branch waving the computer disk over the head of the two assistive technology trainers. "Take this disk and inssstall it," hissed the snake, "for it isss full of knowledge!"

"Um, really, snake?" said the first assistive technology trainer. "I'd love to install it but you see, I was told that we're not allowed to. Sorry, but no."

"Oh come on!" said the second assistive technology trainer. "It's just one piece of software. I want to see what's on it."

"Yesss," urged the snake, lowering the disk, "take the disssk and inssstall it. You will sssee that it will help ssstudentsss."

"Something doesn't seem right about this," said the first trainer, beginning to turn away. "What if we hurt the computer?"

"Hurt the computer?" laughed the second trainer. "How are we going to hurt the computer? It's a computer, not a fuzzy little creature running around in the garden. It can't be hurt! Let's have that disk!"

"Here it isss," said the snake, uncoiling a bit further and dropping the disk just inches from the second trainer's outstretched fingertips. "The sssoftware isss very ssspecial. Very ssspecial indeed."

"Listen," interrupted the first trainer. "It's not that we don't trust you, but there are rules that we are supposed to follow. There are all sorts of things that could go wrong. The computer could crash, or even worse the entire network could crash. We'd be blamed. People would get angry and we could be banished. I want to help the students as much as the next person, but I think we should follow the protocols and…"

"You've got to be kidding!" said the second trainer, snatching the disk from the snake. "None of that is going to happen. You said it yourself. You want to help the students. Well then, help them. Stop standing in the way of progress. Geez, it's just one lousy, stinking piece of software. Just install it already. If you don't, it obviously means that you don't really want to help students."

"Ssstudent needsss are mossst precccciousss," agreed the snake, with a reptilian smile. "Insssstall the disssk. You will sssee how it will sssupport ssstudentsss and give them sssuccesss."

"Well, I guess when you put it that way," relented the first trainer, "it sort of makes sense to get the tool to the student faster. All right. I'm in. I want to help, not hinder. Let's do it."

"Excellent! It's about time!" hooted the second trainer, sliding the disk into the drive. "And away we go!"

It took only a moment for the error message to appear on the screen that read "Corrupted File. System Destroyed." And it took only another moment for the faces of both assistive technology trainers to turn bright red. The computer blinked once and went blank just as the snake disappeared into the underbrush of nearby bushes. Before the assistive technology trainers could even think about running after the serpent, a voice boomed from the speakers of the computer. "Do you know what you have done? You have attempted to install software even after you were told that you were not permitted to do so. The software has destroyed this computer along with several others. All of your privileges are revoked and your previous accomplishments forgotten. You are hereby banished from this garden and can never return. Leave now." Deep within the computer something whirred, sputtered once, and then fell silent forever.

As the assistive technology trainers walked away, the second began to speak, only to be cut off by the raised index finger of the first. "Save it," said the first trainer angrily. "All I wanted to do was help students. Now you tell me—just how are we supposed to help students if we are banished?" The second assistive technology trainer had no reply.

■ ■ ■ ■ ■

As a rule, the assistive technology team should not install software on computers that access the school's network. You do not want that responsibility, no matter how computer-savvy you are. There are just too many opportunities for complications to arise. Instead, work together with the network computer expert(s) responsible for maintaining the computers for the school or district to develop a system where the assistive technology trainer can request installations through the instructional technology department. Even if it's faster to have the assistive technology trainer perform the installation, it is far better to wait to have a network specialist do it.

Solutions for All: Add UDL to the Network

Learning about the existence and applications of new software titles is a continuing responsibility of the assistive technology team. Whether browsing websites, lurking on discussion boards, attending conferences, or flipping through magazines, assistive technology trainers educate themselves about tools that have potential. Every once in a while the team may find a gem that sparkles so brightly that it demands closer attention. Then, after analysis and in-depth scrutiny, a realization hits that this software title might fill a void in the software existing on the computer network. In this scenario, the assistive technology team can propose the purchase and installation of such a software title across the district.

For example, if a school district is lacking software that provides auditory feedback, the assistive technology team could spearhead an initiative to find comprehensive software to perform that function. The assistive technology team could collect and analyze a series of software titles, inspect them for functionality, and compare licensing and cost structures. The team would then submit a proposal to administration for consideration. If approved, the assistive technology team would assist the district in implementing a training plan and offer workshops to assist educators and students in the integration of the software into daily classroom lessons. When the assistive technology team is on the lookout for software solutions that fill gaps in the district, the team promotes the education of every student, not just those in special education.

freeware

Not all software solutions are expensive. In fact, there are a number of free software titles (freeware) or add-ons to existing software titles that can be downloaded from the Internet to help differentiate instruction. Furthermore, because these are free titles, if a student has a computer with Internet access at home, parents could download and install these same programs, providing the student with the same tool across the home and school environments. The following is a list of examples of freeware that could be added to a school network.

Talking Calculator
www.readingmadeez.com/products/TalkingCalculator.html

Talking calculators are great educational aids in math class. This particular one can be expanded to full-screen and provides auditory narration to the calculation entered. The step-by-step calculations can also be copied and pasted into a word processing document. It is a fully functional talking calculator for all basic math functions, with multiple areas of display for the current total, the history of current multistep calculations, and any numbers in memory.

ReadPlease
www.readplease.com

This is free text-to-speech software for Windows operating systems. There are paid versions with more options, but the free version has a variety of voices to choose from; adjustable font size and speed; as well as choices of font, highlighting, and background color. It will read aloud any text that can be pasted into the text window. ReadPlease is handy for readers struggling with document or web page content and can be used as a self-editor for written compositions.

Audacity

http://audacity.sourceforge.net

Audacity is open-source software for recording and editing sounds. It is available for Mac OS X, Microsoft Windows, GNU/Linux, and other operating systems. Audacity is an audio recording, editing, and mixing program offering special sound and mixing effects for several tracks simultaneously. The only memory limitations are those of the computer on which the software is installed. Recordings can be exported in several file formats, including MP3 files, and are readily editable to be used for creating podcasts, recording lessons or assigned reading assignments, brainstorming, pre-writing, measuring and maintaining a record of reading fluency, or rehearsing and self-editing oral presentations.

PowerTalk

http://fullmeasure.co.uk/powertalk

PowerTalk automatically speaks the text on any presentation or slide show running in Microsoft PowerPoint for Windows. PowerTalk is able to speak text as it appears on the screen and can also speak hidden text attached to images. This permits a reader struggling with curricular vocabulary to hear a narration of not only PowerPoint presentations but also lecture notes or presentations available from a variety of sources on curricular topics.

WordTalk

www.wordtalk.org.uk

WordTalk is a plug-in developed for use with Microsoft Word. It will speak the text of the document and will highlight it as it goes. It contains a talking dictionary to help decide which word spelling is most appropriate. It is accessible in the toolbar and is customizable, allowing adjustment of the highlight colors, the voice, and the speed of the speech.

■ ■ ■ ■ ■

AT and IT Roles Overlap

Every school has a technology "go to" person. In some schools, there is a dedicated position with a title such as "technology teacher," "technology resource teacher," or "instructional technology resource teacher." Other schools might simply have a staff "guru," who is relied upon to answer questions about technology. No matter what their formal title, one of their roles is to provide technology solutions and training to students and educators. This role is bound to overlap the role of the assistive technology team. Because of these common responsibilities, it is important for the assistive technology trainer to work closely with the technology resource teacher to minimize duplication of service and support endeavors, while maximizing solutions for all students.

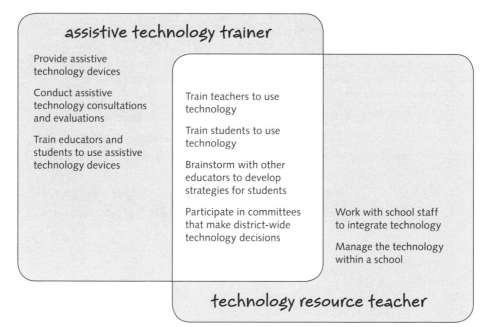

assistive technology trainer

Provide assistive technology devices

Conduct assistive technology consultations and evaluations

Train educators and students to use assistive technology devices

Train teachers to use technology

Train students to use technology

Brainstorm with other educators to develop strategies for students

Participate in committees that make district-wide technology decisions

Work with school staff to integrate technology

Manage the technology within a school

technology resource teacher

Figure 9 Overlapping roles of the assistive technology trainer and the technology resource teacher

part 4

assistive technology
services

chapter 10

assistive technology
consultations

It Begins with a Struggle

Every great story has conflict. Conflict leads to action, which leads to resolution, which leads to a happy ending. Conflict comes in different forms. Sometimes the hero faces an archnemesis, such as Spiderman versus the Green Goblin, or the Three Little Pigs versus the Big Bad Wolf. Maybe the hero must face some sort of environmental challenge, as in the films *Twister, Armageddon,* or *The Poseidon Adventure.* The protagonist might also face off against inner demons as in the film *A Beautiful Mind.*

In the story of a student working toward educational goals, the conflict (or problem, or barrier, or roadblock) is anything that is hindering or even preventing that student from meeting these goals. It is the job of the assistive technology trainer to aid the members of that student's educational team in determining strategies that will result in a happy ending to that story. This conflict should be the only thing that brings an assistive technology trainer into that student's story. That line bears repeating, so let's say it again in another way:

> The only time a student needs assistive technology is when that student is struggling to meet educational goals.

If the student is not experiencing difficulty, then assistive technology is not necessary. The instant the student begins to demonstrate difficulty meeting educational goals is the time to start thinking about what technology might help. When the student continues to struggle and the educator working with that student is out of ideas, it's time for that educator to pick up the phone, type an e-mail, or open the window and yell really, really loudly to contact the assistive technology trainer. If the student is making progress, then let sleeping dogs lie, don't rock the boat—just plain leave things alone.

Numbers as Indicators: Specific Data Is the Only Way

There are times when members of an educational team may not agree about whether a student is experiencing conflict. The student may be demonstrating one set of behaviors in one environment and different behaviors in another, each having an impact on that student's education. This sort of discrepancy may make it difficult for an educational team to know what direction to take. One strategy that provides a compass to the lost educational team is concrete, empirical, quantitative data. For example: How long does a student attend to a writing task when able to first brainstorm using voice recording? Is the resulting paragraph more robust? Are there longer sentences? More details? Does a particular seating assignment away from distracting peers, fluorescent lighting, or noisy air conditioning promote increased attention to task? Similarly, does offering a student a choice of methods to complete an assignment increase productivity given the same amount of time? It is so much easier to make decisions and so much harder to dispute a case when steadfast numbers are presented. None of this wishy-washy "He does well in …" or "He seems to have trouble with …" nonsense, either. Cold, hard numbers mean way more than gut feelings and hunches when it comes to making tough decisions that impact the life of a student. If the data indicates that a student is struggling to meet an educational goal, then get on the horn to contact the assistive technology trainer for suggestions. If the data indicates that a student is *not* struggling to meet an educational goal, then pat that student on the back, say, "Great job! Keep up the good work!" and move onto to another student who is actually struggling.

Preventive Maintenance versus Preventive Measures

It is a good idea to check the dam every once in a while to make sure there are no cracks. It's an even better idea to put a thin coating of concrete on that dam every once in a while to prevent cracking. It is a waste of time, money, and space to build another dam 100 yards away just in case the first dam breaks.

It is a good idea to have the conversation "Everything is going great—what can we do to make sure it continues to go great?" but that shouldn't include new technology unless a known conflict is looming. Even then, it's better to wait to see how the student handles the roadblock rather than assuming there will be a struggle. Unless a student has a degenerative impairment, there is no crystal ball predicting the educational demise of a student who is being successful. If the strategies and tools in place are working for the student, then *yippee-ki-yay!* It is unnecessary to have a conversation about implementing additional strategies if the current system is working.

The Comfort Zone: Defense against Complacency

You're traveling through a consistent dimension—a dimension not only void of insight and creativity but lacking an open mind—a journey into a stagnant land whose boundaries are etched by routine. That's a signpost up ahead. Your next stop: The Comfort Zone!

Most teachers (and individuals in general) live within their technology comfort zone. From day to day, month to month, and year to year, people tend to use what is familiar to them and employ the same tools that they have become comfortable using. For example, a teacher will create a poster with Microsoft

Word instead of Microsoft Publisher if that is the program the teacher is most comfortable with (not even an expert, just comfortable). Along those same lines, if a person who has a working knowledge of Microsoft Excel is presented with the challenge of managing multiple sources of data, that person will tend to use Excel rather than learning Microsoft Access or some other database program. In general, this works for educators. They are productive and build confidence with a few tools at a time. If a student starts struggling, these familiar tools will be the ones a teacher will turn to first to help that student.

There are only two times when educators are forced out of their technology comfort zone. The first is if the tool they are accustomed to suddenly vanishes. For example, if an educator is an accomplished user of AppleWorks on Mac computers but the entire district shifts to a Windows-based platform with Microsoft Word, that educator must learn something new. The second time is when a student is struggling and every familiar tool or strategy has been tried. The educator is then faced with both locating and learning new technology. The problem is that the number of strategies that can be used to assist struggling students is infinite. This is when educators must use their insight, creativity, and open-mindedness and consult with their assistive technology trainer. This consultation can help develop strategies, usually using tools that are already available in the student's customary environment.

The Person with the Imaginary Office: Become a Regular

It is very likely that the assistive technology team and any associated assistive technology trainer will not have an office in a school. Unless the school is Hogwarts, space is usually too limited to justify an onsite office for an individual who isn't there full time. However, if the assistive technology trainer were housed in a school, teachers could just walk on down the hall during a planning period, brainstorm with the trainer, and walk away from that conversation with new ideas for tools and strategies to try with a student.

Just consider that for one moment. At 8:00 a.m. a student is struggling to meet an educational goal, and an educator has tried everything he or she knows to assist that student. At 10:00 a.m., the educator informally talks to the assistive technology trainer, who in turn offers a handful of strategies using technology already existing in the school. By noon, that student is trying a new strategy based on suggestions from the assistive technology trainer. There was no paperwork involved, and the potential for student achievement is realized rapidly without the delay associated with a formal evaluation.

Encourage educators to think of the assistive technology trainer as the person who has an imaginary office down the hall. If educators brainstorm with the assistive technology trainer in the same way they brainstorm with their friends at lunch, they will find new strategies and new tools they can use to benefit all students without having to complete additional paperwork.

Anytime any educator or student approaches an assistive technology trainer with any question, this is called an "assistive technology consultation." It is not documented in the IEP. It is not written as a service on any formal document. It's just a term the assistive technology team can use to represent any informal contact with an educator or student.

Taming Our Nemesis

www.bitstrips.com

action plan committees

The assistive technology trainer has knowledge of tools and strategies to help students who are struggling to meet educational goals. Although the trainer's primary responsibility is to provide tools and strategies for students with disabilities, in many cases these same solutions could be used to assist *any* student who is struggling, not just students who qualify for special education services. There are students, lots of students, who struggle in school. School districts use different methodologies to assist students who demonstrate learning difficulties.

These methodologies generally center on a committee of concerned individuals to develop some plan of action. Assistive technology trainers could serve as adjunct advisors to these committees by providing insights about technology that could be used to assist the struggling student.

Because the majority of funding for an assistive technology team comes from the special education department, the assistive technology trainer may be limited to making recommendations using technology that already exists in the educational environment. That is, the assistive technology trainer might not have the ability to purchase or provide additional technology because funds from the special education department are reserved for students with disabilities. Even if the trainer is restricted in this manner, the trainer can always brainstorm with educational teams to find solutions using technology that already exists in the student's environment. If it is determined that a student who does not have a disability needs some piece of technology that does not already exist in the educational environment, then these tools could be purchased using funds from a source other than special education.

■ ■ ■ ■ ■

Tools at Hand: It's Not "What's Out There," It's "What's In Here!"

A statement assistive technology trainers hear all too often from educators requesting an evaluation is, "I just wanted to see what's out there to help this student." For sure, there will be times when the assistive technology trainer will need to turn to some outside resource in order to meet the needs of a student, but that step comes after exhausting all of the possible resources available within the school. School districts are filled with resources that go untapped everyday. Battalions of tools and strategies, eager to be discovered and put to use, live inside classroom cabinets and inside the circuitry of digital devices. As if in a twisted game of hide and seek, assistive technology trainers help teachers search for these tools and strategies to put them to work in meeting the needs of students. Before looking for what's "out there," begin by looking for what's "in here." Olly, Olly, Oxenfree!

Locating and implementing tools that are already available within the school provides students with the tools that are least restrictive. That is, a student is not restricted to using a unique outside resource but is instead learning to use a tool that could be used by peers in the school. Oh, yeah—and it probably costs less, too. We wouldn't want to forget that point. Implementation of a tool that is already available in the student's environment provides a "Johnny on the spot" solution that is least restrictive and costs less, all without a lick of paperwork.

the great eight

Here are eight lesser-known tools and strategies for assistive technology solutions using Universal Design for Learning principles already available in most classrooms.

1. High Contrast Features

For Windows. By using the keystroke combination Left ALT + Left Shift + Print Screen, the Windows computer display is reconfigured for high contrast and easier visibility. Preferences can be set by individual users to display larger font sizes and background color for any websites or files displayed.

For Macintosh. Mac OS X includes flexible system-wide adjustments for controlling the characteristics of what is displayed on the screen. Contrast can be adjusted by switching the screen to white-on-black or black-on-white or set anywhere in between using a slider.

2. PhotoAlbum

The PhotoAlbum function in PowerPoint on PCs provides a way to quickly and easily make a slide presentation of gathered photographs. It offers several design templates, picture layouts, and frame styles with or without text boxes and captions. No more resizing a giant photo of the close-up of someone's eyebrow to include in a PowerPoint slide. One dialog box guides the user through a simple process of inserting, arranging, and orienting photos, giving quick results. The ability to add formatted text boxes makes it the perfect choice for a great variety of projects including the review of curricular images, community-based instruction lessons, field trips, school orientations, and on-the-spot lesson review. Students are engaged and responsive to their own photographs, and the result of their work is a permanently available recording that can be used to review activities and curricular concepts. For Mac users, iPhoto offers a slide show component, but you would have to use iMovie to add captions. There are also some PhotoAlbum add-ins available to produce similar results.

3. Visual Schedules

Providing students with a pictorial representation of the activities of their day offers necessary structure and expectations in a concrete format. Students will learn by manipulating these images (e.g., moving a picture symbol to a "finished" column) that there are distinct limits to their participation and expectations. Visual schedules also assist in the knowledge that a nonpreferred activity is temporary and can be immediately rewarded by an alternate activity or one of their choosing. Similarly, visual schedules can provide cues to step-by-step directions for routine activities such as washing hands and morning classroom routines (Fig 10.1).

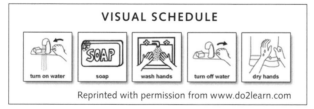

Reprinted with permission from www.do2learn.com

Figure 10.1 Photos, picture symbols, or text can be organized in a sequence of expectation. Students can manipulate these symbols as activities are completed.

4. Text-To-Speech

Macintosh computers have text-to-speech functions as part of the operating system through System Preferences. You can set up a keyboard shortcut to initiate Speech. As an alternative, you can select text you want your Mac to speak, then choose Speech from the application's Services menu. Recent Macintosh operating systems also provide a fully functional screen reader, called VoiceOver, with a synthesized voice and many features to provide access to users with low vision. Narrator, the Windows equivalent to

VoiceOver, can be located in the Accessibility Features. Auditory feedback of text displayed on a computer provides help to those struggling with reading vocabulary. It also offers students a method to self-edit their work when they review their written compositions.

5. Social Situation Stories

Students may need to be taught how to behave or react in certain situations. Social situation stories offer a script to provide this insight. The situation, as well as expected behaviors, should be described along with possible contingencies should the experience not go according to plan. These can be augmented by picture symbols to assist in comprehension or created digitally for review on a device or computer.

6. Insert Sound Feature in Microsoft Word

A voice recording can be inserted into a Microsoft Word document on PCs by using Insert > Object > Wave Sound, which brings up the sound recorder. This feature can provide students with the opportunity to record their thoughts on a topic before they begin the daunting tasks of composition and typing. Educators can also use this feature to offer helpful hints or clues in an assignment or exam. This can also be a quick way for educators to record spelling reviews or tests for those students who may have missed the initial instruction.

7. Graphic Organizing Templates

Graphic organizers, also called mind maps and story webs, can help students classify ideas and communicate more easily and effectively. A graphic organizer can offer structure to that scary blank page for writing projects. It can help in problem solving, decision making, studying, planning, research, and brainstorming. There are a number of free online graphic organizers as well as some dandy software programs that provide a nice variety of applications. Some of these programs allow the user to incorporate graphics and voice recordings, both of which are helpful strategies in scaffolding the assignment to meet the varying needs of students. Some can also incorporate graphics for cues. A search engine will help you find a nice assortment with one sure to meet your student's needs.

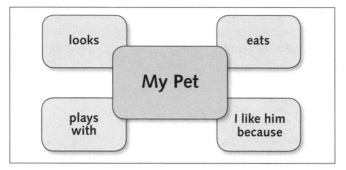

Figure 10.2 Sample graphic organizer

8. Pacing Boards for Communication

This marvelous strategy is ingenious in its simplicity. The pacing board is a visual–motor cuing system that uses dots, picture cues, or word cues to help students learn the concept of multiword combinations. The pacing board provides a visual representation of the units of speech and can be faded to just include physical prompts. For example, if you would like a student to use the full sentence "I want juice" rather than "Juice," three circles could be used and pointed to while modeling the sentence. The student, in turn, uses the prompts to repeat all three words (Kumin, Councill, & Goodman, 1995).

■ ■ ■ ■ ■

I'll Think of Something …

Failure is not an option. There is no such thing as an "unwinnable" situation. To emphasize the point that contacting the trainer before requesting a formal evaluation is *never* a waste of time, it is imperative that at least one (more if possible) tool or strategy be agreed upon before the end of the consultation. When an educator comes to you, the assistive technology trainer, with a problem, there should always, always, always be something you can recommend that is available in the customary educational environment. There will always be something that the educator looking for assistance hasn't tried. There will always be some tool or strategy that can be attempted, even if it is only used temporarily. Like a sequence in an action movie where the hero is trapped and facing impossible odds but still makes an incredible escape, so goes the assistive technology consultation. The assistive technology trainer should never leave a consultation without providing at least one strategy that can be tried, even if it isn't *the* strategy that will ultimately help meet the outlined goal.

the parent trap: when to keep parents in the loop

"Geez, I really liked Mrs. Nurky before that meeting. She's always been so helpful and communicative but, whoa … after that meeting I'm starting to think twice," said Jason's mom to Jason's dad as they pulled out of the school parking lot. They had just met with Jason's teacher and the AT trainer to discuss Jason's writing.

"I know what you mean. She's always good about writing in Jason's homework journal, and she always returns our calls—but that meeting, I have to admit, filled me with doubt," agreed Jason's dad as he adjusted his bottom in the passenger seat.

"I just don't understand how you could have four computers in your classroom and not know what software is on them. At least two of those software titles could already have been helping Jason with his writing. If it wasn't for that AT lady, Mrs. Nurky still wouldn't have known about them." Jason's mom huffed. "I mean, isn't it a teacher's job to know that stuff?"

"I did like those suggestions that AT lady came up with, though," Jason's dad offered, trying to steer the conversation to a more positive note. He knew when his wife was getting revved up and ready to go on a tear. Usually, he tried to dissuade her from ranting, but after tonight's meeting he was almost ready to hear it … almost.

"Yeah, I know. Don't get me wrong. The meeting went well. That AT lady had lots of good suggestions. I think Jason will take to those tools to help him write better, like the three-ring binder turned horizontally so he is writing on a slanted surface," said Jason's mom.

"Oh yeah, that was a really good suggestion, because we can do that one at home, too," agreed Jason's dad, thinking, a little too soon, that he had side-tracked his wife from ripping into Jason's teacher.

"But what I still don't understand," began Jason's mom, "is how Mrs. Nurky can work there for four years and not know those programs existed or that those other programs did all that stuff. She couldn't bother to learn a few programs on the computer? Gimme a break! I mean, if she had known that stuff, Jason could have been using those programs from day one!"

"Honey, teachers are busy, and they…"

"Don't give me that excuse. She's never had a student with writing difficulties before? Come on. She should have known to use a slanted surface. It was so obvious once that AT lady mentioned it. So simple."

"And here's another thing!" continued Jason's mom. "What the heck does the technology teacher do all day? Certainly not training teachers. If she did, Mrs. Nurky would be a wiz on the computer, but as it turns out, she doesn't know diddly-squat!"

"Dear, now, come on. It isn't the fault of the technology resource teacher. I mean, how was she supposed to know…"

"You know, you're right!" agreed Jason's mom, bobbing her head furiously up and down. "It isn't Nurky's fault or the technology resource teacher's fault. It's the administration's fault. If they were doing their jobs they'd know they have incompetent teachers working for them!"

"Hon. Mrs. Nurky isn't incomp…" tried Jason's Dad, knowing, as he was saying it, that this was a bad move.

"Don't you dare defend them!" shouted Jason's mom. "This is our son we are talking about! He deserves a teacher who knows how to teach him and who knows strategies that can allow him to learn! This school, obviously, isn't doing that for him. In fact, I'm thinking I need to write the superintendent and let him know how incompetent this school is!"

Jason's father recognized the lost cause when he saw it, and truthfully, deep down, he wasn't so sure his spouse was wrong on this one. Sure, his wife had the temper of a hungry wolverine stuck in a cage on a sunny day, but that didn't always make her wrong. Maybe Mrs. Nurky was an unfit teacher. Maybe the job performance of the technology resource teacher should be questioned. Maybe the administration didn't have a grasp on who were good educators and who were not so good. Maybe, just maybe, his wife was right.

"You know something, sweetie? You've got a point there," conceded Jason's father. "In fact, I'll write the letter to the superintendent. I'll let him know that he should pay a visit to that school and that he should do it super quickly!"

"Right! He's bound to do something!" smiled Jason's mother.

"But if I'm writing the letter, what are you going to do?" asked Jason's father.

"That's easy," Jason's mother said as an anticipatory smile spread across her face. "I'm going to call the other parents."

■ ■ ■ ■ ■

Don't get caught in the parent trap! Parents, typically, do not sit in on the lunch-room conversations of teachers. Parents, typically, don't go out with teachers on Friday night happy hour. Parents, typically, don't wander haphazardly into a classroom during a teacher's planning time. All of these times that parents aren't present are ideal for an educator to consult with an assistive technology trainer. Why is this? The consultation with the assistive technology trainer should be an informal one and should not involve the parents … at first. This consultation is not an IEP meeting. This consultation is not a child study committee meeting. If a student continues to struggle after implementing the tools and strategies generated from the consultation, then the school can share with parents all of the strategies that were put in place to address the concerns while discussing the next step, which might include a formal assistive technology evaluation.

This should not be misinterpreted as saying that parents should never be involved. Of course, the parents should be included during ongoing discussions about strategies that were successful and those that were not. However, the parents need not be involved in the initial discussions between two colleagues brainstorming tools and strategies that already exist in the school building and which could be tried without convening the IEP team. Whenever possible, it is best to keep initial assistive technology consultations as conversations between educator and trainer before you have the superintendent and an army of angry parents knocking on your classroom door.

Portrait of a Consultation

As the assistive technology trainer, your role in the consultation is not that of the artist. The educator working with the student in question is the artist. This is the person painting on the canvas, molding the clay, or spinning the pottery wheel. The role of the assistive technology trainer is to offer advice to the artist about which brushes to use, which sculpting tools work best with different types of clay, and which firing technique to use for the pot. When an artist walks into the art store and asks the clerk about which tools to use, the painting, sculpture, or piece of pottery doesn't come along. The artist just describes the endeavor in as much detail as necessary to provide the clerk with sufficient information to provide thoughtful advice on the completion of the project. Similarly, the assistive technology trainer does not actually need to see the student to provide meaningful advice on the tools that might provide assistance. Educators know the strengths, the areas of concern, and the strategies already attempted for each of their students. Through a simple conversation they usually can provide enough information about a student for the trainer to make informed recommendations about which tools and strategies could be tried.

Consultations Are Not Services Listed on the IEP

The only assistive technology service that should be listed on an IEP is the assistive technology evaluation. Assistive technology teams and IEP teams may be tempted to write "assistive technology consultation" as a service on an IEP. Sometimes educators will say, "Nah, we don't need a formal evaluation, but we just want someone to talk to the case manager about the student" and then write "assistive technology consultation" on the IEP. Any service included in an IEP requires documentation of the completion of that service. For example, if a student is receiving speech and language therapy as a service, the person providing that service logs the sessions and provides information for a progress report to be reviewed by everyone on the IEP team. Similarly, a request for an assistive technology evaluation requires the assistive technology trainer to conduct an evaluation and provide an evaluation report. That report is then reviewed by the IEP team to decide which recommendations will be implemented. If a consultation is written on the IEP, then the trainer must conduct the consultation and provide a subsequent report to be reviewed by the IEP team. To put it plainly: if a consultation is written into an IEP, it is no longer an informal conversation and becomes identical to an assistive technology evaluation.

jot and scribble

There is a saying that "cleanliness is next to godliness." Who knows—that may be true. What we do know is that "preparedness" is even closer to "godliness." When you walk into a consultation or an evaluation having read all the relevant information on a student, you do yourself a great service. Not only will you feel more confident about your abilities during the consultation or evaluation, but you maximize the possibility that others will see you as an expert. As you read through the student's information, jot down ideas you have about potential tools or strategies that could work as recommendations for that student. Scribble down any questions you have for the educators working with the student to help paint a complete picture of the student's educational environment. If you read through all the specifics of the situation and take some notes on them prior to the visit, you'll also be giving your subconscious mind the opportunity to work on the problem. There may be times when those initial strategies you considered won't be appropriate, but with each ensuing consultation or evaluation you'll find that those initial, potential tools and strategies are the ones that end up being the recommendations that work most frequently for students.

■ ■ ■ ■ ■

Singled Out: Staff Talk

An assistive technology consultation is an informal dialogue among educators—specifically, among those working with a student and the assistive technology trainer. The process does not require any formal paperwork. The process does not require parental approval. Parents might not be involved or even aware of the consultation. If the consultation is, in essence, two peers talking about educational strategies or tools to help a student, there is no need for a parental involvement. However, at no time during the assistive technology consultation should the trainer ever single out the student. That is, the student should never be removed from class, isolated, interviewed individually, or in any other way spotlighted by the assistive technology trainer without prior parental permission. If it is believed that the assistive technology trainer should interact with the student directly, then an assistive technology evaluation should be conducted and prior parental permission should be obtained via the IEP process.

consulting in paradise

A gentle breeze caresses your skin as you sit on the beach letting the warm, crystal-clear water lap at your toes. You reach down and pull the cool beverage out of the bucket of ice. All tension has ebbed out of your body, and you ponder the prospect of staying in this paradise forever. You look over at your friend lounging beside you, and without uttering a word, the message "This is the best spring break ever" is conveyed between you. You think, could things be any better? It's then when the third person in your trio returns with another bucket of beverages.

"I was just talking to the most interesting man in the cantina," she says, temporarily interrupting the luscious sound of the tide, "and guess what? He's a teacher at another high school in our same school district!"

"That's a shocking coincidence," says your neighbor lazily. "Now pass me another bottle of the good stuff."

"He was telling me how much he enjoys teaching algebra and feels like he's really connecting to his students, like I cared about that. You should see this guy's eyes!" says Captain Interruptus. "Anyway, he kept going on and on about what a tough time this one student is having with algebra. Apparently this student was very good at math when he could use manipulatives, but algebra is just whipping his behind. When he found out I was a teacher in the same school district, he asked me if I knew any strategies he could use to help that student."

"You certainly had a detailed conversation with this stranger you just met in the cantina. No wonder you were gone so long," you say, hoping this comment will put an end to the discussion so you can go back to dreaming about living in a hut by the water.

"Well, yeah. We talked quite a bit, but I didn't know what to tell him about algebra. I'm an English teacher. So I told him you might be able to help him. Here he comes now," your oh-so-lovely friend says as she waves her hand to the man strolling down the beach.

Just when you thought you could relax, take a break, and enjoy yourself without thinking about students or problems or anything other than palm trees and coconuts, your "friend" (might have to move her down the list) invites some guy to come talk about algebra. Who talks about algebra in paradise? When you open your eyes and see the gorgeous specimen standing in front of you, you find the answer to your question. *You* talk about algebra in paradise.

■ ■ ■ ■ ■

Where It's AT: Anywhere, Any Time

A consultation can happen anywhere at any time through any media. A consultation can take place in a classroom, meeting room, hallway, or parking lot, or even on a remote island beach in Bora Bora. All different forms of communication can be used to conduct a consultation. Consultations can take place in a face-to-face environment where everyone participating sits around a table and discusses a student. A consultation can also occur on the phone between two people or as a conference call. Although typically reserved for less complex issues, e-mail is another form of communication for consultations. Videoconferencing retains the ability of meeting face-to-face without having to be in the same physical space, eliminating travel time. Even three-dimensional, virtual environments, such as Second Life, can be used to conduct a consultation. Any means of communication is acceptable as long as the outcome results in strategies that assist the student in meeting educational goals.

The Appalachian Paper Trail: Documenting Consultations

The Appalachian Trail is 2,174 miles (3,498 km) long, stretching from Georgia to Maine. The main trail is marked with solid white rectangles (blazes) painted on trees and posts, and hikers use them to follow the entire route. Solid blue rectangles mark the many side trails that are used for a variety of purposes, including finding fresh water sources, seeing interesting sights, or walking to nearby towns.

Some students have a cumulative folder containing enough paper that it seems as if, laid end-to-end, it might cover the entire Appalachian Trail. Assistive technology trainers create their own blue-blazed paper trails, including e-mail correspondence and notes about telephone conversations. A summary of the consultation should also be included as part of the assistive technology paper side trail. The following is a list of reasons, each with a brief description, as to why the assistive technology trainer should send out a summary of what went down in the consultation:

CYA. If you're not sure what this acronym means, well, do a quick Internet search and you'll see soon enough. Essentially, by sending out a summary of the consultation, the assistive technology trainer has successfully eliminated the opportunity for someone to come back and say that the consultation was never done.

Educators are busy and typically responsible for more than one student. By the end of a consultation, a number of strategies may have been discussed. Even the best educator, who took notes during the meeting, might forget some of the tools and strategies discussed or misinterpret what was discussed. By sending the summary of the consultation, the assistive technology trainer provides that educator with a way to go back to check (and recheck) every recommendation that was discussed.

Share and share alike. If the consultation was effective and resulted in tools and strategies that resonate with an educator, that person might share what was learned with other colleagues. In that way, the assistive technology trainer is providing strategies to multiple teachers via proxy. Having the trainer's summary of the consultation in hand makes sharing the information easier, and the educator doesn't have to rely solely on memory. When educators share strategies that have worked for them, it means fewer consultations to conduct in the future and more students finding easier access to education.

To whom it may concern the most. By sending the summary of the consultation to an educator, the assistive technology trainer provides a means of communicating with the parents of the student who is struggling. The summary serves as proof that a discussion took place between the educator and the assistive technology trainer. It also serves as a guide to what strategies are going to be implemented to help that student achieve the outlined goals. When parents receive a summary passed along by the educator, it shows that the school district isn't out of answers, that the people involved in educating their child are invested in their child, and that an effort is continuously being made to achieve the outlined goals.

The long drive home. Inevitably, as the assistive technology trainer drives away from a school following a consultation, additional tools and strategies will pop into that trainer's mind that weren't originally discussed during the consultation. The subconscious had a chance to work on the problem, thumb through the old cerebrum, retrieve additional ideas, and push them within reach of the conscious mind. By sending a summary of the consultation, the assistive technology trainer has a chance to incorporate any thoughts, tools, strategies, and ideas that popped into the noggin between the end of the consultation and the time the summary is sent.

The defense rests. The number of consultations and recommendations provided to educators will be a handy little piece of quantitative data to convince administrators that an assistive technology team is necessary or to prove that the team has been effective. By sending a summary of the consultation to the educator and keeping a copy for reference, the team can add up just how many students have been impacted by the assistive technology consultations along with how many recommendations have been provided. For the particular number-crunching, money-squeezing administrator, you can even calculate a dollar per student ratio to provide evidence of just how much money you have *not* spent. If the assistive technology team has conducted 200 consultations, all yielding no-cost recommendations, then the dollar per student ratio will decrease. This data can provide credence to the value of having an assistive technology team in your district for any lurking doubters.

There may be times when you are tempted to just skip the summary of a consultation. You might feel like you don't need to create the side trail off the main trail. You might feel like the consultation was too brief with recommendations made that don't warrant documentation. It might seem like blazing a side path to nowhere sometimes—but the reason to write the summary is the same reason why you'd bring your extra water on a hike on an extra hot day. Wouldn't you rather have it and not need it than need it and not have it?

generating better, faster, stronger summaries

Ah, there is this great little function in most word processing programs that can help you create better consultation summaries faster: Find and Replace. Let's say you complete a summary of consultation for a student named Tommy who has writing difficulties. You, being totally efficient, have separate folders set up on your computer for each area of concern, such as writing difficulties, communication challenges, and organizational issues (Fig. 10.3). You save a shortcut to Tommy's summary to your "writing difficulties" folder. Then, a few weeks, months, or years later when an educator requests a consultation for a student named Timmy who has difficulties similar to Tommy's you can go to the appropriate folder, pull up Tommy's old consultation summary and do a quick "Find and Replace" swapping "Tommy" for "Timmy." This, of course, only serves as a start, and it will be necessary to individualize the consultation based on Timmy's needs and the specifics of the consultation. But this will save you time because you don't have to create a new consultation summary—and also it helps ensure that you haven't accidentally left out a useful strategy that worked for Tommy that might also work for Timmy.

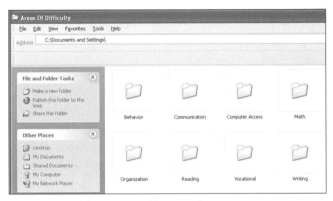

Figure 10.3 Folders organized by area of concern

■ ■ ■ ■ ■

E-mail Nation

Paperwork. Who doesn't like to toil away at the computer documenting cases, archiving notes, and writing reports? After all, isn't your love of jamming away at the keyboard the reason why you became an educator? The truth is, paperwork is unavoidable and necessary, but it doesn't have to be a terrible burden. There are ways of decreasing paperwork to maximize the time spent on the other (possibly more fun) responsibilities of being an assistive technology trainer. One major way to decrease the amount of paperwork is by accepting e-mail as a valid form of communication. The consultation was informal, so the follow-up can also be informal. The style of the summary can be informal, friendly, and professional all at the same time. Tutorials and websites can be attached or embedded respectively.

Here is a sample e-mail sent to a teacher after a consultation for a student named Melissa.

> *Hey there, Super Teacher,*
>
> I just wanted to thank you for having me out to talk about strategies for Melissa. I definitely appreciate getting together to brainstorm. I'd also like to summarize what we talked about so you have something to reference in the future. Please feel free to share this with anyone interested in Melissa's education (parents, other educators, related service, etc.).
>
> You mentioned that Melissa is a fifth grade student who has difficulty processing information quickly and has difficulty remembering facts. You mentioned that Melissa does extremely well with routines. You explained that Melissa presents the most difficulty when completing math activities, retaining memorized facts beyond one day, and formulating thoughts for writing. You stated that she receives services in a self-contained setting for both math and language arts. You explained that Melissa does better when she has a picture to represent concepts or when she has physical manipulatives to use. You also explained that Melissa demonstrates some motor coordination difficulties and receives Adaptive PE services. You mentioned that Melissa really focuses and tries hard while working but that she does fatigue throughout the day. You also explained that Melissa has been diagnosed as having seizures and that it is not apparent when she is having a seizure. You also mentioned that her comprehension increases when materials are broken down into steps. You stated that Melissa participates in the Successmaker software program for math and is currently approximately on a second grade level according to the data on the program. You explained that she is adept at using a calculator but relies on this as a tool for all math calculations.
>
> The following are suggestions of things to possibly try based on our conversation:
>
> Consider Melissa's participation in sequencing activities at school and at home. Sequencing activities can be split into two categories: numerical sequencing and non-numerical sequencing. Numerical sequencing activities ask the student to sort pictures that contain images where each picture in

the sequence increases by a numerical factor. An example of a numerical sequencing activity would be organizing pictures of rings on a pole where each picture represented an additional number of rings on the pole. Numerical sequencing can be in factors of one or more (two things added each time, etc.). Numerical sequencing can also be organizing in reverse order to indicate that items are being taken away. Non-numerical sequencing activities ask the student to sort pictures that contain images of events. An example of a non-numerical sequencing activity would be organizing images that represent a person bowling. Sequencing activities might assist Melissa in understanding mathematical concepts. Describing the pictures in a series of images following a sequencing activity might also assist Melissa in increasing her ability to tell a linear story as well as make pictures in her head about events that have happened when telling about past events.

Using a digital camera Melissa could take pictures and print them. Then, Melissa could manually slide the pictures into an order that makes sense.

Some software titles available on instructional computers have sequencing exercises built right into them. Sammy's Science House is one such program where a student is asked to slide pictures into an appropriate sequence to make a movie play.

Consider reinforcing the use of transition words such as "First," "Second," and "Then" with Melissa. These words could be placed on her desk as well as reviewed with each vocabulary or spelling list.

Consider Melissa's participation in activities where she independently reviews information provided on multimedia presentations, such as Microsoft PowerPoint presentations. PowerPoint presentations made by other educators are readily available for download. Using the PowerTalk add-on (a free download for PowerPoint but already installed on all instructional computers) she could listen to the text on the PowerPoint presentations. The following are a list of sites that contain educational PowerPoint presentations available for download:

> http://jc-schools.net/ppt.html—Many educational presentations for download

http://tinyurl.com/edgames—Many educational games and templates

http://tinyurl.com/gravesppt—Many educational presentations for download

Consider Melissa's use of a graphic organizing template in the writing process where visuals representing topics about which she can write are provided. Melissa could be asked to describe each picture to help her formulate ideas about that topic. Graphic organizers can be created using a variety of software titles including Inspiration, Microsoft Word, and PowerPoint. One picture could be placed on a slide, and she could be asked to describe what she sees. Pictures can be quickly added to PowerPoint presentations using the Photo Album function.

Consider Melissa's participation in interactive math websites. The following are a list of interactive websites that may contain relevant mathematical applications.

http://illuminations.nctm.org—A great place to find lessons, activities, and materials related to math, easily searchable by grade level and content

www.aplusmath.com—Interactive flash cards and games for practicing mathematical concepts (including multiplication)

www.coolmath.com—Interactive games for practicing mathematical concepts

www.ictgames.com/resources.html—Interactive "Flash"-based games for practicing mathematical concepts

http://tinyurl.com/oswegomath—Multiplication practice with a built-in timer

http://nlvm.usu.edu/en/nav/vlibrary.html—Tons of virtual manipulatives

I hope these suggestions and recommendations are helpful. If you need me to show you or anyone else how any of these strategies work, just let me know. We can arrange a time for me to do training. If you try these and find that they are not working, or if Melissa's educational needs change, just let me know. I can come back out and we can brainstorm some more.

Thanks so much!

Assistive Technology Trainer Extraordinaire

The Consultation List: Step-by-Step

For those of you who like lists, the following is a step-by-step account of what happens during a consultation:

1. A student is struggling with an educational goal as documented by collected data, or a member of the IEP team believes additional technology may support a student.

2. The educator contacts the assistive technology trainer.

3. A meeting time is scheduled between the assistive technology trainer and the educator. Other educators may be invited to this meeting, but it is not an IEP meeting.

4. The assistive technology trainer jots down some notes on potential strategies based on the nature of the problem.

5. The assistive technology trainer and the educator(s) meet to discuss student strengths, areas of concern, and tools and strategies already in place or previously tried. Recommendations are generated.

6. The assistive technology trainer provides a summary of the consultation to the educator.

7. The educator decides which strategies to try and in what order.

8. Data is collected on student progress toward achieving the educational goals

The Evalummendation: The Next Step

During a consultation with an educator, there may come a time when the assistive technology trainer believes that a tool above and beyond what is already available within the school may be necessary for a student to achieve the targeted educational goal. The rule still applies for the assistive technology trainer to share at least one strategy in order to provide the educator with something to try. However, because the solution tool of choice is not available to the student, the ultimate recommendation resulting from this consultation will be to request an assistive technology evaluation. At that point, the consultation can shift from a brainstorming, idea-generating meeting to an explanation of the process for requesting an assistive technology evaluation.

The Win–Win–Win–Win Scenario

If every educator follows the rule of "Never request an assistive technology evaluation without consulting an assistive technology trainer first," students will get strategies faster. That's a no-brainer. The strategies provided during an assistive technology consultation will be universal because they will be things that can be used by anyone. That essentially means that these tools are least restrictive in nature. Therefore, not only will the student who is struggling become aware of least restrictive strategies, but so will every other student who works with that teacher. Because these strategies use tools that are already available, nothing needs to be purchased and there is no extra cost. This results in a "Win–Win–Win–Win" scenario. Teachers win because they get a new rabbit to pull out of their magic hat of tricks when they come across a student who is struggling. The administration wins because achievement scores go up without the need to spend any additional funds. The assistive technology team wins because formalized paperwork has been minimized. And most importantly, students win because there is now a way to reach their educational goals with no restrictive impact.

chapter 11

assistive technology
evaluation
requests

If we've been suitably convincing, then you agree that the first level of service the assistive technology trainer can provide is a consultation, an informal discussion with educators about strategies a student can use to meet educational goals. Providing assistance to an educator begins with communication. Whether the assistive technology trainer is contacted via e-mail or telephone, stopped in the hall, or summoned by a spotlight shining into the night sky with a silhouette of the AT team logo, the educator needs to know that the trainer will be right there to help.

Table 11.1 Differences between a consultation and an evaluation

	Consultation	Evaluation
Where?	Anywhere	Customary educational environment
When?	Anytime the educator is free	During an activity where the student is working on a goal as outlined by the IEP team
Who?	Any educator working with the student (educator can include parents)	Any educator working with the student (educator can include parents) The student
Interaction	Conversations with educators	Conversations with educators Observation Student interaction
Duration	As long as it takes. Typically one visit with an educator is enough, but it can be as many conversations as necessary	As many visits as it takes as long as IEP team reconvenes to review the evaluation report within the time frame written on the IEP
Initial Paperwork	None, nil, zippy	Formal request documented in IEP Request for Individual Assistive Technology Evaluation form
Concluding Paperwork	Nothing officially, but a Summary of Consultation for every consultation is encouraged	Evaluation Report IEP team reconvenes to review report and decide which recommendations become accommodations
Outcomes	Strategies using tools already available in the school or tools that are free Recommendation to conduct an assistive technology evaluation (additional tools possibly needed)	Any tool, any cost
Outcome Framework	Tools and strategies can be implemented the very same day	Tools and strategies are provided after IEP team reconvenes and after tools are acquired

But what does a consultation look, feel, and smell like? What are the differences between a consultation and an evaluation (Table 11.1)? Is each its own animal, or do they have similarities? What is required when a consultation is conducted versus when an evaluation is conducted? This chapter is meant to paint that picture for you so that when you're all done reading, you can hang it up on the wall of your office for everyone to look at.

Student Observation

Chicken fingers and chicken wings have similarities and differences. They are both taken from parts of a chicken and they both taste great with hot sauce, but one has bones and other does not. It is a subtle delineation, but it makes a difference. You'd feed chicken fingers to your two-year-old without fear of the toddler choking, but the bones in the chicken wings probably would make you think twice about plopping them down on the Dora the Explorer plate. The differences between an assistive technology consultation and an assistive technology evaluation are also subtle. However, one big, glaring, strobe-errific difference is that an assistive technology consultation should *not* contain an observation of the student, whereas an assistive technology evaluation *absolutely* needs to contain an observation of the student.

It may seem obvious that the assistive technology evaluation should require an observation of a student. You need to observe the student demonstrating difficulty in the area of concern to justify the recommendation of a tool, or to be frank, to justify the purchase of a tool. What is not so obvious is why the consultation should not include an observation. After all, both consultations and evaluations involve providing strategies, interviewing educators, and providing a written summary of the service. The actual way in which the services are conducted is very similar. But these similarities may cause confusion between the two in the minds of the people for whom you're providing the service. By leaving the observation to an evaluation, you further delineate the two services.

When you strip away the similarities between a consultation and an evaluation, you are left with the differences, which are few. The consultation is an informal process requiring no preliminary paperwork or IEP meeting, while the evaluation is a formal process consisting of timelines and official documents. The consultation yields recommendations and strategies using only tools that are free or currently available in the student's customary educational environment, while the evaluation can yield a recommendation for any tool or strategy in existence. Notice how the differences are related to the outcomes and the process and not related to how the service is conducted. Let's pose it in the form of a question. If you were to include an observation as part of a consultation, what's the big difference? Just outcomes, IEP documentation, and paperwork. The process of actually providing the service is no different, and that can cause confusion. Therefore, it is best to leave the observation as a part of the evaluation and not the consultation.

Consider the following scenario where an observation is *not* part of the consultation.

> Heather is a student who is struggling to meet an educational goal. Heather's parents begin to wonder about technology that might assist her and mention this to Heather's clean-cut teacher. The teacher explains to Heather's parents that the first step in considering assistive technology is for the teacher to meet with the assistive technology trainer to discuss tools and strategies. Heather's teacher explains that this process is called an assistive technology consultation. Heather's teacher explains that this is an informal conversation to brainstorm possible solutions. Heather's parents agree and wait patiently to hear back from the teacher about the results of the meeting. Heather's teacher then organizes a meeting with the assistive technology trainer and some related service providers. During the meeting the trainer and Heather's educators decide on some strategies to try, but they also agree that it sounds like Heather might need some tools that are not already present in the school. Therefore, one of the outcomes of the meeting includes recommending that an assistive technology evaluation be conducted. Heather's teacher shares the consultation summary provided by the assistive technology trainer with Heather's parents, explaining the recommendations that were developed during the meeting. Heather's teacher also shares that one of the recommendations was to conduct an assistive technology evaluation. When Heather's parents ask what an assistive technology evaluation entails, the teacher responds by saying that it entails the assistive technology trainer observing Heather in her customary educational environment and possibly interviewing Heather.

Now, consider the following scenario using the same student in a different, crazy, mixed-up parallel universe where an observation *is* part of the consultation and people feed their two-year-olds chicken wings.

Heather is a student who is struggling to meet an educational goal. Heather's parents begin to wonder about technology that might assist her and mention this to Heather's scruffy-looking teacher. The same preliminary scenario ensues, except that before the consultationmeeting, the assistive technology trainer observes Heather in her customary educational environment. During the meeting, the assistive technology trainer and Heather's educators come up with a few things to try but also agree that it sounds like Heather might need some tools that are not currently available at school. Therefore, one of the outcomes of the meeting includes recommending that an assistive technology evaluation be conducted. Heather's teacher contacts the parents and explains that the meeting took place. Heather's teacher shares the summary of consultation provided by the assistive technology trainer, detailing the recommendations that were developed. Heather's teacher also shares that one of the recommendations was to do a formal assistive technology evaluation. When Heather's parents ask what that entails, Heather's teacher responds by saying that it entails observing Heather in her customary educational environment and possibly interviewing Heather. Heather's parents then ask what will be the difference between the first time the assistive technology trainer observed and the next time the assistive technology trainer observes.

As the scruffy-looking teacher in this parallel universe, what do you say to Heather's parents? How do you explain the difference between the assistive technology consultation and the assistive technology evaluation? For the sake of argument, let's explore the options:

Answer: The observation during the evaluation is more detailed than the observation during the consultation.

Possible parent response: Detailed? How is an observation detailed? You're either observing or you're not observing. How can one observation be more detailed than another?

Answer: The observation during the evaluation is longer than the observation during the consultation.

Possible parent response: How much longer? Why wasn't the observation during the consultation as long as it needed to be?

Answer: The observation during the evaluation has already been completed. The assistive technology trainer did the observation during the consultation.

Possible parent response: Let me get this straight: you did what is essentially an evaluation without my consent? Where's my lawyer's number?

Honestly, we don't know what we'd say to satisfactorily answer the question, which is why we think it best to save the observation for evaluations only and not consultations.

Following the One Rule = Good Will

People need rules. Rules guide us, keep us safe, and attempt to keep society at large running smoothly. IEP teams in particular crave rules—rules make them happy. They want rules that make the process efficient and effective. You can help every member of the IEP team by making one rule: all requests for an assistive technology evaluation will be honored. Even if you think that an assistive technology evaluation is completely unnecessary, never let a request be your "hill to die on" (proverbially speaking). Don't squabble, wrangle, quarrel, or bicker over whether an assistive technology evaluation should be conducted. Even if the assistive technology trainer hasn't been consulted prior to the request, if someone is insisting on an evaluation, go ahead and make the request. This rule will decrease the stress on the case manager, administrator, related service providers, and parents.

This rule might mean more work in the long run for the assistive technology trainer because the time spent conducting the evaluation and writing the report might not have been necessary. However, the good will generated by eliminating a potential stressor at the IEP meeting will pay off in the long run. By making this rule, you have won an everlasting place in the hearts of the case manager, administrator, and related service providers. By enforcing this rule, you have immediately created the first ounce of trust between yourself and the parents of the student. These two intangibles cannot be measured and cannot be replaced.

my house is on fire

911 Operator: "Please state the nature of your emergency."

Caller: "Please. Please. My house is on fire. You've got to send someone immediately!"

911 Operator: "Remain calm, sir. Do you have a fire extinguisher on the premises?"

Caller: "No. Please ... I need help!"

911 Operator: "Please sir, remain calm. Do you have a fire extinguisher anywhere in the house?"

Caller: "What? I already told you. No. Now please call the fire department. The fire is spreading!"

911 Operator: "Sir, please remain calm. I can't help you if you're screaming at me. I need to gather information about your situation. Did you know that fires could occur in your house?"

Caller: "Are you kidding me? What are you talking about?"

911 Operator: "It's a very simple question, sir. Prior to this particular fire, were you aware that fire existed and that one could happen in your home?"

Caller: "Well, yes. Of course I knew what a fire was but, <cough> I didn't expect one in my house."

911 Operator: "Have you completed the second grade?"

Caller: "What? <cough>."

911 Operator: "Sir, please try to pay attention. The sooner you answer my questions the sooner I can process your request. Have you completed the second grade?"

Caller: "<cough> Of <cough> course. What does that have to do with … <cough>."

911 Operator: "Sir, so you were aware fire existed, knew it was dangerous, knew one could occur in your home, and you have completed basic fire safety that every child who has made it past the second grade should know, yet you don't have a fire extinguisher handy?"

Caller: "No <cough, cough>. I don't <cough>."

911 Operator: "I'm sorry sir. Your request has been deemed unworthy of our services. Good luck with your fire."

<click>

■ ■ ■ ■ ■

Every Request Is Appropriate

As the assistive technology trainer, you're a 911 operator. Someone has a problem. You collect data and send out the necessary tools to help address that problem. Like a 911 operator, you might get some calls that are pretty off the wall and yet still need to be treated with respect. There may come a time when someone requests an assistive technology evaluation that you feel is unwarranted, but to the person making the request, it holds some level of importance. After all, it took valuable time to make the request. Take it as a compliment that the assistive technology team was even considered as a resource even if you, personally, don't agree with the perception of the problem. If every evaluation request is treated equally, without judging the request itself, it will be easier to remain objective about every situation. If someone is asking for help, it is the job of the assistive technology trainer to provide that help, and not give the impression that "this isn't worth my time."

As an assistive technology trainer, you don't have the option to refuse a request for an evaluation. It's one of the services you provide. Just like a 911 operator, you don't get to hang up on people because you don't think they're worth your time or because they didn't follow proper procedures. The assistive technology trainer perseveres until the student no longer needs assistance.

Let's compare two different scenarios:

> **Scenario 1.** Barry is a student with a mild learning disability who thinks he might like to play an instrument. He once saw Bugs Bunny bonk Elmer Fudd over the head with a French horn, and so now he thinks it might be fun to play that instrument. The problem for Barry is that, because of his disability, he has trouble reading the notes on the printed page. Instead of contacting the assistive technology trainer first, the IEP team requests an assistive technology evaluation even though "playing the French horn" is not listed as a goal on the IEP.

> **Scenario 2.** Claire is a nonverbal student with an identified disability of autism who does not have a consistent method for expressive language. The IEP team consulted with the assistive technology trainer early in the school year, and a communication board was provided. Claire took off with the communication board, pointing to different visuals, and the IEP team is beginning to believe that a more sophisticated voice output device might be warranted. Therefore, the IEP team requests an assistive technology evaluation.

Which scenario warrants the attention of the assistive technology trainer? Which evaluation is the assistive technology trainer obligated to conduct? Which one will make a difference in a student's life? Which one warrants assistive technology support?

The answer is both. Both scenarios warrant the attention of the assistive technology trainer. Both scenarios require that the assistive technology trainer conduct an evaluation. Both scenarios could make an important difference in a student's life, and both scenarios warrant assistive technology support.

With assistive technology to help Barry read notes, the assistive technology trainer has provided access to Barry's full potential. To put it simply, with the technology, Barry is given a choice and given a chance to become the world's best French horn player. Without the technology, Barry's choice and chance is taken away from him. It should be up to Barry to decide—not his disability, and not his assistive technology trainer.

If you had the power to control (not just shape, but control) a student's destiny, would you want it? If you deny the student the opportunity just because you've deemed assistive technology support unjustified, then you've played a role well outside your scope of power.

First Come, First Served

The line at the fast food drive-through has one golden rule. The first car in line is the first car to be served. The line does not care how hungry you are. The line does not count the number of people in your car. The line does not hear the cries of the two-year-old wanting his fries and chocolate milk. If you get behind a minivan full of curmudgeons who change their order 10 times, it is not the fault of the line. The line is. The line does. The line works.

As evaluations roll into the assistive technology team's lap, there may be a compulsion to triage each case, giving priority to "more severe" situations and saving "less severe" cases for later. The line would disapprove. The line would be disappointed. The line would be right.

There is no fair and just way for the assistive technology team to prioritize one student's needs over another. Would you ever want to be in the position of trying to justify to a parent your decision to place a student on the back burner? "Uh, yeah, see, we didn't think your kid was as important as another kid, so we did that other kid's evaluation first. Um, so, in the meantime, your kid is still struggling with goals. Yeah, um, sorry about that."

The line provides the answer that is universally understood. "Yes, I understand it has been a few weeks and we haven't been out to see your child yet because, well, we take the evaluations on first come, first served basis. Every student is important to us, so please understand, we will take every evaluation seriously in the order of submission."

Trust the line. The line is never wrong.

keep it secret; keep it safe

Through the dark forest infested with rabid ogres, over jagged mountains swarming with dragons who breathe scorching cones of blistering flame, beyond the murky moat filled with crocodiles, piranha, and huge man-eating leeches, exists a castle. The walls of the castle are guarded by ghoulishly gruesome goblins brandishing poisonous spears made from the fangs of giant venomous serpents. Inside the castle, a putrid giant, wearing a necklace adorned with three keys carved from scorpion tails, sits upon a throne of crackling bones and rotten carcasses. Under the throne is a hatch, covered with black widow spiderwebs, which leads to a room filled with a sea of gems, gold, and diamonds. An oak chest sits in the center of the treasure trove, secured with three adamantine padlocks and protected by a boobytrap that shoots jets of toxic, flesh-dissolving gas. Inside the chest lies the most precious of parchment inscribed by the wisest wizards in all the land. On the parchment is the process of how to request an assistive technology evaluation in your district.

Once you have developed the process for requesting an assistive technology evaluation, lock it away. It is not necessary to share the process with the entire district. Keep it a secret. By locking up the procedures, the team promotes the key concept of contacting the assistive technology trainer prior to requesting a formal evaluation. If educators don't know the process, they have no choice but to contact the assistive technology trainer to discover the process. As a result, the assistive technology trainer can provide recommendations that might eliminate the need for an evaluation. Therefore, once your process has been established, give it to the ogre, who can give it to the dragon, who can fly it over the moat to give it to the goblins, who can deliver it to the giant, who can open the hatch, disable the trap, open the locks, and place it inside the oak chest for safekeeping. When it is time to make a formal request for an evaluation, the assistive technology trainer can be the knight in shining armor who guides the IEP team step-by-step through the process.

■ ■ ■ ■ ■

The Nature of the Beast

An assistive technology evaluation is one of the primary services provided by assistive technology trainers, and it serves two main purposes. The first purpose is to identify tools and strategies that would potentially assist the student in reaching educational goals. The evaluation process takes place in order to analyze the educational situation and to generate recommendations that could alter that situation with positive outcomes. The second purpose of the assistive technology evaluation is to justify the allocation of funds for technology. In this way, the assistive technology trainer acts as the individual who is saying, "Yes, this technology is warranted. Go ahead and buy it."

"Justification of funds" may not sound like a very educationally relevant reason for conducting an assistive technology evaluation, yet this is the same reason for any educational evaluation. For example, when a student participates in a speech-language evaluation, it is to determine whether a speech-language impairment exists. Why? Because if the speech-language impairment exists and it is impacting his education, then the student has a right to speech and language therapy, and therapy costs money. Stating that a student has a speech-language impairment impacting the education of that student is the same as saying that funds will need to be allocated to pay for speech-language therapy.

How do educators know when it's time to make a request for an assistive technology evaluation? Here are some guidelines.

- Data on student goals shows that the student isn't making sufficient progress, and every tool and strategy available in the student's customary educational environment has been exhausted as possible interventions.

- Every technique every educator can think of has been implemented with the student, and the student is still demonstrating difficulty.

- Someone on the IEP team is demanding an assistive technology evaluation.

- A student who is struggling to meet a goal indicates that there is a piece of technology he would like to explore.

- An assistive technology trainer has been contacted and believes it is time to conduct an evaluation.

Opening the Procedural Door for Evaluations

Assistive technology evaluations should be requested at an IEP meeting and should be documented on a page in the IEP that outlines the services the student will be receiving. The assistive technology evaluation is the only service provided by the assistive technology trainer that is documented in the IEP. The assistive technology evaluation documentation should include specific information about the service, frequency, location, and duration of the service. Let's examine each condition of the service individually:

Service. An assistive technology evaluation is a service provided to a student that includes an observation of the student, interviews with educators working with the student, and possibly some interaction with the student. We recommend that the service be listed as "Assistive Technology Evaluation."

Frequency. Although an assistive technology evaluation can occur over multiple days (conducting multiple observations, interviews, and interactions), all of those visitations fall under the purview of one assistive technology evaluation. Therefore, we recommend that the frequency be listed as "One Time" on the IEP.

Location. The location of an assistive technology evaluation is related to the goals the student is having trouble achieving. The evaluation should be primarily conducted in the location where the student is demonstrating difficulty. The location could be at school, at home, in grocery stores, and so forth, depending on the specific goal needing further support. However, the catchall term for all of these places is the student's "Customary Environment."

Duration. An assistive technology evaluation needs to be completed within a reasonable time frame. However, since "reasonable" is a relative term, we recommend that your assistive technology team list a more specific time frame for the duration of the service on the IEP. One strategy for selecting a time frame is to use the same one as the related service providers. For example, if occupational therapy, speech therapy, and physical therapy evaluations are all due within 65 days from the date requested, then it might be easiest to adopt a policy that assistive technology evaluations also follow that 65-day time frame. Using this example, the duration would read "within 65 days."

A narrative version of the entire request might state: "The Individualized Education Program Team requests an assistive technology evaluation be conducted one time in the student's customary environment within 65 days."

Parental signatures on the IEP provide the necessary consent to conduct the assistive technology evaluation, which may include observing a student in the customary environment, removing a student from a class to participate in an interview, and interviewing any relevant educator associated with the student. Once the IEP is signed, it should be provided to the assistive technology trainer to begin the process of evaluation. In this way, the IEP team has opened a procedural door. Within the period of time specified on the IEP, the assistive technology trainer must conduct the evaluation and generate a written report of it, and the IEP team must reconvene to discuss which recommendations outlined in the report are going to be implemented as accommodations on the IEP. The act of discussing the evaluation serves as the closing of the procedural door and documents that the assistive technology evaluation has been completed and reviewed by the IEP team.

Swimming with Sharks: Requests Should Be Specific

Brody, Hooper, and Quint climbed onto the deck of the *Orca* at the end of the movie *Jaws* with one specific mission in mind. Kill the shark. They weren't going pleasure boatin' or day sailin', and they weren't talkin' about hookin' some poor dogfish or sand shark. Their goal was the great white. Not just any great white, but the one that ate Chrissie Watkins, Ben Gardner, Alex Kintner, and the dog Pippin.

Similarly, a request for an assistive technology evaluation shouldn't be a fishing expedition where the IEP team throws out a line just to see what they can catch in the deep blue sea. It is imperative that IEP team members understand that if the student isn't demonstrating difficulty meeting a goal, there isn't a need for an evaluation. The request for an assistive technology evaluation should be directly related to specific goals that the student is having difficulty achieving. Once the AT team knows which goal isn't being met, they can get the job done, just like the trio on the *Orca*. As an assistive technology trainer, if you don't promote a process of IEP teams requesting evaluations for specific goals, the number of evaluations might eat you alive!

A Request for Information:
Targeting the Goals in Need of Support

Requests for assistive technology evaluations should be made to address specific goals that the student is having difficulty achieving. Like a hit man (laser) awaiting instructions from his employer (an oncologist) on his next target (which are the nasty cells in the body that need eradication), the assistive technology trainer needs to know which goals the IEP team wants the evaluation to address. If a student is struggling to meet a goal, then that goal becomes the target of the evaluation. In some instances, the student might be struggling to meet several or all of the goals listed on the IEP. No matter how many goals are targeted, the IEP team needs to have some way of communicating which goals are to be targeted during the assistive technology evaluation.

Documenting the goals to be addressed by the evaluation can take many forms. The simplest way to document these goals is to indicate them on the IEP as part of the request for the evaluation. For example: "The Individualized Education Program team requests an assistive technology evaluation to be conducted one time in the student's customary environment within 65 days to address goals 1 and 4 as outlined in this Individualized Education Program."

The simplest way, however, may not be the best way. In the example above, the IEP team has requested that the assistive technology evaluation address goals 1 and 4, but there is no indication as to what tools and strategies are already in place to meet those goals. The assistive technology trainer could, no doubt, gather hints from other areas of the IEP such as the present level of academic and functional performance page or the accommodations page, but there is still a modicum of guesswork involved on the part of the trainer. Again, like a doctor treating a patient, you'd want to know what interventions have already been tried and proved ineffective. The doctor could rely on a review of the medical records alone, but that takes time and there is a chance of missing something.

Another way to document the target goals would be to add fields for this information on the IEP form. These fields could also contain information relating to strategies previously used to meet the targeted goals. Although it would be beneficial for this information to be included within one document, there are some drawbacks as well. First, requesting this information within an IEP may serve as an invitation to request assistive technology evaluations, prompting members of an IEP team to say, "Oh yeah, an assistive technology evaluation! That sounds good. Let's do that!" This would be counterproductive in terms of the "only use when needed" approach the team has worked so hard to promote. Second, the number of students requiring an assistive technology evaluation would be very small in comparison to the actual number of IEPs being completed. It is not necessary to include information in an IEP form that will benefit only the small percentage of the student population that requires an assistive technology evaluation. Third, increasing numbers of districts are adopting digital IEP systems that are developed by contracted firms. Altering these digital forms might result in additional costs and require coordination between the firm and the district.

Yet another way (and possibly the best way) to indicate which goals should be targeted during the assistive technology evaluation is to develop a separate form containing specific questions that will aid the assistive technology trainer in knowing exactly which tools and strategies have previously been tried. The form could be called the "Request for Individual Assistive Technology Evaluation." The form could be completed at the IEP meeting, with the IEP team making a mutual decision on the goals to be included. The questions on the form serve a dual purpose: indicating which information the assistive technology team needs to complete the evaluation, as well as reminding the IEP team about best practices. The following is a list of the questions that can be asked on the form, along with a brief description:

Have you contacted a member of the assistive technology team prior to requesting an evaluation? This question serves as a reminder to IEP teams that completing a consultation before requesting a formal evaluation allows the assistive technology team to provide strategies faster and with less paperwork.

Which goal has the student demonstrated difficulty in achieving? Which goals does the student need assistive technology support to achieve? These questions serve as a reminder to IEP teams that assistive technology evaluations are focused initiatives that target specific goals, along with re-emphasizing the fact that an assistive technology evaluation is not warranted unless a student is having difficulty meeting at least one goal.

Describe the tools and strategies already used to address the goals targeted for assistive technology support. This statement could mention additional references to include work samples, notes, pictures, or other student artifacts that emphasize what has already been tried with the student. A question could be added to provide insight as to why those tools and strategies have not proved effective.

Are there any additional factors the evaluators need to know before conducting the evaluation? This question is an open-ended question allowing the IEP team to include any additional relevant information such as medications, allergies, and environmental impacts.

What are the best times to observe the student working on the targeted goals? This question again emphasizes the point that specific goals should be targeted as well as provides information to help schedule the evaluation.

This type of form requires the IEP team to thoughtfully and thoroughly examine the purpose for requesting the assistive technology evaluation while providing necessary information to the evaluator. Detailed answers to the questions on the form can save the assistive technology trainer time during the evaluation.

Before Recorded History: Addressing Known Challenges

Assistive technology evaluations can be requested during an annual IEP meeting or during a Review/Revision meeting. But is it appropriate to request the evaluation during the initial IEP meeting? Wouldn't it be prudent to assess student performance on the goals before requesting an assistive technology evaluation? After all, if it is appropriate to request an assistive technology evaluation only when a student has demonstrated difficulty achieving a goal, then how can that occur during an initial IEP? Conducting an assessment before requesting an evaluation might seem to be a logical sequence of events, but there is an alternate way to look at student goals.

Things existed in our world before humans named them: trees, rocks, rivers, clouds, and much more. As we developed language we identified all these things and gave them names. Just because we haven't named something doesn't mean it doesn't exist, does it? Of course not. Right now there are still undiscovered things such as planets in a distant galaxy and animals hidden in the deep dark depths of the ocean. These things are just waiting to be given names as soon as we discover them.

The same thing is true for the educational goals for a student who is found eligible for special education services because of a disability impacting educational performance. The student was demonstrating difficulties before they were detailed in the initial IEP. The educational goals were always there—they just needed to be discovered and named by the IEP team. It can be inferred that a student has been struggling with goals, albeit previously unnamed goals, prior to the initial IEP and, therefore, an assistive technology evaluation could be requested during that initial meeting.

The Eligibility Concoction

Pull out the big lobster pot that your mother-in-law gave you for a wedding present, the one taking up all the space in the back of the cupboard. Add all of these ingredients: artichokes, quail breast, marshmallows, four rice cakes, chopped (not diced) tomatoes, scallions, prawns, curd, olive oil, yogurt, syrup, ketchup, some pickles (sweet, of course), flour, yeast, sugar, honey, thyme, a few eggs, just a bit of parsnip, and some love. Let it cook until it smells just about right (you'll know it when you smell it), cool it down, and invite the local preschoolers over to play with it in your living room. Do you know what you get when you do all of that? The same thing you get when you try to combine assistive technology evaluations and the eligibility process for special education services. A big honkin' mess.

During the process to determine whether a student presents a disability, a student receives numerous evaluations to determine if that student qualifies for special education services. This process has nothing to do with providing tools that might assist the student in meeting educational goals and, therefore, has nothing to do with assistive technology evaluations. When a district is initially deciding to incorporate assistive technology evaluations into their special education practices, some individuals might mistakenly lump assistive technology evaluations with other evaluations that pertain to eligibility. Like oil and water, assistive technology evaluations and the eligibility process for special education services just don't mix.

the easier, the better

Increased documentation resulting in more paperwork is not what teachers and IEP team members hope for when they request an assistive technology evaluation, but it is the best way to gather essential information. To keep the amount of additional paperwork to a minimum, keep the fields on the "Request for an Individual Assistive Technology Evaluation" to a minimum. Even though it is an additional form to complete, if you streamline the form by asking only for the information you can't readily find somewhere else, you'll save everyone time. When crafting the form, keep the following question in mind for each field: "Is this information readily available elsewhere?" If the answer is yes, then omit that information on your form. If a teacher and other IEP team members have that information in another place, don't make them supply it again. Teachers will appreciate the effort to keep the form short, IEP teams can move through the IEP more rapidly, and the assistive technology trainer will have less to look at when the form is sent.

■ ■ ■ ■ ■

Web-It!

Content management systems are specialized templates for controlling and maintaining websites. If your school district has such a system, or if someone in your district has the know-how, consider making the Request for an Individual Assistive Technology Evaluation an interactive web page. Instead of filling out a paper form, the teacher and IEP team go to the web page, fill out the fields digitally, and hit a submit button. Upon submission, the information can go to any number of e-mail addresses as well as be recorded into a database. In this way, the information for the request can be shared automatically with relevant staff, such as the assistive technology trainer and the leader of the assistive technology team. Information from the request could also be collected into a database for analysis. The assistive technology team can use this data to generate information such as the number of evaluation requests made without prior assistive technology trainer assessment, and the types of requests (supports for communication, writing, reading, etc.) that are most prevalent. Ultimately, this data is useful for measuring the assistive technology team's own progress toward team goals.

Cut-Off Date

Assistive technology trainers should certainly be involved with students during the summer, but it might be more appropriate to delay any assistive technology evaluations until the beginning of the next school year.

It is generally not appropriate to conduct an assistive technology evaluation over the summer because evaluations should be conducted in the student's customary environment. If a student receives his education in a jungle, then you grab some bug spray and head into the wild. If a student receives his education on an iceberg, then you throw your parka into the kayak and hope you don't run into any polar bears. If a student receives her education 20,000 leagues under the sea, then you slip on the scuba gear or take a deep breath. The observation portion of the evaluation should take place in a setting where the student typically works on the targeted goal. The educator interview portion of the evaluation should be conducted with educators directly and regularly involved with that student. Also, the student's customary educational environment may change from the end of one year to the beginning of the next.

The fact remains, though, that students may demonstrate difficulty at any time, including the last few weeks of school. If a student requires an assistive technology evaluation, then it should be conducted. There is no way to dispute that fact. But if the school district has adopted a 65-business-day time frame for when evaluations should be completed, then an evaluation requested in late May would be due in late August (or even sooner if the district adopted a 65-calendar-day time frame). The evaluation would have to take place outside of a student's customary environment.

To ensure that the student receives an assistive technology evaluation and that it is conducted in the student's customary educational environment, we suggest promoting a suggested "cut-off" date for requesting evaluations each year as summer approaches. It can't be mandated by the school district that all assistive technology evaluations be conducted in the fall, but if everyone on the IEP team agrees it is best for the student to postpone an evaluation, the request can be specified that way on the IEP. The following is an example of how a request for an assistive technology evaluation could be written late in the school year:

> The IEP Team requests that an assistive technology evaluation will be completed one time in the customary educational environment by October 15, <insert year>.

Changing the due date of the evaluation to a few weeks into the following school year allows the assistive technology trainer to conduct the evaluation in the student's new customary environment. This also provides new educators working with a student the time to get to know the student and collect some additional data on the targeted goals. In this way, the evaluation will be conducted with the student's current educators, resulting in more detailed and pertinent recommendations.

Rescinding Requests

On occasion, believe it or not, people change their minds about what they think is best for a student. This applies to educators, parents, and, in general, IEP teams as a whole. It is possible that an IEP team thinks that an assistive technology evaluation is warranted and then, a few weeks later, believes that an assistive technology evaluation is not necessary. For instance, a student might be struggling to meet a goal at the time an assistive technology evaluation is requested, but then have a breakthrough moment a week or two later and master that goal. In that scenario, an assistive technology evaluation may no longer be necessary. For whatever reason, if an IEP team decides that an assistive technology evaluation is no longer necessary, the request should be rescinded. This can be documented on the IEP or on an IEP Review/Revision by writing something like, "The IEP team agrees that the request for an assistive technology evaluation is rescinded." This documentation should then be sent to the assistive technology trainer so the trainer knows that the evaluation is no longer necessary.

chapter 12

conducting
the
evaluation

Scheduling the Evaluation

If the IEP team's request for an evaluation comes after a consultation with the assistive technology trainer has been conducted—hooray! for the IEP team. The trainer will start the evaluation process with more information. If a request for an assistive technology evaluation comes out of the blue, that is a signal to remind the IEP team of the advantages of making contact with the trainer prior to requesting an evaluation.

Before scheduling an evaluation, be sure that you have secured permission to do the evaluation and that all necessary documentation has been collected as outlined by the policies established by your assistive technology team. This should include all of the following:

- Complete version of the signed IEP or IEP Review/Revision requesting the assistive technology evaluation

- Documentation listing the specific educational goals to be targeted during the assistive technology evaluation

- Most recent progress reports conveying an accurate picture of the student's current level of academic and functional performance

If you don't have the proper documentation, then wait until you do before conducting the evaluation. It should be noted that although the trainer needs to have the proper documentation before conducting the evaluation, this does not mean that the documentation needs to be completed properly. If an IEP team mistakenly documents the request for assistive technology evaluation in the wrong place on the IEP, the assistive technology trainer is still obligated to conduct the evaluation.

The trainer should schedule the evaluation to take place during a time when the student is working on the targeted goals. Although there may be some benefits to observing a student in an area of relative strength, it is more apparent which tools and strategies might be appropriate when the student is observed struggling. Therefore, if a student is struggling in math, then observe the student participating in a math activity. If a student is struggling while reading, then observe the student reading. If a student is having difficulty expressing emotions appropriately during recess, then schedule the evaluation during recess. If a student is having trouble finding items in a grocery story, then schedule the evaluation during a community-based instruction lesson at the grocery store.

SETTing Yourself Up: A Framework for Success

To effectively conduct an evaluation, the assistive technology trainer needs to know what to do when actually observing the student. Rather than re-inventing the wheel here, we will direct you to a resource that best describes how to

conduct an evaluation. We invite you to explore the SETT (student, environment, tasks, tools) Framework, developed by educational specialist Joy Zabala as
a four-step methodology for conducting an evaluation. More information on the
SETT Framework (along with a whole array of AT information) can be found at
the Assistive Technology Training Online Project from the University at Buffalo
(http://atto.buffalo.edu/registered/ATBasics/Foundation/Assessment/sett.php).
Beyond the SETT Framework, here are descriptions of different aspects of an
evaluation.

Document review. Prior to the onsite visit the assistive technology trainer
reviews all of the documentation provided by the IEP team and makes notes
about possible recommendations.

Student observation. The first part of the onsite visit is when the assistive technology trainer lurks in the classroom taking notes on what the student is doing.
Difficulties being demonstrated by the student as well as possible recommendations for tools and strategies that could assist that student should be noted. The
role of the assistive technology trainer during the observation is to be an impar-
tial observer of what is happening in the classroom. The observation can take
place in any setting and over multiple days if necessary.

Student interaction. The second part of the onsite visit involves student interaction. The assistive technology trainer gleans information from the student about
difficulties in school along with tools and strategies tried. Examples of student
interactions are interviewing a high school student about his daily activities in
and out of school and attempting to elicit communication from a student who
has the targeted goal of expressive communication. This portion of the evaluation is optional and at the discretion of the assistive technology trainer, who will
determine if it is warranted. The student interaction can take place in any setting
and over multiple days if necessary.

Additionally, student interactions will look very different based on the specifics
of each setting and each student. For example, during some evaluations it will
be important to remove the student from class to obtain candid and insightful
information. Some questions that might be asked are: "What does your typical
day look like from start to finish?" "What are your favorite and least favorite
classes and why?" "If you could change something about school, what would
it be?" "If there were an item that could be pulled out of a magician's hat that

instinctive interactions

As an assistive technology trainer, teaching pumps through your veins and may come as easily as breathing. Assistive technology trainers are also a caring lot who seek to help whenever possible. For these two reasons, you may find it extremely difficult to hold back during the observation phase of the evaluation. Whether you pretend to be a fly on the wall, a chameleon, or the invisible man, it is important that you merely witness what is happening without interfering so that an uncontaminated picture of the educational environment can be obtained. This becomes even more difficult when you see teachable moments pass or witness a teacher struggling with a student. If you are just itching to dive in and help, take solace in the fact that you will get your chance to interact and that your ultimate purpose can be better achieved by providing thorough recommendations and training in the future.

would make school better, what would that item look like?" Each can provide relevant information about what tools and strategies can be implemented to assist the student. However, if you are conducting an evaluation for a preschool student, an interview might not be as appropriate as observing the student interacting in play, circle time, or snack.

Educator interview. The assistive technology trainer interviews relevant educators working directly with the student in an attempt to capitalize on their expertise. Every educator holds a unique perspective as to how a student is performing, so it is important to gather information both from staff and from related service providers and paraprofessionals. The educator interviews can take place in any setting, over multiple days, and using various forms of communication (including e-mail).

By the end of the evaluation, the assistive technology trainer should have sufficient information to provide recommendations for tools or strategies that will potentially assist the student in meeting the targeted IEP goals. As the assistive technology trainer, when you can say to yourself, "I think I've got some solid recommendations that can help this student," then you know that you can end the evaluation.

Once you feel like you've gathered all you can from observation, then it is time to dive in and work with the student. Notice that we used the phrase "feel like." Every evaluation is subjective and unique. There are no concrete criteria to determine when you should jump in and when you should hang back. However, if you start working with a student during the evaluation, it is very difficult to stop, pull back, and reassume your position as passive observer.

noteworthy note-taking notes

Every assistive technology trainer has a unique style of taking notes, but the following are a few strategies and tools to consider:

Create a list of questions. While reviewing documentation prior to the school visit, prepare a list of questions. This will allow you to keep on track without forgetting any information you wanted to find out.

Use a portable word processor. Bring a portable word processor for taking notes. As long as the tapping of keys isn't distracting in the educational environment, there is no reason not to get notes into digital form right there during the evaluation. Most portable word processors allow you to quickly switch between files and documents. Different files could be used to take notes on separate observational topics such as "tools already in place," "participation in lesson/observation," "student interaction," and "evaluator interview." Not only does it save you time, but it also demonstrates that you're willing to use something with batteries.

Divide paper into quarters. If you need your trusty pen and paper to take notes, divide the paper into quarters. Each resulting quadrant can denote different topics (Fig. 12.1). Quadrant 1 can include a list of tools already in the environment. Quadrant 2 can be where key points are noted during the observation. Questions you plan to ask educators along with their responses can be listed in Quadrant 3. Quadrant 4 can house ideas that will become your recommendations.

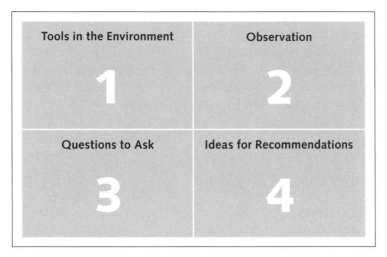

Tools in the Environment	Observation
1	2
Questions to Ask	Ideas for Recommendations
3	4

Figure 12.1 Quadrant Strategy

Highlight possible recommendations. Whether you're taking notes on paper or typing them into a word processor, highlight the ideas that will later become your recommendations by circling them on the paper or bolding them on the word processor. When you're writing the evaluation, you'll be able to easily spot the ideas that can become recommendations.

Use a checklist. When first starting to do evaluations, use a checklist to ensure that you thoroughly examine all of the pertinent issues. The list can be customized for each evaluation, but some generic items that could go on the list might include all of the following:

- Listed tools already in environment

- Observed student working on each goal targeted by IEP team

- Asked questions of educators

- Explained the rest of the evaluation process to the educators

Showing Off: Business as Usual

Most educators are accustomed to being observed. There always seems to be someone popping into classrooms, whether it is related service providers, administrators, other educators, or parents. Some educators go about their business just as they always do, as if you weren't even there. Conducting an evaluation in this sort of environment is ideal because the observer can get an accurate snapshot of what takes place on a typical day. There are other teachers who pounce on the observer with questions such as "What do you want to see?" or "What can I do for the evaluation?" The answer is always the same—"Just do what you'd normally do"—and that usually helps dissuade any contrived situations. As long as the assistive technology trainer witnesses the student working in an area of difficulty as outlined by the IEP team, then the educator has provided what is necessary for the evaluation.

Classroom Technology Hunt

Educators can't make it through the day without using tons of technology to assist students. The technology can range from low-tech tools such as posters on the walls or visuals on a desk, to high-tech strategies such as computer software programs or personal digital assistants (PDAs). As part of the observation, it is important to take note of the technology currently implemented along with technology available in the environment. The assistive technology trainer can later incorporate this information into the report, thus highlighting the technology already in place for a student. This offers evidence to the educators and the student that they have been using technology and are comfortable with such strategies. Taking an inventory of technology already in place for a student can actually begin prior to the observation by studying the accommodations outlined on the IEP that have been deemed necessary by the IEP team to guarantee a free and appropriate public education.

The Related Service Gold Mine

When you've got a problem with your computer and you've tried everything you can think of to fix it, you seek help from the person in your life who has the most knowledge about computers. When you've got a rash that breaks out all over your body and just itches incessantly, you seek the aid of a person who has some expertise in treating rashes. When you're conducting an assistive technology evaluation for a student, you search out the people with expertise developing strategies for students with disabilities and ask them for their input.

For most students who require an assistive technology evaluation, there is usually a group of related service providers serving that student. Speech-language pathologists, occupational therapists, and physical therapists are the most common related service providers. These professionals can provide invaluable information and recommendations to help the assistive technology trainer generate a holistic picture of the student's educational environment. Collaboration with multiple members of the student's IEP team will foster collegiality and collaboration, resulting in relevant recommendations that the team will consider their own. To put it simply, if some of the ideas for new tools and strategies come from discussions with the related service providers, then the related service providers will be even more willing to apply the new tools and strategies.

Professional Courtesy

Professional courtesy is a concept you don't hear about that often in the world of education, but it exists nonetheless. As an assistive technology trainer trying to forge a relationship with the educators in the district or within a school, it is imperative that you extend some simple professional courtesies. However, the cues for when and how to extend the courtesy don't always come flying over to you with hands waving, screaming, "Now's the time! Do it this way!" Luckily for you, there is a simple strategy that can help you know how and when to extend some professional courtesy—and it's something your momma taught you a long time ago: "Treat others the way you would like to be treated."

For example, when you're asked to do a consultation or evaluation for a student who is having communication difficulties, be cognizant of the fact that the speech-language pathologist has been working like crazy to institute a communication system for this student. Your presence in that environment may be considered judgmental of the work already being done. If you were that speech-language pathologist, would you like it if someone came barging in telling all the educators you work with that it's time for a change? Probably not. This is one of those times when you need to extend a professional courtesy. Collaboration among all team members will produce the most relevant recommendations while fostering a positive ongoing relationship.

Minimally, an e-mail should be sent to all related service providers requesting thoughts and opinions about tools and strategies that could be implemented for a student being evaluated. This way, if there is no response, at least you've tried. You've covered your bases and extended the necessary professional courtesy.

Professionals working in the business of shaping student's lives get extremely invested in their work. They put in countless hours and toil over decisions because they give a hoot about what happens to their students. Remember that these professionals will spend way more time with the student than the assistive technology trainer will. Therefore, when you step into their world, tread with respect.

judge dread: be supportive at all times

"What are you feeding that boy?" asks old Aunt Ida in her thick, raspy voice. "Looks like pure lard by the looks of that belly."

Aunt Ida, the gruff, obnoxious, know-it-all sister of your grandmother, always makes irritating comments, and just the sound of her voice makes the hair on the back of your neck stand up. However, today is your son's fourth birthday party, and you refuse to let this ancient bag of cynicism bring you down.

As much as you want to slug her, you respond coolly, "Now, Auntie, it's winter time. We all pack on a few more pounds in the winter."

"Bah! Too many video games and too much television. That's his problem. A good mother would get him outside every once in a while so he can work off some of those pounds," Aunt Ida growls. As if she should talk. Who's the one who sits in front of the television all day watching reruns of *Barnaby Jones*?

"Well, he'll be starting gymnastics in a few weeks again. I'm sure he'll slim down then," you reply calmly as you slice another piece of birthday cake. Calm, remain calm.

"Gymnastics? You put him in a sport for girls? No wonder, though—just look at the clothes you dress him in. What boy wears a yellow shirt?" Ida says with scowl on her face.

You reply through gritted teeth "Ida, yellow is a neutral color. Plus, he looks handsome in that yellow shirt."

"Handsome? Maybe at midnight during a power outage in a room with black windows to someone who's blind. If ya ask me, that boy is homelier than a tick on a rat."

It's then you feel the final straw break. No one insults your son like that, not even your beloved grandmama's sister. Afterward, you'll reflect on how odd it was that losing control of your senses in that moment of pure insanity actually sharpened your aim. The freshly cut piece of birthday cake smashes dead center on the old woman's sour face. Instantly a mixture of elation and satisfaction washes over you. "Gosh, that felt good!" For years to come, even at Aunt Ida's funeral 15 very long years later, the story of your heroics lives on as legend in the family.

■ ■ ■ ■ ■

Leave Judgments to Others

When conducting an assistive technology evaluation, don't be Aunt Ida. It's not the job of the assistive technology trainer to judge the abilities of the educators or judge the decisions of the IEP team. The assistive technology trainer's role during a student evaluation is to be a neutral observer. Leave the judgments to the grouchy old lady sitting in the corner by herself at the family party. This is important during the observation as well as in the report. By reporting only facts, the assistive technology trainer maintains a level of objectivity that will provide credence to the report while strengthening the relationship between trainer and IEP team. The educators on the IEP team will be much more willing to call on the trainer for assistance in the future if the trainer is there to help, not judge. Educators are scrutinized often enough in their professional lives by administrators and parents as well as by their own Aunt Idas. By concentrating on assisting educators with tools and strategies and leaving the judgments to others, the trainer maintains a positive relationship with everyone.

Who's Got Your Back? Taking a Partner Along

Batman and Robin, Shrek and Donkey, Holmes and Watson, and WordGirl and Captain Huggyface are all examples of heroes and sidekicks. A sidekick provides the hero with a partner for meaningful dialogue. When the hero needs help in solving the problem, the sidekick may find the clue that reveals the answer. If the action becomes too intense, the sidekick provides some necessary comic relief. What hero wouldn't want a sidekick? Of course, as important as sidekicks are, we wonder if Robin, Donkey, Watson, and Captain Huggyface enjoy being called sidekicks. The term "sidekick" implies that they can be "kicked to the side" without really being missed. Do they really think of themselves as any less important to the story than the hero? Probably not. Therefore, out of respect, we're going to refer to these partners as "backups." It's a euphemism, for sure, but the sideki… er, backup doesn't need to know that.

Here is how a "backup" can be used to enhance assistive technology services. An assistive technology evaluation is requested for a student and assigned to a primary assistive technology trainer who is responsible for corresponding with the case manager, scheduling the evaluation, conducting the evaluation, writing the report, and training the student and educator. The primary trainer is the individual who is ultimately responsible for ensuring that the assistive technology services are provided to the student. At the time the primary trainer is assigned, a backup trainer can also be assigned.

The backup trainer's role, just like the sidekick's role, includes coming along during the adventure as another set of eyes, ears, and hands, as well as providing unique insights into the situation. The backup trainer participates in the evaluation by taking notes, making observations, interacting with the student and educators, and generating ideas about what tools and strategies might be recommended. The extra hands are especially useful for taking detailed notes during the student interaction portion of the observation while the primary trainer interviews the student. The extra brain working on the case can lead to recommendations that the lone assistive technology trainer might miss. A dialogue or brainstorming session between the primary and backup trainers can lead to a refinement of recommendations for increased effectiveness.

Once the evaluation report is written, the backup trainer can act as a proofreader, reminding the primary trainer of missed details, or noting embarrassing grammer or spalling errors. Furthermore, the backup trainer can call upon personal experiences to suggest additional resources, making the evaluation report as detailed and as comprehensive as possible. Post-evaluation, the backup trainer can continue to support the primary trainer by assisting in training or developing any necessary resources or materials.

Having a backup trainer has other benefits, including having a second person knowledgeable about the case in the event that the primary trainer goes on leave for any reason. When primary and backup trainers work together effectively to come up with solutions for a student, it provides opportunities for professional growth and strengthens the bonds within the assistive technology team. Together, the backup and primary trainers can serve as an effective mini-team within the larger assistive technology team.

Backup Selection Process

When assigning the backup assistive technology trainer to a case, the same rule applies as when assigning the primary trainer: *discipline and experience don't matter.*

To put it another way, don't distribute cases based on the disciplines or experiences of the assistive technology trainer. We know it's tempting. It's like the candy house for Hansel and Gretel. Oh, how good that house must have looked to the two starving children lost in the woods! But as good as it looked, there was a witch in that house waiting to turn unsuspecting, naive children into dinner! Want another analogy? How about that cute little mouse that found its way into your kitchen for a few days? His nose was tickled by that peanut butter on a cracker, just sitting there waiting to be eaten. Just as the mouse went to fill his belly with that tasty morsel … WHACK! No matter how tempting it looks, remember, it's a trap set to go off when you least suspect it.

We can see you're going to need some convincing not to lick the candy cane railing or nibble on the Jif, so the following is a list of reasons why not to assign the backup role based on discipline or experience:

Opportunity lost. Everyone on the assistive technology team who doesn't get to be your backup loses an opportunity to learn from you. The flip side is also true—you lose an opportunity to learn from anyone who is not your backup. If the assistive technology trainer who has an occupational therapy background is always chosen to be the backup trainer for a student who has fine motor concerns, then the trainer with a background in speech-language pathology loses the chance to learn more about fine-motor issues. Likewise, if a backup trainer is chosen based on previous experience with a particular tool, the other trainers lose an opportunity to learn from the experience of implementing that tool. This is crucial when a student might need a tool that is an infrequent recommendation.

For example, two years ago Moe, an assistive technology trainer, conducted an assistive technology evaluation that resulted in the student using a rare computer software program named N'yuk. Prior to this student, no one in the district had used N'yuk. In the ensuing two years, no one else in the district has needed to use N'yuk. Now, an IEP team member for a different student has suggested that N'yuk be explored and an assistive technology evaluation has been requested. Moe has the most experience with that software, but should he be chosen as the backup for the evaluation? It would actually be more appropriate to pick one of the other assistive technology trainers, such as Curly or Larry, so that they have the opportunity to learn about N'yuk as well.

Putting the "we" in team. Even if Moe is not chosen as a backup, he is still a member of the team. During the evaluation if you and Curly (or Larry) need to bounce ideas off of Moe because of his experience, well, then, by all means, consult with Moe. One of the beautiful things about having a team is being able to access and use the collective experiences of every colleague on the team!

Unbalanced. Some types of disabilities have a higher rate of incidence. If backup trainers were selected based on discipline, some assistive technology trainers would be much busier than others. Nothing breeds resentment and contempt faster than having more work to do than someone else.

The absent discipline. If backup trainers were chosen based on disciplines, then there would need to be an assistive technology trainer for every related service discipline. What do you do if you don't have a teacher of the visually impaired on staff and the student who needs to have an assistive technology evaluation is visually impaired? Who becomes the backup trainer when the discipline is not represented on the team? To avoid the question, avoid assigning backups based on discipline.

The adjunct assistive technology team/duplication of effort. Many students who require assistive technology evaluations already have a team of different educators and related service providers working for them. Collaboration with the professionals working with the student fosters a sense of trust. When discipline-specific questions arise, asking the professional already working with the student, rather than choosing a backup assistive technology trainer with a background in that discipline, will result in a more detailed answer specific to that student.

If backup trainers are not based on discipline and experience, then what process should be used? Backups could be assigned by school. If the team has established a policy by which each primary trainer has a set number of schools, then the primary trainer would have one backup trainer for one school and a different backup trainer for another school.

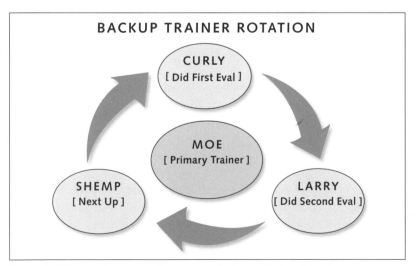

Figure 12.2 Backup trainer rotation ensures that every trainer is treated equally

Another fair way to ensure that every assistive technology trainer is treated equally is to set up a rotation (Fig. 12.2). Using a rotation, every trainer would get a turn working with every other assistive technology trainer in a set order. Each assistive technology trainer could maintain a table containing a list of everyone on the team. Each trainer could then cycle through the list, checking off people as each are used as a backup.

Are Two Heads Better Than One?

Although there are a number of positives that come along with having two assistive technology trainers conduct an evaluation you should also recognize the potential disadvantages.

Jeopardizing your reputation. When a speech-language pathologist conducts an evaluation with a student, it is done alone. The same typically goes for any other related service evaluation; it takes only one professional per discipline to conduct the evaluation. Therefore, why should assistive technology trainers use backups? Some people could interpret the use of two assistive technology trainers to conduct an evaluation as an indicator that assistive technology trainers aren't as good at their jobs as other related service providers. This perception could jeopardize the reputation of assistive technology trainers and their team.

Limiting future expansion. If you are attempting to expand the assistive technology team in years to come one question a budgeter might ask is, "Why should we support the hiring of additional assistive technology trainers when it takes two of you to do the job of one? If the assistive technology team needs more people, why not just conduct evaluations separately?"

Increasing workloads while reducing time for other endeavors. Being a backup trainer takes additional time and energy away from other team initiatives as well as away from the backup's own primary caseload. With the addition of a backup trainer, the primary assistive technology trainer now needs to account for an additional person's schedule, potentially increasing the amount of time it takes before the evaluation is conducted, resulting in a greater amount of time before a student is provided with a tool or strategy that might assist that student in achieving the targeted goals.

Creating opportunities for disagreement. Whenever an evaluation is conducted with a backup trainer there is potential for disagreement. For example, a backup trainer could disagree with a recommendation made by the primary trainer. This internal strife could manifest itself in many ways later on and none of those ways would be fun. Feelings could be hurt and egos could be bruised. Although people tend to be able to get over one incident, over time, discontent can grow. After all, weeds grow best on rainy days. Without hyperbole it can be said that disagreements between primary and backup assistive technology trainers could severely damage the productivity and effectiveness of the assistive technology team as a whole.

Table 12.1 Pros and cons of having a backup trainer

Pros	Cons
There's an extra set of hands during the evaluation that models a best practice.	Other related services don't have or need backups. Having a backup potentially hurts the reputation of AT trainers.
Brainstorming ideas leads to better recommendations.	It increases workload and takes time away from other initiatives and primary caseload.
It's a form of internal staff development—trainers learn from one another.	The primary trainer has another person to include in the schedule, causing potential scheduling difficulties.
It strengthens team bonds.	It can cause strife amongst team members.
Proofreading leads to better written reports.	Requesting more AT trainers can lead to questions about doing evaluations in pairs.
How much was spent per assistive technology trainer?	How many devices were checked out based on classroom evaluations?

Stuck in the Middle with or without You

Tick tick tick tick. The clock is ticking. Your time is almost up! Quick—decide! Backups or no backups? What's it going to be? Oh, Toto, the hourglass won't turn over! It won't turn over! Auntie Em, oh, Auntie Em! BUZZZ! Time is up. What's your answer?

When two roads diverge in a yellow wood, you always have the option to just leave the road altogether and forge your own path. The decision about whether or not to incorporate backups does not have to be cut and dried. Take out the machete and start hacking your way through the brush, carving out a trail that works best for you. You can create a system for having a backup assistive technology trainer on *some* assistive technology evaluations without insisting on having a backup trainer for *every* evaluation. For example, a backup assistive technology trainer could be required for the first 50 assistive technology evaluations conducted by a primary trainer. A variation could be that a backup assistive technology trainer is required for the first 25 assistive technology evaluations involving students who need writing support, the first 25 evaluations that need math support, the first 25 evaluations that need communication support, and so forth. (Please note that the numbers 25 and 50 were selected arbitrarily—there's nothing magical about them.) Whatever system is decided upon, remember to outline the pros and cons of that system before making it final. Every assistive technology team will have to decide which practice will work best in its own school district.

Believers and Skeptics, Trials and Tribulations

When it comes to conducting trials for assistive technology devices, trainers fall into two general categories: believers or skeptics. It will be up to you to decide in which camp to pitch your tent. Don't worry, though—if your campsite gets flooded, you can always pack up and move. Furthermore, if you find that the new campsite is infested with ants, you can always move yet again.

Believers

Believers think they know what tools and strategies will assist a student, without initiating student trials, prior to including them as recommendations in the evaluation report. Armed with expertise and experience, they believe that the recommendations outlined in an evaluation will work. Their belief is that the information gathered through observation, student interaction, and educator interviews combined with logic has led to a series of recommendations that will assist the student in meeting the targeted goals. The believer feels the trial period for recommendations comes *after* the evaluation is written. Essentially,

"could do" recommendations

Believers write recommendations in terms of "Could Do's." The believer does not make a statement about what will definitively assist the student. Rather, the believer begins recommendations with phrases such as "Consider using …" or "Explore the use of…." By using these guiding, nondefinitive phrases, the believer subtly alludes to the fact that the IEP team is the ultimate body making decisions about what is best to implement for a student.

the believer says, "With everything I've seen and with everything I know, I'm pretty darn sure these recommendations are the right tools for the job." To the believer, the trial of a tool or strategy begins only after it is written as an accommodation. The trial runs continuously throughout the life of the current IEP. At the next annual IEP meeting, every accommodation will be scrutinized for its effectiveness, including the accommodations that were added based on recommendations from the assistive technology evaluation. If the IEP team determines that the accommodation is still necessary, then the tool or strategy will be included and used again throughout the next year. If the IEP team determines that the accommodation is not necessary, then the trial ends and the tool or strategy is removed.

Believers have confidence that reasonable and effective deductions can be made based on the information collected during the evaluation. It is important to point out that the believer is still making decisions based on data. Quantitative measurements based on observing the student performing certain tasks such as typing at a computer, reading words, or speaking sentences are just a few examples of empirical data collected during the evaluation. Believers have confidence that this data is sufficient to justify recommendations without conducting trials of the recommendations.

Being a believer allows the assistive technology trainer certain luxuries. Namely, the believer does not spend valuable time developing a scientific experiment for each idea that occurs during the evaluation. With no trials, the believer can expedite the process of the evaluation and provide the IEP team with recommendations sooner. The believer also eliminates questions and scrutiny regarding the accuracy, duration, and implementation of the trials themselves. If none of the recommendations are trialed, then every recommendation has been treated as equally important, and IEP team members don't have cause to question why and how a particular recommendation was chosen. Believers exude a sense of confidence about their abilities to make decisions. Believers do not blindly take leaps of faith based on unsubstantiated evidence, but, rather, trust in their own ability and the abilities of those around them.

To be a believer is also to be a gambler. If a recommendation turned accommodation costs money, then the believer is going "all in," betting the school district's money that the tool purchased is going to work for the student. If it turns out that the student continues to demonstrate difficulties achieving the targeted goal, then tweaks to the tools and strategies, or different tools and strategies altogether, need to be implemented. Either way, the assistive technology trainer advocated for money to be spent without the desired outcome coming to fruition. The believer wagers the school district's money with the expectation that making the recommendations without conducting a trial will assist the student in meeting the targeted goals sooner.

Skeptics

Skeptics believe tools and strategies need to receive a trial with a student for a period of time prior to being written in the report as recommendations. To skeptics, a recommendation cannot be formulated based on observation, experience, and logic alone. They believe empirical data on the effectiveness of a tool or strategy needs to be collected prior to the generation of a recommendation. Before writing the recommendations, the skeptic systematically experiments with the use of different tools and strategies, collecting data on the student's use of each. Once this data is collected and analyzed, recommendations are written in the evaluation report. Essentially, the skeptic says, "With every tool and strategy tried along with everything I've seen, I have proof that these recommendations are the right tools for the job." To the skeptic, the trial of a tool or strategy takes place both before and after the recommendation is written as an accommodation. The trial of a tool or strategy takes place during the evaluation in order to make a recommendation and continues as it becomes an accommodation.

The skeptic proves that a tool or strategy is going to assist a student before it becomes a recommendation on the evaluation report. The skeptic takes time to develop a systematic trial of the tool or strategy where the student spends a specified amount of time using each while being observed. Based on the results, the skeptic formulates a recommendation. It is important to point out that the skeptic is still making initial decisions based on experience, expertise, and logic. After all, the skeptic still needs to choose which tools and strategies will be involved in the trial by analyzing the data collected during the observation, student interaction, and educator interview portions of the evaluation.

Being skeptics allows assistive technology trainers to rest assured that the tools they recommend money being spent on are worth the cost. The skeptic writes recommendations in the assistive technology evaluation report without fear that the recommended tool might not actually work for the student. The skeptic's confidence comes from the proof that what is being recommended works for a student.

To be a skeptic is also to be a question answerer. The following is an example of the questions the skeptic will be forced to ponder when developing a trial prior to a tool or strategy being written as a recommendation:

- How long will each trial last? Was the duration determined arbitrarily, or was there a reason for the length? Are holidays, sick days, assemblies, and other hiatuses taken into account in making this determination? If a trial of five days was selected and the student demonstrated difficulty using the tool, can one be certain that a sixth or seventh day of a trial wouldn't have made a difference to that student?

- How many tools or strategies will receive a trial period? Is there enough time to complete the number of trials within the time frame allotted on the IEP?

- What data will be collected during the trial? How will it be collected? Who is collecting the data? How often will data be collected?

- How are recommendations determined if the trial period results in data showing that a student could use any of the tools or strategies?

- Does every idea that might become a recommendation receive a trial? If not, which recommendations receive a trial? Do only the recommendations that cost money receive a trial? Consider the following: Does a pencil grip get tested before you make the recommendation, or can you discern just through observation that the student might benefit from a pencil grip? Does a calculator need to be evaluated for effectiveness? Does moving a student closer to the blackboard require a trial before it's adopted as an intervention? Does placing a visual that reads "raise hand" as a reminder to not shout out in class need to be subjected to a trial? Does every accommodation receive a trial period before being implemented? If not, how do you decide what requires a trial and what does not?

- If a tool is used conditionally with a student for a trial period and found to be effective, is it then removed for a time to determine if the next tool would be even more effective? Can the elimination of an effective tool be justified even for a short period of time?

- Because every variable cannot be controlled during the trial, can one ever be certain that the tool being evaluated with a trial was the determining factor for student success? Could factors such as nutrition, maturity, environment, and mood (which are all variable) skew results of a trial? What if a student was just going through a slump in abilities the same week a trial occurred? Can all of those factors be controlled? If not, how accurate is the data being collected?

> ## "should do" recommendations
>
> Skeptics write recommendations in terms of "Should Do's." The skeptic, armed with data from the trials, is able to make statements about what will definitively assist the student. The skeptic starts recommendations with phrases such as "Use …" or "Implement …" By using these definitive, nonwavering phrases, the skeptic highlights the decision the IEP team should make about what should be implemented to assist the student in meeting targeted goals.

For some of these questions, skeptics will need to develop answers specific to each trial and evaluation. At any time, the skeptic might be forced to answer all of these questions to justify the procedures used to conduct the trial that determined a recommendation.

Mix and Match

Now that you have read descriptions of believers and skeptics, which one are you? Don't worry—we're not trying to pigeonhole you or pin you down to one or the other. Luckily, choosing between believer and skeptic does not have to be a forever decision. With each evaluation, you can determine what would be the best approach for a student. Some situations call for the assistive technology trainer to take the role of the believer, expediting the process and getting tools and strategies to students more quickly, whereas other situations require the assistive technology trainer to take the role of the skeptic, scientifically experimenting with tools to ensure success. The following examples show how a situation might call for a particular approach.

Ahmad is a student who is having difficulty writing a complete sentence that includes every word. Ahmad tends to leave out smaller words in his writing that he does not leave out in his speech. During the evaluation Ahmad typed the sentence the "The ferret slept the bed." When asked to read the sentence out loud Ahmad said, "The ferret slept on the bed" as if the word "on" were in his typed version. In this case, it seems like a reasonable recommendation for Ahmad might be the use of a program with auditory feedback as part of his editing process. In this way, Ahmad would be able to hear mistakes he has made in his writing. In this case, it is probably not necessary for Ahmad to participate in a trial to see if this system will help him write complete sentences. It is reasonable to expect that integration of auditory feedback will assist in increasing his writing abilities.

In another example, Sara is a student who is having difficulty communicating. She is nonverbal because of a motor dysfunction. She also demonstrates motor difficulties impacting her ability to target a selection with her index fingers. Targeting is difficult but not impossible for Sara. To determine what communication system would be most efficient for Sara, two trials are set up. Sara spends two weeks trialing a dynamic communication device with a cell guard where she attempts to target large cells that each contain a message. Sara spends the following two weeks accessing the same communication device using a single switch next to a part of her body where she has consistent control. With each click of the switch Sara starts and stops a scanning array, allowing her to make selections on the communication device. During each two-week period, the number of utterances and the speed at which she makes those utterances are collected. Using this data, a recommendation for one system is then established.

Trial by Fire

Just like Grover, we're going to warn you that there is a monster living in this section of the book. It's scary at first sight, but we were compelled to include it anyway. Upon gazing at this monster of an idea, some readers may promptly toss the book into the fire or run to the bathroom to scrub their eyes out with baby shampoo. Others will get kinks in their necks from vehemently nodding as they whoop and holler in agreement. In fact, you may just want to skip ahead to some other section of the book. Not going to bail? Okay, but don't say we didn't warn ya.

> **In most cases, you should start out with the intention of being a believer. Believers are more prevalent than skeptics.**

There we said it. RAAARGH! That's that monster. If you're still reading this and not currently dropping this book into a barrel of acid, then we'll tell you that the remainder of this section explains the rationale behind those statements.

trials versus assessing

Trying a device for a few minutes during the evaluation isn't a trial—it's part of the assessment. For something to be considered a "trial," it needs to take place over an extended period of time—that is, at least over one day. Trying different tools and strategies such as switch placement, access to a computer, and functions on a computer takes place during the student interaction portion of the evaluation and is a component of the assessment. Conducting a trial for different tools and strategies with a student takes place over an expanse of time, extending the student interaction portion of the evaluation.

Assistive technology devices that are necessary for a student to receive a free and appropriate public education are listed as accommodations. Most accommodations that are put in an IEP are not based on trials or concrete evidence. Most accommodations are based on what the IEP team *thinks* the student needs for a free and appropriate public education. The IEP teams use their experience and student observation to determine accommodations. Ultimately, most accommodations are best guesses, albeit educated guesses, for what the student will need to ensure a free and appropriate public education. If only proven tools and strategies are written as accommodations, then initial IEPs wouldn't include any accommodations at all. In this way, the method the IEP team uses to determine accommodations correlates with the believer's method of generating recommendations (which have the potential to become accommodations).

Time is precious, and extra time is hard to come by. Developing trials prior to generating recommendations takes time to coordinate, implement, and analyze. Would all of the time spent on constructing trials in order to develop "proven" recommendations be better spent working on implementing recommendations that will "most likely work"?

Skeptics have numerous questions to answer about the nature of the trials in order to make the trials effective and, possibly, in order to satisfy IEP team members. For a believer, the only trials the IEP team need to consider take place once the accommodation is part of the IEP. The IEP itself answers many of the questions about using trials. For instance, the duration of the trial is the length of the IEP.

Whenever in doubt, initiate each assistive technology evaluation with the intention of being a believer. The trainer can switch to being a skeptic at any time if that is what the situation calls for. The trainer is never locked into being a believer. The trainer can always jump ship and do a trial if it is ever unclear what should be recommended. However, once the trainer dives overboard, there's no going back for that student. Once the trainer has started a trial, it needs to be completed with that student. But, for the next student, that trainer can go right back to being a believer again.

chapter 13

the
assistive technology
evaluation
report

The Report Dissected

Got your scalpel in hand? Good. Now make one long vertical incision. Pull the flaps back and pin them to the cork. With your magnifying glass, take a look inside. Using the following handy-dandy guide, see if you can identify all of the following parts of the assistive technology evaluation report.

Student and Report Information. Fields of data about the student including name, identification number, case manager name, grade, attending school, people present at the time of the evaluation, and date(s) of the evaluation.

Background Information. Any relevant information about the history of the student including any or all of the following: Summary of the present level of academic and functional performance, assistive technology consultation summaries, and the reason(s) why the evaluation was requested.

Existing Supports. A list of assistive technology already in place for a student including accommodations and any other tools and strategies currently being used. Accommodations may be listed separately from other existing supports to distinguish strategies put in place by educators that are just good teaching practices from what the IEP team has already deemed absolutely necessary for the student to receive a free and appropriate pubic education.

Observation. A description of what occurred during the observation, student interaction, and educator interview(s).

Recommendations. Suggestions of tools and strategies that could be implemented with a student, each relating to a goal that was targeted by the IEP team as well as relating to something witnessed during the observation.

Resources. Books, magazines, websites, and other additional materials the IEP team might find useful for addressing the goals outlined by the IEP team.

Appendixes. Tutorials, diagrams, and examples of tools and strategies referenced in other locations throughout the evaluation. These items provide the first step, and in some cases the only step, in providing training to those who will be implementing the recommendations.

digital photos in reports

Assistive technology evaluation reports don't have to be drab, visually boring documents. The readers of an evaluation report don't need to feel like they are reading something from the reference section of the library. Thanks to digital photography, you can take as many pictures as you need, and you don't have to be Ansel Adams to take a good picture. Digital photos can be used to enhance an evaluation report, clarify a point, or draw attention to a particular section of the report. Photos can be added to break up long sections of prose, making the page visually stimulating to the reader. Examples of the types of photos to take include existing supports, furniture arrangement, screenshots of software, and a scanned version of a student's work. When you see an opportunity, snap the photo. Then, when you're writing the evaluation report, you can decide whether you want to insert the photo, house it in a folder for future reference, or just delete it from existence. You might also find that the digital photos taken during the evaluation act as memory joggers that remind you to include additional resources or recommendations to the report.

■ ■ ■ ■ ■

Reasons for Recommendations: Justify!

A good rule of thumb to use when writing an assistive technology evaluation is to imagine that it will be scrutinized in a court of law. As a matter of fact, that possibility exists for every evaluation written, so, it's not so far a stretch to imagine an assistive technology trainer on the witness stand being grilled by a young hotshot lawyer straight out of a John Grisham novel. When the lawyer leans over the stand, face flaming red with intensity, pointing his finger in the face of the trainer and yelling, "Why did you put this recommendation for word prediction software with an auditory feedback function in the evaluation?" there had better be a way to justify the answer.

To ensure that each recommendation can be justified, the trainer should ponder the following question: "Can the reader go back to the observation portion of the evaluation report and pinpoint why I am making this recommendation?" If the answer is yes, then the recommendation passes inspection. If the answer is no, then the trainer has three options. The first option is deleting the recommendation on the grounds that it is unjustified. The second option is altering the wording of the recommendation so that it makes sense based on something witnessed in the observation. Or, the third option is adding content about the observation that justifies the recommendation.

For example, consider the following recommendation: "Consider Alex's use of a document holder during activities where he is typing information from paper into a computer."

Somewhere in the observation portion of the evaluation report something like the following would need to be written: "Alex placed his draft copy on the table next to the mouse. As Alex typed his draft copy into the computer it was noted that he shifted his head position, shifting his visual plane, after each word. That is, he would look down, read one word, look back up at the screen, and then type that word into the computer. Alex repeated this action for every word on the paper."

In this example, the reader of the evaluation report would be able to see the justification for the recommendation in the observation section. Each recommendation should have a similar justification in the observation section of the final evaluation report. So as the hotshot Clarence Darrow wannabe pivots dramatically with a coy smile on his face, thinking he caught the trainer in a flub on the evaluation report, the trainer can confidently respond by saying, "Well, sir, if you had read the entire report, you'd know that in the observation section I noted that the student demonstrated difficulty identifying the correct spellings of words from the spell check function of the word processing program; hence, providing a word prediction program with auditory feedback would provide the student a mechanism to hear the words typed rather than relying on reading ability." The trainer can then sit back and relax in confidence as she watches the lawyer's mouth drop open in surprise. Case closed.

Facts and Opinions: Sworn Enemies

The content written in an assistive technology evaluation report can be broken down into two major categories: facts and opinions. Facts are objective statements that can be proved, and opinions are subjective statements that can be disputed. Facts and opinions are like mongooses and cobras—they don't like each other, and it is best to keep them apart.

The assistive technology trainer authoring the report is the zookeeper who gets the fun responsibility of keeping those two combative enemies away from each other. Luckily for the trainer, the zoo has separate habitats for these creatures. The facts live in the student information, background information, existing supports, and observation sections of the report, while the opinions reside in the recommendations, resources, and appendixes sections of the report (Fig. 13.1). Housing the opinions and facts in their respective places helps the reader understand what is currently happening in the educational situation and what the trainer thinks should happen to help that student meet educational goals.

Every once in a while a fact tries to sneak over the wall to take up residence in a recommendation, resource, or appendix. Likewise, every so often an opinion attempts to burrow a tunnel and pop up in a piece of student information, in the background information, or, especially, in the observation. It is the job of the assistive technology trainer writing the report to make sure that all the facts stay with the other facts and all the opinions stay with the other opinions, ensuring peaceful harmony. When these two creatures mix, the reader of the report becomes confused as to what is a fact and what is an opinion.

The observation is the most likely place where the trainer could mistakenly or accidentally insert an opinion. Opinions in the observation will confuse the reader or, worse, raise questions as to what is fact and what is opinion in the whole report. If you catch an opinion in this section and strongly believe that it will make a difference in the report, move it to another location within the report.

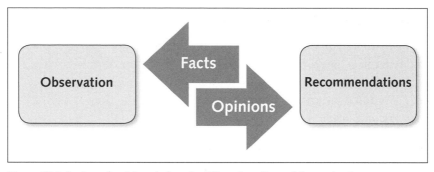

Figure 13.1 Facts and opinions belong in different sections of the evaluation

Observation Section Style

The observation section of the report can take the form of an action-by-action account of the events that occurred while observing the student. It can also take the form of a summation of the overall events that transpired during the observation of the student. The action-by-action account is useful when attempting to provide a detailed account of what happened during the observation. When you're trying to convey the overall gestalt of an educational situation, the summative account is more useful. In some cases, it is appropriate to mix the styles when reporting the actions during a specific activity while also capturing the overall experience in an educational setting. The following are examples of portions of observation sections representative of each style.

Action-by-action style. At the conclusion of the math worksheet activity, the teacher instructed all of the students to take out their math workbooks. She then instructed the students to tear specific pages out of the workbook, put the workbook away, and put their heads down. After a few moments of watching other students open their math workbooks and tear out the pages, Alex retrieved his workbook from inside the desk. Alex then looked at which pages the other students were pulling out of their workbooks. Alex began to carefully tear the pages out of the book. After Alex's pages were torn out of the book, he placed the pages on the desk and placed the workbook partially on his lap and partially propped up against the desk. When the teacher said, "I'm looking to see who has their math books in their desk," Alex continued to thumb through the math workbook. Alex was then prompted by another student in the cluster to put the book away and to put his head down like the rest of the students. Alex quickly put the book away and put his head down on the table. While the students were putting their workbooks away, the teacher came around the room stapling the removed pages. When the teacher said, "Did I staple everyone?" Alex, whose papers were not stapled, did not respond. The teacher then announced to the class which problems on the worksheets they were expected to complete. Alex marked some of the problems as indicated by the teacher. When instructed to begin working, Alex looked straight ahead with pencil in hand, without writing.

Summative style. Alex participated in at least five other activities during the remainder of the time while the evaluators were present. These activities included sentence repetition and completion. Alex repeated aloud a sentence stated by the teacher and then wrote a word to complete the sentence. Alex used a standard pencil to write his name in cursive within provided boxes. He wrote legibly and stayed within the confines of the boxes. He also used a large calculator to complete math problems that were provided orally by the teacher. Alex read aloud different sounds and words from a workbook as well. Alex appeared to demonstrate the understanding of spatial concepts by properly placing a pen in various locations as directed by the teacher. During these activities Alex worked diligently and earned two minutes of video watching after each activity.

Cover Letter

Educators working in special education have tons of procedures to learn. For most educators an assistive technology evaluation might occur infrequently, especially if their school district has adopted the "let's do an informal consultation first" approach. To assist the case manager of the student, the assistive technology trainer can provide a cover letter to the evaluation report explaining step-by-step what needs to occur to complete the process. The cover letter to the report can be short, containing a checklist of actions that should occur. Consider the following example of a letter to a case manager.

Dear Case Manager:

To complete the evaluation process, please follow the steps listed in the checklist below. Once these steps are completed, items recommended in this evaluation can be provided.

Steps to be completed by the Case Manager:

☐ Contact me to discuss the evaluation.

☐ Send a copy of the evaluation to all members of the IEP team.

☐ Schedule an IEP meeting to discuss which of the recommendations, if any, are needed for a student to receive a free and appropriate public education.

☐ On the IEP please write, "The IEP team has reviewed the Assistive Technology Evaluation dated <date>, and the following accommodations have been added to the IEP: <list accommodations>."

☐ Send a copy of the entire signed IEP to:

　☐ Me, at the Assistive Technology Office

　☐ Special Education, at the Central Office

　☐ Student's School File

Important Note: Recommendations to be implemented are at the discretion of the IEP team. The IEP team is ultimately responsible for initiating use of the accepted assistive technology recommendations as well as collecting data. Please forward a copy of future progress notes to the Assistive Technology Office.

Should you have any questions, please feel free to contact me at 123-456-7890 or by e-mail at SuperATTrainer@greatschooldistrict.k12.st.us. Thank you for your assistance in this process.

Don't Procrastin... Ah, We'll Finish That Later

If you're one of the few people who enjoy writing evaluations, then you are very lucky indeed. But if you're like most of us, writing up a report falls somewhere between going to the dentist and shoveling the driveway on a below-zero day on our list of favorite things to do. Don't get us wrong—we know assistive technology trainers live to provide tools and strategies to help; it's just the process of writing the observation and recommendations that isn't all that fun.

You might be tempted to procrastinate. After all, don't the sages upon mountains so high say that you are hurting only yourself by procrastinating? Apparently those sages don't know everything, because in the case of an assistive technology evaluation, procrastination hurts everyone. There is an educator waiting for your report. There is an IEP team waiting to reconvene and write accommodations. Most importantly, there is a student struggling to meet an educational goal who is depending on you for tools and strategies. Take the time you need to make the right recommendations. You won't be doing anyone any favors by speeding through a report just to get it done and not providing useful recommendations. Keep in mind, however, that the sooner you get a report done, the sooner that IEP team can reconvene to decide what is going to be implemented. In turn, the sooner you get a report done, the sooner a student gets a tool or strategy that will facilitate meeting the goal. Getting the report done as soon as you can, without Dilly or Dally getting in your way, benefits the educators, the student, and you!

chapter 14

assistive technology
recommendations

Bringing the House:
Unlimited Recommendations

When writing an assistive technology evaluation report for an individual, it is the responsibility of the assistive technology trainer to generate and list as many thoughtful recommendations and resources as possible. If the recommendation is justified by the observation, it should go into the report. When reviewing an individual assistive technology evaluation, the IEP team needs to be made aware of every potentially effective tool and strategy justified in the observation section. That is not to say that the trainer should include frivolous recommendations just for the sake of adding recommendations.

There should not be recommendations unless the assistive technology trainer thinks there is a potential benefit.

If a trainer is writing a report and finds that there are too many recommendations to be implemented at one time, then he or she should include a caveat message in the recommendation section that suggests that the IEP team prioritize the recommendations, implementing only a few at first. It then becomes the responsibility of the IEP team to decide how to prioritize each recommendation.

The Right Tool for the Job

"Oh, I just saw the greatest little techno-wizzy-majobber at this conference I went to. It sorts socks, checks e-mail, brushes teeth, changes diapers, and cuts the lawn all at the same time! Let's buy it! We'll find someone who can use it later."

It happens. Someone finds the greatest, newest toy and buys it just to see how it works. Then it sits on the shelf or closet or in the trunk of a car, waiting for the mythical perfect student to come moseying along who can use that fantastic Wizjammer 5000. The money is wasted, and the device collects dust and becomes more outdated with each passing minute. Then the next conference comes along, and that same someone picks up the Wizjammer 6000 to repeat the entire scenario. A short-haired lady once yelled "Stop the madness!" That's good advice for this situation.

By adopting the "right tool for the job" approach instead of an "I have this tool. Who is doing a job?" approach, the assistive technology team places the needs of the student above all else. To create and foster this philosophy, start by defining the needs of the student to narrow the search for a tool. After the needs of the student have been considered, describe the properties of a tool that will be needed for student success. For example, if you decide you need a tool to help you hang a picture of dear ol' mom, you would probably look for something that pounds nails. You can use that criterion to hunt for the proper tool from the tool chest. Which tool pounds things? Saw? No. Sledge? Possibly, may be overkill though. Put it in the "Maybe" pile. Claw hammer? Don't need the claw, but the head of the hammer would do nicely for pounding. Let's try that. Voila! The right tool for the job has been found! This same principle, when applied to considering assistive technology devices for students, can eliminate waste. Furthermore, using this approach decreases the risk of supplying a student with a device solely because of its availability in the existing inventory.

You may be concerned that you don't know about every tool that exists out there. You could spend all day, every day, exploring the latest and greatest assistive technology devices on the market. Technology is being developed, right now at this very instant; so by reading this sentence you are missing out on some new piece of technology that just hit the market. So how can you maintain a current knowledge of all the newest gadgetry and strategies? You can't. We give you permission to stop trying. You're off the hook, free and clear. You don't have to know every new techno-wizzy-majobber that comes out. Just let it go … let it go. You'll still be able to find the right tool for the job.

The Generic Accommodation

Kleenex is a brand name for facial tissues, Q-Tips is a brand name for cotton swabs, and Band-Aid is a brand name for bandages. Yet people refer to any type of facial tissue, cotton swab, or bandage by these brand-specific names. Keep this in mind when writing recommendations. Recommendations shouldn't be written using specific product names and brands, but, rather, using generic descriptive terms. For example, rather than recommending an "Alphasmart," you recommend a "portable word processor," or rather than recommending a "Springboard Plus," you might recommend a "voice output device with a dynamic screen and touch interface." There are both philosophical and practical reasons for writing recommendations using generic descriptive terms.

Philosophically, is it the trainer's absolute recommendation that a student use this particular brand of device and only that brand? That is, does the trainer firmly believe that this specific brand-name device is the only tool that the student could use successfully? Would the student likely fail to meet the goals targeted by the IEP team if given a similar device but not the brand name outlined in the recommendation? It is a unique situation (in fact, so rare that it is unknown to us) that student success is dependent upon the implementation of a specific brand of device. Philosophically, students need a type of device, not a specific device.

promotion via recommendation

If the assistive technology team has been working diligently on a project that would be beneficial to the student or useful to the IEP team members for that student, then by all means include that project as a recommendation or resource referenced in the assistive technology evaluation report. For example, if an evaluation was completed for a student who had a targeted goal of increasing communication, the assistive technology trainer might include a recommendation in the evaluation report for members of the IEP team to attend an upcoming staff development workshop being offered by the assistive technology team on the topic of "Strategies to Elicit Communication." Promoting the endeavors of the assistive technology team by including them in evaluations can increase the attention given to the work of the assistive technology team while simultaneously providing useful resources to every member of the IEP team.

Practically, think of the nightmare that would occur if a specific device were named in an IEP as an accommodation and then that device were to break. Unless very specific technical contingency clauses are included in the IEP, the second that device ceases to function, the school would be out of compliance with the IEP. It is unlikely that an assistive technology team would be able to replace the exact type of device immediately. The device may need to be shipped out for repairs. The device may be unable to be repaired and a replacement may need to be ordered. These circumstances remove necessary access to an accommodation listed in the IEP. However, if the accommodation is written generically, describing the attributes of the tool that is necessary, then there is a greater likelihood that a device meeting the description of that accommodation can be provided immediately.

If a trainer feels that the IEP team will be confused by a generic description instead of a brand name, the recommendation could mention the brand name as a point of clarification. For example, the trainer could write, "Consider the use of graphic organizing software that has voice recording capabilities, such as Inspiration." In this way, the assistive technology trainer is using the brand name as an example, but not specifically recommending the brand name.

How Much Wood Could a Woodchuck Chuck If a Woodchuck Could Chuck Wood?

Assistive technology recommendations are often a tangible object such as a device or software that has to be purchased. As a result, it is easy for someone to read a recommendation in an assistive technology evaluation and say, "You've got to be kidding! That's going to cost a fortune!" However, when reading the very next report that calls for speech-language, occupational, and/or physical therapy, that same person might not even bat an eyelash.

Let's take a look at some cost comparisons. According to a 2006 survey conducted by the American Speech-Language-Hearing Association (ASHA, 2006), the average speech-language pathologist working in a school setting earned approximately $45 an hour depending on the location of service. If a student were to receive 60 minutes a week of speech therapy for just one year (the length of an Individualized Education Program) that would cost approximately $1,800 per school year ($45 per week for 40 weeks). What if we were to bump that up to 90 or 120 minutes a week? The dollar amount increases to $2,700 and a whopping $3,600, respectively. Comparatively, how many assistive technology devices or software titles cost even $1,800? Not many. One other marble for us to shoot into the circle is that assistive technology devices and software titles are usually a one-time expenditure, whereas speech-language therapy costs another $1,800 (or more) the following year.

Please don't get the wrong impression. The point here is not to say that speech therapy costs too much or that school-based speech language pathologists are overpaid (quite the opposite in our opinions). It is simply to point out that every service listed in an IEP has an associated cost (the total cost may not be readily apparent), and assistive technology devices and software titles are often a bargain when compared to the cost of other services and are typically a one-time expenditure rather than a yearly cost.

It's All about the Benjamins: Justification of Expenditures

When assistive technology trainers write recommendations, they are essentially saying that purchasing the devices outlined in the recommendations is justified. The school district is relying on the expertise, knowledge, and ethics of the assistive technology trainer to make only recommendations that might assist the student in meeting the targeted goals. Rather than asking a special education supervisor or school-based administration to justify a tool and its related expense, the school district is placing that responsibility in the hands of the assistive technology trainer. Assistive technology trainers have the training and experience to make recommendations for tools that will assist students; so they are the natural choice for authorizing the release of funds. To put it simply, when an assistive technology trainer makes a recommendation in an evaluation, it means that the assistive technology trainer belives that "This is the right tool to do the job, and it is okay to go ahead and spend the money for it."

When an IEP team agrees that a recommendation is necessary for a student to receive a free and appropriate public education, it is included as an accommodation on that student's IEP. Again, to put it simply, when an IEP team turns a recommendation from the assistive technology evaluation into an accommodation for a student, they are essentially saying, "We agree with the trainer that this sounds like the right tool for the job. We think the student needs it. It's time to purchase it and train us and the student on how to use it." That IEP is then sent to the assistive technology trainer, who has the responsibility of acquiring the device referenced in the accommodation. After acquiring the device, the trainer will train the educators and the student in using the accommodation to meet the goals outlined in the IEP. Note the timing of delivery. A device is not delivered and no training is provided until *after* it is written as an accommodation. Until a description of a device is in the IEP, it should *not* be provided to a student. Up until the acceptance as an accommodation, the device lives only as a recommendation and, therefore, does not need to be purchased.

If it seems like a strange idea that the assistive technology trainer is the individual to justify the purchase of tools and the IEP team is the entity that ratifies the recommendation, we invite you to consider a parallel situation with which you might be more familiar. Every student could benefit from speech-language therapy, but only a few qualify for the actual service. Why have a qualification service? Why not just give every student in school speech-language therapy? Wouldn't that be a way to increase the language abilities of every student? You bet your patootie it would, but why isn't providing speech therapy carte blanche to every student, regardless of need, a common practice? The answer: Because speech therapy costs money, that's why. There is an eligibility process to determine who *needs* the therapy and who doesn't. When you consider speech therapy in this way (or any special education service for that matter), any student would benefit from that service, but only those who qualify as having a need receive it. It is easy to see that a driving force behind services is cost. That is, in order to justify spending the money on speech therapy, a student needs to qualify for it. The IEP team is the entity that ultimately determines if a student receives speech therapy based on the recommendations of a speech-language pathologist. Therefore, the IEP team is the entity that determines if the school district is going to spend money on speech therapy. Assistive technology devices work in much the same way. The IEP team has the final say in determining if a student needs an accommodation (i.e., assistive technology device) based on the recommendations of an assistive technology trainer. Therefore, the IEP team is the entity that determines if a school district is going to spend money on an assistive technology device (i.e., accommodation).

Every Penny Counts

When conducting an assistive technology evaluation and making recommendations, it is not the job responsibility of the assistive technology trainer to save the district money. It is the job of the assistive technology trainer to make sure the student gets tools and strategies that will help them meet goals. There will come a time when a trainer will need to make a recommendation for a student that requires the purchase of something expensive and, in some cases, *very* expensive. However, an unwritten, common goal of the assistive technology team should be to recommend strategies that cost as little as possible but still work as effective interventions.

Strategies that are less expensive are typically more universal and least restrictive in nature. The moment a student uses a device that is not already available in the customary environment, it's a step away from an unrestricted environment.

vendors are not sponsors

Don't take candy from strangers. This advice still applies to us adults. Assistive technology teams and individuals on assistive technology teams should not receive funding from vendors selling assistive technology devices. Ethical questions could surface if a member of the assistive technology team began accepting funding or devices from specific vendors of devices or software. Trainers need to maintain their objectivity when making recommendations for students. If an assistive technology team receives funding from a vendor, the trainers on that team might, willingly or unwillingly, make recommendations based on the funding source rather than solely on the technology that would best assist the student. Discounts are fine. Swag is fine. Funding is not fine.

For example, when considering which computer input device would be least restrictive for a student, all attempts should be made for that student to learn to use a standard QWERTY keyboard and mouse/trackpad configuration, because these are the standard ways in which people currently interface with the computer. These methods are widely used in other classrooms, computer labs, public libraries, and other public and private facilities. If a student begins to rely on a different computer input modality, there becomes a need to travel with that piece of equipment just to interface with a computer. In the future the primary human interface with a computer may change to a more Star Trekkian method: speech. For right now, however, the keyboard remains the standard operating procedure in society.

When existing inventory is used, there is no additional money spent. There are a number of reasons why a team might have unused devices in inventory, such as students graduating or abandoning equipment. These items are available and should be used whenever possible. Equipment has a better chance of being used by a student if it resides in that student's classroom rather than the team's inventory closet. Having said that, there is a fine line between giving an educator a device to try in a classroom situation and making a recommendation based on what's available. Recommendations should always be based on what the student could use to meet educational goals and should never be based on equipment availability. However, if a situation calls for a single-hit communication device and a Little Mack happens to be sitting around in the inventory closet, well then, that's a few less clams the team will have to spend.

The third reason to attempt to keep the recommendations as inexpensive as possible is to build administrative trust in the assistive technology team. When trainers consult with student after student, educator after educator, and continually generate recommendations using tools and strategies already available in the customary environment, which, consequently, have no associated cost, they are building administrative trust. If the administration believes the assistive technology team is working hard to provide solutions using items that are already available, then in the future they'll trust the team's judgment when asked for the Hope diamond that the student just has to have it in order to receive a free and appropriate public education.

chapter 15

reviewing the
assistive technology
evaluation report

How a Recommendation
Becomes a Law (Accommodation)

Once the assistive technology evaluation report is
finalized by the assistive technology trainer, it is sent to
the student's case manager. The case manager then has
the fun of reading the report, especially the recommendations, and contacting the assistive technology trainer to
discuss the report. It is imperative that the case manager
understand the recommendations, because it will be
the case manager who will be presenting these recommendations at the IEP meeting. Once the case manager
understands each recommendation, copies are made and
distributed to the rest of the IEP team members.

The case manager also schedules a Review/Revision of the IEP with the other members of the IEP team. Prior to the meeting, any IEP team member can contact the assistive technology trainer to ask questions about the report.

At the IEP meeting, the IEP team reviews the report, asking the following question for each recommendation: "Does this student need this to ensure a free and appropriate public education?" You might remember that question as being the very same question asked when considering accommodations during the initial and annual IEP meetings. If the answer is "yes," then the recommendation becomes an accommodation. If the answer is "no," then it isn't an accommodation. Remember, this doesn't mean the recommendation can't be implemented with a student; it just means that it is not an accommodation.

When the accommodations are written, the Review/Revision is returned to the assistive technology trainer to acquire the tools that are necessary as outlined in the accommodations. The trainer also offers training that is necessary for the student and any educator to successfully implement the accommodation.

Guess Who's Not Coming to Dinner

Assistive technology trainers should not attend IEP meetings. No, you didn't misread that last sentence. But, in case you doubt it, here it is again in big bold print with capital letters and a different font:

ASSISTIVE TECHNOLOGY TRAINERS SHOULD NOT ATTEND IEP MEETINGS

What follows are the reasons why assistive technology trainers should not attend IEP meetings.

The IEP team is capable of making the decisions. The IEP team has the responsibility of determining what accommodations a student needs. At some point the IEP team made decisions about accommodations without an assistive technology trainer present; why should this change after an assistive technology evaluation? If the IEP team was capable of making decisions about accommodations prior to an assistive technology evaluation, then it continues to be capable of making decisions about accommodations after an assistive technology evaluation.

It empowers educators. The assistive technology trainer provides training and follow-up visitations to the educators working with the student, but is not present in the classroom working with the student every day, all day. No matter how much time the assistive technology trainer spends with a student, it won't be as much as the educators working directly with the student. Therefore, it is imperative that the educators directly involved with the student on a daily basis understand the accommodations with regard to implementation. By keeping the assistive technology trainer away from the IEP meeting, educators are empowered to take on the challenge of understanding and implementing new tools and strategies.

All questions are already answered. Everyone on the IEP team has had an opportunity to review the assistive technology evaluation report and to contact the trainer with questions about recommendations prior to the IEP meeting. Because all questions about the nature of the report and recommendations have been answered prior to the meeting, there is no need for the assistive technology trainer to be present during the meeting.

Meetings would dramatically impact service time. If the assistive technology trainer were to attend every IEP meeting where decisions regarding assistive technology are made, then an assistive technology trainer would be required to attend every IEP meeting in the district. The ratio of assistive technology trainers to the number of IEP meetings in a school district precludes the trainer from attending every meeting. If it were the case that assistive technology trainers were required to attend every IEP meeting in the school district, then the amount of time spent attending IEP meetings would dramatically impact the amount of time the trainers have available to perform other responsibilities.

Every accommodation is created equally. In the eyes of the IEP and the IEP team, every accommodation is necessary to guarantee a free and appropriate public education and, therefore, equally important regardless of cost. When a recommendation is made in an assistive technology evaluation, the trainer is placing a stamp of approval on the expenditure for a device. In some cases (fortunately) the cost of the device will be $0 because no purchase is required or because there is a device fitting the description of the accommodation presently in inventory. Other accommodations will cost a little, or a lot, or maybe even boatloads of moolah. By considering every accommodation equally, the IEP team eliminates any ickiness about making decisions based on money rather than student need (Fig. 15.1).

Sample Accommodations	
Accommodation	Access to word processor during assignments longer than two sentences in length.
Implementation	The school already has two computers in each classroom with word processing programs.
Cost	$0 USD

Accommodation	Use of slanted surface when handwriting.
Implementation	Three-ring notebook flipped horizontally on which the student writes.
Cost	$0.99 USD (or free if a three-ring binder is on hand. If a three-ring notebook can't be found somewhere in the school you're not looking hard enough!)

Accommodation	Use of single cell voice output communication device for expressive communication.
Implementation	Big Mack programmed with different vocabulary as needed, placed within reach of a student.
Cost	$104 USD (unless you have some of these devices sitting around in a storage closet, in which case the new cost would be $0 USD.)

Accommodation	Access to a Braille printer/embosser that provides audio commands, prints/embosses in both alphanumeric text and in Braille, works in conjunction with software that converts alphanumeric text to Braille, and works in conjunction with software that converts alphanumeric text to Braille using a standard Qwerty keyboard.
Implementation	Romeo Pro 50 embosser used in conjunction with Canon dot matrix printer controlled by the TranSend LT control unit. Duxbury software used for converting text into Braille.
Cost	Embosser: approximately $2,500 USD Control unit and printer: approximately $2,000 USD Software: approximately $600 USD Grand total (estimated): $5,100 USD (and that is all for one accommodation for one student!)

Figure 15.1 Sample accommodations

A Statement of Conclusion: Closing the Door

Once an IEP team has met to discuss an assistive technology evaluation, the team should document that fact. Every service on an IEP includes proof that the service was provided. For most services, this comes in the form of progress notes written either collaboratively or separately by the individuals providing the services. Once the IEP team has met to discuss the evaluation, a statement similar to the following should be written on the Review/Revision or on the section of the IEP where assistive technology is noted as being considered:

> The assistive technology evaluation requested on <insert date> was reviewed by the IEP team. The following accommodations have been added to the IEP based on the recommendations outlined on the assistive technology evaluation dated <insert date>:

The accommodations, usually numbered, can then be listed. On the other hand, if the IEP team has met and agreed that no recommendations from the assistive technology evaluation need to be added, then something like the following statement should be inserted:

> The assistive technology evaluation requested on <insert date> was reviewed by the IEP team. No accommodations have been added to the IEP based on the recommendations outlined on the assistive technology evaluation dated <insert date>.

This step, documenting the discussion of the assistive technology evaluation, is a vital step in the process. This ensures that the evaluation was conducted and that the IEP team has reviewed the recommendations. The assistive technology evaluation should not be considered "completed" until the IEP team has documented that it has been reviewed.

Remember when the IEP team requested the evaluation on the IEP a few weeks ago? When that occurred, the IEP team stated a deadline for the completion of the assistive technology evaluation. That deadline wasn't for just submitting the evaluation report; it meant that the IEP team needs to reconvene to discuss the recommendations prior to that due date. This implies that the assistive technology trainer actually needs to get the report written and out to the case manager a few days before the deadline established on the IEP.

For example, the IEP team writes during an IEP Review/Revision, "The Individualized Education Program team requests an assistive technology evaluation to be conducted one time in the student's customary environment within 65 days." This means that the case manager should receive the evaluation report from the assistive technology trainer in no later than 60 days. That would allow the case manager 5 days to schedule the IEP meeting, distribute copies, and conduct the IEP meeting. Of course, as mentioned earlier, the sooner the evaluation is completed, the better it is for everyone involved—but by allowing at a minimum 5 days' time, the case manager is provided with some time to complete the meeting within the 65-day time frame.

Recommendations That Are Not Accommodations

That poor, poor, sad and lonely recommendation. Look at it over there in the corner, crying and wishing it could have made the cut to become an accommodation on the IEP. But, alas, the IEP team did not think the student needed that recommendation in order to guarantee a free and appropriate public education. But, what's this? The case manager is plucking the little recommendation from the corner of the room. Now what is she doing? Why, she's applying that recommendation and using it to assist the student. Is she allowed to do that? The recommendation doesn't care! It's so pleased at being used it's got a huge smile plastered on its face and … and … was that a giggle? It seems that the recommendation is happy enough being wanted even if it isn't needed.

Recommendations that do not guarantee a student a free and appropriate public education are not included as accommodations. This does not mean, however, that they need to be totally discarded. A good recommendation should be implemented, assuming that it doesn't cost any money. Remember, the IEP team outlines what is needed. Educators are still free to use strategies and tools as appropriate.

May I Take Your Order?

When you know what you want to order at a restaurant, you close the menu and set it on the table. That is your nonverbal signal to the server that you're ready to place an order. Likewise, when it is time for the assistive technology trainer to acquire a device, a nonverbal signal is sent from the IEP team in the form of the Review/Revision or new IEP. After the assistive technology trainer receives this documentation, acquisition of materials can begin. The IEP team should be cognizant of the fact that it might take some time to obtain the device. Devices need to be ordered, paid for, shipped, unpackaged, and catalogued, all before delivery to the student can take place. Therefore, when writing the starting date for the accommodation that includes a device, it is wise for the IEP team to give some leeway. The IEP team should understand that the device will be delivered as soon as it is acquired; however, there needs to be an acknowledgment as to when that will occur. One possible way to avoid a conflict between acquisition time and the wording on the IEP is by using the phrase "no later than" along with a date that is as far off in the future as can be agreed upon. This way, there is sufficient time for acquisition, and the device can be implemented upon arrival.

The Loophole Riddle

Everything described so far for requesting, conducting, and considering an assistive technology evaluation is a procedure or a process. What would a good procedure be without a loophole? And this one is no exception. Sure, we could just explain what the loophole is—but what fun would that be? Instead, we've decided to make it into a game. The loophole is not described on this page. Rather, it is hidden on another page in this book. Which page? Well, that's the game. You need to break the code below in order to find the loophole. Don't bother looking in the table of contents, either, you cheater—we purposely left it out of there!

2 12 6__4 18 15 15__21 18 13 23__ 18 7

6 11 8 18 23 22__23 12 4 13__26 7

7 19 22__22 13 23__12 21__7 19 22__25 12 12 16

The Evaluation List

For the list lover in you, the following is a list of each step of an assistive technology evaluation.

1. An assistive technology consultation is conducted and an assistive technology evaluation is recommended.

2. The IEP team requests an assistive technology evaluation by documenting the request as a service on the IEP.

3. The IEP team documents which goals the student is struggling to achieve.

4. A representative of the IEP, most likely the case manager of the student, sends the required documentation to the assistive technology trainer.

5. The assistive technology trainer reviews the documentation and schedules the evaluation, including an observation of the student, interviews with relevant educators, and possibly an interview of the student.

6. The assistive technology trainer conducts the evaluation, gathering sufficient information for effective recommendations.

7. The assistive technology trainer writes a report documenting justified recommendations.

8. The assistive technology trainer provides the report to the representative of the IEP.

9. The representative of the IEP distributes copies of the report to all IEP team members.

10. The IEP team members individually review the report and ask questions for clarification from the assistive technology trainer.

11. The IEP team reconvenes to review the report, decides which recommendations will be implemented, and documents which recommendations will become accommodations.

12. The IEP team sends the updated IEP, including recommendations, to the assistive technology trainer.

13. The assistive technology trainer acquires and provides any necessary tools and related training.

14. Educators collect data on the student's performance as outlined in the IEP.

15. Accommodations are scrutinized for their necessity during each successive IEP meeting.

chapter 16

assistive technology
classroom
evaluations

Johnny AT-Seed: Growing an Orchard

Assistive technology trainers feel more confident with each evaluation. They begin to feel like Johnny AT-Seed, crossing the district planting seeds of solutions that will bear the fruit of knowledge in the form of learning strategies. They see those seeds sprout, reach out for more sun, and then branch out. As word spreads from educator to educator about the good work being done by the assistive technology team, more folks will begin to make inquiries about how assistive technology can be used to support their own educational practices. As Johnny AT-seed travels from school to school, an ever-increasing number of students discover new ways to learn and demonstrate knowledge. Leaving each student and educator excited about new tools and strategies, Johnny can see the fruits of diligent labor. Educators are smiling. Students are happy. When conducting an assistive technology evaluation and making recommendations, invariably educators will remark, "Gosh! I can use that same solution with Tanya and Josie, too!" That's a few more AT seeds, planted, watered, and ready to grow! Which leads to an idea. Instead of planting one seed at a time, maybe there is a way to plant an entire orchard. Maybe there is a way to provide tools and strategies that aren't already available in a classroom—to the entire classroom. How can this be accomplished? Through assistive technology classroom evaluations!

Tilling the Classroom Soil

Let's say an educator is working with a number of students receiving special education services who have good verbal skills, but demonstrating their knowledge on curricular topics is a thorny issue. These students, collectively, are having similar difficulties. Initially, perhaps the educator would like to schedule a series of individual assistive technology evaluations because all known strategies have been exhausted. Because all the students are experiencing similar difficulties, there may be a faster, more prudent method for addressing these concerns. The first step for the educator should be to contact the assistive technology trainer to raise some concerns about students in the class. After the assistive technology trainer expresses gratitude to the educator for making contact without requesting individual evaluations, the trainer and the educator can begin to work collaboratively to develop ideas to assist the students in need. The conversation should start with an exploration of the problems that exist, just like a consultation for an individual student. The trainer scratches around in the soil to get some basic information about the concerns and previously tried, but not completely successful, interventions. Using this information the educator and the assistive technology trainer begin to weed the soil to make room for the new ideas to grow. From this conversation a series of ideas will sprout. Some of these ideas may be in the form of tools and strategies already available in the classroom, but there may be times when the trainer and educator feel that additional tools may be beneficial. When this is the case, the assistive technology trainer could recommend that a classroom evaluation be conducted.

To Benefit the Many

Because the classroom evaluation is not related to individual IEPs, it is not governed by any law. There is no law stating that assistive technology classroom evaluations are a necessary service in a school district. Although not dictated by law, an assistive technology team may wish to consider this practice for introducing tools and strategies to a classroom. The practice of conducting classroom assistive technology evaluations is a fast and simple way to provide justification for the purchase of additional tools. Similar to an individual evaluation, the classroom evaluation provides a way of determining which tools should be implemented in a classroom while simultaneously providing a justification for these tools. For each recommendation in a classroom evaluation, the assistive technology trainer is essentially saying, "I think the students in this environment would benefit from this tool. It's okay to go buy it." It is important to realize that the assistive technology classroom evaluation centers on the word "benefit" and not "need." If a student needs a particular tool, well, that is a decision made by the IEP team—but if students (note the "s") could benefit from something, well, that's a decision made by the educators working with those students.

Less Is More: Streamlining Paperwork

Making it as easy as possible for an educator to request a classroom evaluation maximizes the possibility that the educator will want to use this service of the assistive technology team. Educators have enough paperwork to do, so streamlining the process is important. When developing a "request for classroom evaluation" form, keep in mind that the astrological sign of every student in the class is not necessary information. Just start with the basics, and any additional information can be discovered while conducting the classroom evaluation. The following is the short list of information necessary before conducting an assistive technology classroom evaluation:

* What are the educator's concerns?

* Which tools and strategies, in general, have already been tried?

* When is the best time to observe the students in order to see them working in the area of concern?

One for All: The Needs of One Benefit All

A classroom evaluation can be conducted in any educational environment provided that there are at least two students receiving special education services presenting similar difficulties. When the students are included in the general education classroom, the assistive technology trainer can conduct the evaluation in the general education setting. If a recommendation is made for an additional tool—for example, an additional software title added to the computers within the classroom—when this tool is implemented in the classroom, it becomes available for any student in that environment to use. When training the students in the class on the new tool, the trainer could start with the students with disabilities. Depending on the disability, those students could then model the tool's use and possibly demonstrate to classmates how the tool works. It's thrilling to see a student who was struggling turn around and demonstrate the tool used to overcome that challenge. In many cases, the new tool in the classroom also becomes an avenue to differentiate instruction. Universal design for learning becomes a reality when any student in the class has access to the tools they need to be successful. In this way, the assistive technology classroom evaluation is a powerful method for reaching many learners. Students can be impacted with immediate, at-their-fingertips solutions. The assistive technology classroom evaluation is a quick, easy, and effective best practice using the principles of Universal Design for Learning all rolled up into one tidy package.

High-Yield Planning: Visiting the Classroom

Following the initial consultation with the educator, the assistive technology trainer visits the classroom or other environment during a time when the students are working on an area where the challenges are being exhibited. There are many similarities in how classroom evaluations and individual evaluations are conducted (Fig. 16.1). During a classroom evaluation the trainer observes what is already being used, witnesses students demonstrating difficulties, watches student coping strategies, possibly interacts with the students to glean more information, interviews the educators working in that environment, and generates ideas for tools and strategies. As long as no student is being singled out, the trainer may work with the class, trying different techniques and strategies to get an idea of what might be effective recommendations.

classroom AT evaluation

Pertains to more than one student receiving special education services

Interact with multiple students in a classroom (optional)

Share strategies among students (generally)

Write evaluation using friendly language

Referral source reviews recommendations and determines implementation

Initial consultation: Note challenging issues and strategies tried

Visit environment to observe student work and challenges

Observe classroom supports and strategies in use

Generate/Demonstrate ideas and recommendations

Provide AT supports, training, and equipment as warranted

Involve related service staff

Receive formal request for evaluation via IEP team

Review individual's IEP

Interact with or interview student (optional)

Write evaluation using formal language

IEP team reviews and accepts recommendations

individual AT evaluation

Figure 16.1 Similarities and differences between classroom and individual AT evaluations

But Wait, There's More! Even Less Paperwork

Order the free assistive technology classroom evaluation and receive absolutely free, at no extra cost, a beautiful "No IEP Meeting Pass" good for *all* participants! Because the observation is being conducted in a classroom setting and no particular student is being evaluated, the assistive technology trainer can proceed without a formal meeting. Shall we repeat that? No IEP meeting is necessary! The assistive technology trainer is offering suggestions for the entire classroom. The suggestions and recommendations will offer solutions for best-practice teaching techniques. When the assistive technology trainer makes recommendations, these will become tools of the trade needed to meet the needs of that particular set of students. The assistive technology trainer is not making individualized recommendations for individual students, but, rather, making global recommendations that can be used by the majority of the students in the environment.

Early Bird Special

When educators first hear about the almost-too-good-to-be-true assistive technology classroom evaluation, they often jump at the chance to have one. Why shouldn't they? Minimal paperwork, no additional meetings, and solutions for the majority of the students in the environment are a winning combination. Eager to get tools and strategies in place, many educators request classroom evaluations as early in the school year as they can, just as soon as they get a feel for the students' strengths and weaknesses. Conducting classroom evaluations early in the school year will help to establish a set of strategies that can be tweaked and fine-tuned throughout the entire year.

Easy Does It: The Classroom Evaluation Report

Once the observation is complete, the assistive technology trainer generates an assistive technology classroom evaluation report. Assistive technology evaluation reports for individual students need to be written formally as an official document because the report is going to be reviewed by the entire IEP team. In contrast, assistive technology classroom evaluation reports can be written in a friendly, informal style in order to foster the relationship between trainer and educator. Whether that documentation is placed on an official letterhead, sent electronically, or scrawled on a bubble-gum wrapper doesn't make much difference as long as the receiver can understand and keep the message. E-mail is the perfect way to write and send assistive technology classroom evaluations because e-mail lends itself to using a more friendly tone. E-mail can also be archived, retrieved, and converted into other file formats whenever necessary. A report completed in an e-mail is a valid way to document the completion of the classroom evaluation, because the service of an assistive technology classroom evaluation is not governed by anybody other than the assistive technology team (and possibly the special education department of the school district). What follows is an example of how an e-mail classroom evaluation might begin:

Dear Super Teacher,

My goodness, what a treat it was for us to have the opportunity to visit your class! It was such a pleasure watching a professional who loves her work. Every interaction served to engage each student in a positive learning and communication experience. We wish we could have stayed longer. It really seems like you have a fun class. I may have mentioned that whenever we come out and do classroom evaluations, we end up learning new ideas that we can spread around the county. The visit to your classroom was no exception. Each student appeared to feel welcomed and at ease in a positive learning experience. They demonstrated respect for each other and engaged in self-directed activities based on established routines. We were able to watch a language arts activity where the students engaged in an assignment of daily sentences and then used color-coded magnetized sentence strips in a cooperative learning vocabulary exercise.

The strategies and organization in your classroom are models for all. The existing strategies include a plethora of technology such as the clever low-tech reminder for students to return their permission slips, the daily agenda on the board, the use of highlighters, organizational strategies in the form of student cubbies, paper clip work tasks, and use of graphic organizers, just to name a few. It is abundantly apparent that you recognize and address the individual needs of each of your students, seeming to challenge each of your students at their individual skill level, on both an academic and communication skill level. Each student appeared engaged and involved throughout your lesson.

> As I noted, you are already using a lot of technology in your classroom. Just a fraction of the strategies are mentioned above. We are hoping that you will share some of your math websites and PowerPoint treasures with us to pass along to other lucky teachers. I suspect that there are many strategies you use that were not exhibited in our "snapshot" observation. I will not be surprised if you say, "We already do that" for at least one of these suggestions.

Within this introduction, note the assistive technology trainer stating how much technology the educator already had in place in order to emphasize the fact that every tool is considered technology, not just items with electricity. The trainer also maintains a positive tone throughout the introduction that is friendly, encouraging, courteous, respectful, and professional. Finally, the trainer points out that because of the nature of conducting evaluations in small chunks of time, only a snapshot of what really happens throughout the day was observed. This statement lets the teacher know that the assistive technology trainer realizes that the short amount of time to conduct the evaluation does not lend itself to getting a complete picture of what happens all day, every day and that the resulting recommendations are based on the snapshot.

I Want It All … and I Want It Now

After the classroom evaluation report is written, it is shared with the educator(s) who made the request. It is the responsibility of the educator to read the report and consider the recommendations. The educators may wish to meet with the assistive technology trainer to review the report, ask questions, and clarify the recommendations because, just as in an individual evaluation, the recommendations will be written using descriptive, generic terms rather than specific brand names. After the educator reviews the report, it is the educator's decision which recommendations to implement and in what order. In many cases the assistive technology trainer and the educator will work together to establish the order of implementation. Based on these decisions, the assistive technology trainer acquires the necessary tools and provides training. What follows is an example of an introduction to recommendations in a classroom evaluation report:

> … let us offer some recommendations. We ask that you take them into consideration with the knowledge that you have demonstrated

excellent perception of your students' needs. There is quite a list here, so you might think of prioritizing the list and then implementing one at time.

The following is an example of a conclusion to a classroom evaluation report:

> When you get this e-mail, if you have any questions about what is described here, let me know and we can go over them together. After your review, let me know which of these you would like to implement. For those recommendations that require specialized equipment or training, we will provide that as soon as you know that you want to use these strategies. Just so you know, the services don't stop here. We can work with you to help implement these strategies. We are always available to brainstorm solutions to any concerns you might be having. Thanks again for having us out, and keep having fun!

Always, Sometimes, Never: Sharing the Report

Just like conducting an individual assistive technology evaluation, when conducting a classroom evaluation, the trainer should collaborate with any pertinent related service providers, working to generate comprehensive recommendations. The written report can then be shared with every educator working in that classroom, so that the entire educational team becomes familiar with what was recommended and can take part in any new initiatives, tools, or strategies being implemented in the classroom. The assistive technology trainer can facilitate whole-team involvement by *always* working with related service providers and the teachers.

However, the assistive technology trainer should carefully consider the ramifications of sharing the evaluation with school administration. Unless specifically asked by administration to conduct a classroom evaluation or to share those reports, it might be best to leave the option of sharing the report with administration up to the teacher making the request. Sometimes, teachers may feel that recommendations in a report, even those written in the most positive manner possible, demonstrate their shortcomings. Again, to foster a positive relationship of trust, it is best to leave the decision to share the classroom evaluation report with administration up to the teacher unless you're specifically told to do otherwise.

An assistive technology classroom evaluation is never for an individual. There may be times where an educator wants to focus in on one student during the classroom evaluation. Of course the trainer should listen and try to offer assistance for that student, but when the conversation turns to one student's specific needs, then that is actually an assistive technology consultation. After brainstorming about this one student, the assistive technology trainer should attempt to redirect the conversation back to the concerns in the classroom as a group. When the assistive technology classroom evaluation report is generated, the recommendations should be only for items that might benefit more than one student.

Portion Control: Limited Recommendations

The assistive technology trainer has to rely on experience and intuition when deciding how many recommendations to include in the evaluation report. In direct contrast to the individual evaluation, where every possible recommendation should be included, an assistive technology trainer may want to limit the number of recommendations listed on the classroom evaluation report. Some teachers may feel intimidated or overwhelmed by a long list of recommendations. In these cases, too much of a good thing can be a bad thing. The goal is to foster a relationship between the trainer and the educator, not cause ulcers from worry and stress. The assistive technology trainer has the option to reserve some recommendations for a classroom evaluation report if the list is beginning to get too lengthy. These reserved recommendations could be written in the trainer's notes but not included in the report so that the trainer can refer to them in the future once a few recommendations have been successfully implemented.

From Classroom to Individual

It is the expectation of the assistive technology trainer and educators that tools placed in a classroom become integrated successfully with students. These tools are for use by anyone in the classroom, but sometimes a student integrates one so successfully to help achieve goals that it might become apparent that the student needs this tool in order to receive a free and appropriate education.

For example, a classroom evaluation was completed for a room full of fifth-grade students, and one of the implemented recommendations was the use of word prediction software for writing activities. The teacher encouraged students to use the software to help them with their spelling when generating sentences. One student, let's call her Chelsea, quickly took to using the software and has expressed how much she enjoys using it. Over time, data has been collected documenting that Chelsea's writing abilities have made great strides toward her writing goal. It appears that Chelsea may need the word prediction software to continue to make progress on that goal. In this scenario, it is best for the IEP team to request an individual assistive technology evaluation to make recommendations that may lead to the acquisition of the software for Chelsea's specific use. In this way, once the IEP team has adopted a recommendation from the individual assistive technology evaluation as an accommodation, Chelsea will be guaranteed access to that software in future educational environments (including when she moves on to middle school and new classroom settings that did not have an assistive technology classroom evaluation).

Conversely, if a classroom tool doesn't work for a student, that also provides additional important information to the educational team. Further investigation on an individual basis becomes streamlined with this data. There will be an occasional student whose needs will not be met completely by a classroom evaluation, and that will be the time for an individual one. The classroom evaluation process has provided valuable information to better pinpoint which direction to take to help that student achieve IEP goals. Regardless of success, the tools and strategies employed as a result of a classroom evaluation can provide valuable data to tailor an IEP to truly meet an individual's needs.

Year to Year

The dynamics in a classroom may change from year to year. Students move on to their next environment, educators move on to their next professional goal, and technology moves onward, ever changing. There will be situations where an educator works with the same group of students from year to year, but for most classrooms the environment changes yearly. For this reason, the majority of classroom evaluations are valid only until the end of that school year. In order to determine whether a classroom should continue to work off the existing classroom evaluation report or a new classroom evaluation report should be generated, the trainer should consider the following:

Is the environment similar? If the environment within the classroom has not changed or has only changed slightly, then consider the existing classroom evaluation report as remaining valid. In this scenario the trainer could provide tools repeatedly to a classroom knowing that the majority of students, and their respective goals, have remained constant. However, if the majority of students have changed, or if the goals of student have changed, then it might be best to conduct a new classroom evaluation to generate more pertinent recommendations resulting in more pertinent tools.

Has the educator incorporated the tools into lessons? If the environment has changed within the classroom but the educator remains constant, the trainer might consider viewing the existing classroom evaluation as valid. If an educator has implemented the tools so successfully that the tools have become integral parts of lesson plans relied upon by the educator, then it might be best to leave the tools in place from year to year.

chapter 17

training
and
follow-up

Do With, Not For

You've heard the old Chinese proverb "Give a man a fish and you feed him for a day. Teach a man to fish and you feed him for a lifetime." It's a great little saying, but wouldn't it be nice to have the fish and learn how to fish later? Who likes to learn on an empty stomach? The educator will be the person ultimately responsible for integrating the technology into a student's environment; therefore, it is best for the assistive technology trainer to provide training in such a way that helps the educator learn the material as quickly and efficiently as possible without doing all the work for an educator. Assistive technology trainers should always follow this rule: Do *with* an educator, not *for* an educator.

Do not make a PowerPoint presentation for an educator—make it with the educator. Do not adapt a storybook for an educator—adapt it with the educator. Do not create a visual schedule for an educator—create it with the educator. We are not advocating leaving educators in the lurch; by trying to minimize the amount being done *for* a teacher and maximizing the amount being done *with* a teacher, the assistive technology trainer empowers the teacher and, ultimately, provides an assistive technology service to every future student that teacher instructs.

Training Wheels: Methods for Training

Providing training and following up with educators is one of an assistive technology trainer's most important responsibilities. Training and follow-up need to be offered after every consultation, individual evaluation, and classroom evaluation to increase the chances that the tools and strategies will actually be used in the classroom. To some educators, implementation of tools and strategies may be as easy as falling off a bicycle. To others, integrating new tools and strategies might be a scary as spending a night alone in the Bates Motel on Halloween. No matter how comfortable an educator is with new technologies, even the most savvy traveler in the realm of assistive technology needs some guidance in order to use new strategies. The job even stresses the importance of this duty right in the title "Assistive Technology Trainer."

Training does not always need to be a face-to-face visit with an educator—it can take many forms. Like an educator differentiating instruction to meet the needs of all of the learners in the classroom, the assistive technology trainer needs to evaluate each case to establish the best methods for providing training. What follows is a list of some different training strategies:

Appendixes. Including training materials as appendixes to the evaluation report provides an opportunity for the entire IEP team to learn how recommendations would actually be implemented. Sample visual strategies, classroom floor plans, graphic organizing templates, or brief software tutorials with relevant curricular topics are all examples of items that could be placed within an appendix. It is helpful to embed the appendixes in the digital copy of the report so that the case manager receives all of the information in one tidy little package. By always including every tutorial and sample in the appendix material, the trainer won't have to try to remember, "Did I put that tutorial on how to insert a voice recording into a Microsoft Word document in the envelope when I mailed it?" Or "What did I attach to that last report I wrote about a student with similar learning issues?" The electronic file will be complete with the cover letter, evaluation, and appendixes.

Electronic resources. Websites can offer a wealth of information. Ready-made templates, activities, slide shows, visuals, and more can be found on the World Wide Web. You name it—the web has it! Why slave away making visuals or communication boards when another wonderful educator has already created and shared that type of resource? Even if it's not exactly what is needed, often it can lead the educator down the right path or provide enough impetus to get started. Educators work hard enough without having to create new materials from scratch. To some, new tools and strategies can sound daunting until the trainer shows them where they can find great ideas to help pique their curiosity and differentiate instruction. When teachers see that resources have already been created, resulting in less preparation time and less work, they'll smother their trainer with appreciation.

Tutorials. Did you ever get a do-it-yourself kit to build a piece of furniture? Did you read the manual or just look at the pictures? If you're like us, you hate to read manuals and the pictures are what you look at first, reading the text only to fill in the gaps. This is how your tutorials should work. When creating tutorials, the assistive technology trainer should bring in graphics and screenshots to demonstrate the step-by-step navigation of computer programs. A picture is worth a thousand words. As a team, assistive technology trainers can collect these gems and provide easy access to them by creating a common folder to house them. Periodically, each trainer can copy this folder to a thumb drive to take while traveling from school to school. This way the trainer can share the tutorial quickly whenever a nifty and timely trick needs to be demonstrated.

Samples. For some IEP team members, a sample will be just the right touch to get started in creating relevant classroom tools. Providing a sample resource to an IEP team is like handing out a free sample of food at the grocery store. Both tantalize the sampler to explore the product further. For example, if a place mat of visuals is a recommendation for a preschool-age student, the assistive technology trainer could find or make a sample and provide a short description of the materials used to create the sample. For tools or strategies that are tangible

just a click away

When you offer website resources in an evaluation or consultation, be sure to provide the IEP team members with the resources in a digital format. No one wants to try to type a long URL into an Internet browser. By providing the resources in a digital format with active hyperlinks, you've made them easy to click and explore, and you increase the chances that the IEP team members will visit those resources.

objects, a digital photograph could provide the inspiration. The sample should lead educators to want to create and use more, or to expand on the sample provided.

Video tutorials. Just as students have unique learning styles, so does each IEP team member. Video tutorials may offer just the solution for visual learners. A program that can capture the movement of the cursor and menu selections can be used to create a short video tutorial on how a student could interface with a software title. Watching the process involved in using a program or creating a classroom support may be the way to hook a student or educator who learns best from visual media. Unlike a live training session, a video can be watched repeatedly to refresh memories or to relearn a concept.

Modeling. Educators may feel like a tool or strategy is too overwhelming for them to successfully implement alone. In these situations, having the trainer model how a tool or strategy can be integrated can go a long way to demonstrating that the technology is there to help, not hinder. Often the trainer will also hook the students, who will bring the teacher along for the ride. Jumping right into the thick of things and acting as the trusty trail guide to explore the mysteries of the new technology will go a long way to reinforce the fact that the educator is not alone on the adventure. As an educator gains confidence in newfound abilities, the assistive technology trainer can slowly tiptoe out of the room. In this way tools and strategies will become part of the routine of the classroom and not something to consciously think about, resulting in best practices in action.

When you offer the menu of training opportunities to educators, try to establish a firm training date right then when their interest is piqued. For example, if an educator shows interest in co-teaching a classroom lesson, don't let that opportunity slip through your fingers. Grab your calendar and say, "How about next Wednesday?" If the educator needs to postpone the appointment, set another date right away. Too often people say, "I'll be in touch with you," and before they know it it's the end of the school year. Writing the dates on the calendar helps educators carve out the time necessary. Then, a day or two before the training, send out a reminder e-mail letting them know that you're excited about the opportunity to train. A preparatory e-mail is just one other way to foster the ongoing positive relationship established with the educator while providing a subtle reminder that the training is coming up soon.

Each One Teach One: Students as Trainers

Each generation seems to partner most easily with the latest technology. We love technology, but can't begin to text message on a cell phone as quickly as the typical teenager. The assistive technology trainer can make the most of these skills by enlisting students into the AT Brigade! The trainer can teach the students strategies while the teacher looks on, we hope with a broadening smile. Even if the trainer starts by training just one student, that one will spread the word of what was learned. It won't be hard to spot the

parents as partners

Parental involvement is integral for student success, but the type of participation necessary varies depending on what tools and strategies are being used. For instance, if a strategy is to give the student the responsibility of feeding the classroom fish, the parents aren't expected to run out and buy an aquarium so the student can practice at home. Instead, the parents could promote the strategy by encouraging active participation and asking the student about the job. Minimally, the parents or guardians of the student should be made aware of the strategies used in the classroom. In most cases, however, it is important for the parents to be active participants using tools and strategies in the home environment as well. For instance, if a student is using a communication device, it is imperative that the communication device be consistently implemented across all environments.

student who is comfortable with a computer or dry-erase marker on a desktop. Showing that student a shortcut and watching that student nudge a classmate to spread the good news will be fun to watch. Any tool or strategy that a student finds interesting, such as text-to-speech software or an editing tool that has jazzy colored transparency windows, will spread from student to student faster than the flu. Before long, small groups of infected students will pass the contagion through the entire class. Even the most reluctant, technophobic educators will be bitten by the bug and succumb to the new best practice born in the classroom.

Paraprofessionals: Diamonds That Sparkle

Every educator working in the classroom makes an impact on students. In many cases a teaching assistant may spend more time with a student than any other educator. Likewise, many teaching assistants may be friendlier with technology, leading the other educators in the use of a new tool or strategy. It's important to provide technology training (be it for low-tech or high-tech tools) to para-professionals as well primary educators. Arming the teaching assistant with the knowledge of how to successfully implement a tool or strategy maximizes the student's exposure to the technology. Investing the time to provide training to anyone supporting students will pay off in the long run for everyone—especially the student.

Curb Your Enthusiasm: Shorter Is Sweeter

Educators are hungry for strategies and tools that have been proved useful for students. It is understandable to want to share your entire assortment of tasty strategies as fast as possible in order to fill that new educator's brain with fantastic new techniques to implement technology. If it were as easy as cranking open the educator's mouth, backing up the dump truck, and letting it all fall in, the job of the assistive technology trainer would be much easier. Unfortunately, too much all at once often leads to AT indigestion. One spoonful at a time is often better than cramming the belly to the point of explosion. Learners vary in the amount they can handle in one sitting, and each will provide signs indicating when it is time to stop. Trying to match the appetite of the learner, whether it is a student or an educator, takes patience. Sometimes curbing enthusiasm, speaking slowly, and exercising some restraint provides for a more palatable experience, leaving room for a future dessert.

Never Underestimate Face Time

The assistive technology trainer should visit with educators and classrooms following consultations and evaluations as needed. The presence of the trainer in the school will often generate important questions and comments that are easily answered face-to-face. Invariably an educator, upon seeing the trainer walking down the hall, will seize the opportunity to say, "I have been meaning to e-mail you about a student" or "I'm so glad I saw you, because I have a question for you." These are great conversations that lead to building rapport and relationships necessary to spread the good news about assistive technology. It never hurts for the trainer to pop into a classroom while visiting a school just to ask, "How is that strategy working? Do you have any questions?" The amount of goodwill generated by these friendly visits will be immeasurable in relation to the time invested.

run, run, as fast as you can! a tale of caution

The frightened teacher sprinted down the empty hallway as fast as her short legs could carry her, whizzing past rows of lockers. She turned the corner and took the stairs two at a time, surprising herself at how nimbly she leapt from stair to stair. Stopping to catch her breath when she crested the top stair, she chanced a glance back down the stairwell. Was her pursuer still coming? Over the sound of her wildly beating heart she strained to hear any footsteps or breathing or any other sign that the … the … *thing* was still after her. What the heck was it? It looked human, but no human could send that many e-mails. No human could make that many phone calls. No human could be in that many places at one time. Unless it was … obsessed!

Things were great at first. One student needed help with some organization skills. The teacher called her assistive technology trainer and they met, brainstormed, and came up with strategies. The student began to use the strategies, and everyone was happy. But then the e-mails started. At first, it was just one. No big deal. Then it turned into one per day. One turned into two, and two turned to four, and before long there was no way to keep up. "How is Johnny doing?" read one e-mail. Thirty minutes later "Here's another resource for you" popped up in the inbox. Twenty minutes after that: "Did you like the resource I sent you? How does Johnny like it?" Ten minutes later: "Oh, one other thing, maybe I could stop by sometime to observe Johnny using the strategies?" Four minutes after that: "I haven't heard from you yet. I know you must be busy. What if I come by tomorrow, or even better yet, later today?" Two minutes later: "I'm going to be driving by your school anyway today. I'm going to pop in." Day after day the e-mails came, followed by phone calls and multiple surprise visits. She couldn't escape.

How had the good working relationship degraded into this onslaught of attempted correspondence? She told that crazy assistive technology trainer that if the strategies didn't work, they would get together again. But the strategies were working! Why was this follow-up machine—that's what she really was, a machine—still stalking her?

The teacher leaned over the railing, but there was still no sign of the warped assistive technology trainer. Had she finally gotten her point across that she wanted to be left alone? The teacher felt the adrenaline rush wane and her heart rate begin to slow. Maybe the assistive technology trainer had taken her hint of tearing down the hallway in the opposite direction as it was intended. Don't call me, I'll call you. Just then the loud, sharp RINGGG of the bell rang through the hallways and she nearly jumped out of her skin.

The hallways flooded with teens headed toward their lockers. Feeling foolish about her nervous behavior, she made her way back to her classroom. Surely it must be safe now. She smiled and nodded at students as she passed them in the busy hall. "Yeah, she must have gotten that point," the teacher thought as she turned the handle of the door to her classroom. You'd have to be really obstinate to not get the poi…

"Hiya!" said the assistive technology trainer, sitting at the teacher's desk in the room. "Looked like you had quite the emergency there, the way you were running down the hall. Does it have to do with Johnny? Anything I can do to help?"

■ ■ ■ ■ ■

As a general rule, assistive technology trainers should try not to chase educators. Every educator has a busy schedule with multiple responsibilities. The role of the assistive technology trainer is to be supportive, not oppressive. Whenever possible, the assistive technology trainer should let educators call for meetings when they are necessary. That is, assistive technology trainers should let the educators know that they will be at their beck and call, but it is up to the educators to make contact. Every now and again a simple e-mail reminder or popping into a classroom to say hello is appropriate, but only occasionally. Like a golfer who hits the golf ball just right, making it rip through the air in a perfect arc, landing just inches from the hole, the assistive technology trainer is looking for the sweet spot. Finding the balance between not enough contact and too much contact is the challenge for every assistive technology trainer (and golfer).

guilty as charged

On visits to classrooms you'll find devices that, for whatever reason, were never implemented. Making educators feel guilty about those devices sitting on a shelf gathering dust isn't a positive way to motivate them to use devices. Trainers should save the guilt for those evil siblings who forgot their birthdays or who ditched them at the last minute when they needed a babysitter. Instead, trainers should investigate the situation to discover why the device wasn't implemented. If the student(s) in the class are making progress without the use of the devices, then they probably weren't necessary in the first place. If the student(s) in the class continue to demonstrate difficulties, work with the teacher to alleviate those difficulties by providing further training.

Keeping Tabs via Progress Notes

A key element in following up with a student is the collection and review of progress notes. Educators should provide progress reports to all IEP team members to document the student's progress or lack of progress toward goals. These reports serve as an indicator of whether or not the IEP is working to meet the needs of the student. By reviewing the progress notes, both the IEP team and the assistive technology trainer can make extrapolations about the relative necessity of accommodations. Upon review of the progress notes, the following two scenarios could occur:

1. Goals are being met. Prior to the involvement of the assistive technology trainer, the student was having difficulty meeting a goal. Following the implementation of the assistive technology trainer's recommendations, the student has started to meet the goals as expected. Hooray! Huzzah! Yippee-ki-yay! The IEP team and the assistive technology trainer might read the following while reviewing the progress notes for a student: "The student has made sufficient progress on goal X, achieving the targeted 75% accuracy." Based on this review the IEP team and the assistive technology team can extrapolate (not 100% know, but infer) that the IEP, including the identified accommodations, is working to meet the needs of the student. By extension, the IEP team and assistive technology trainer can extrapolate (again, not with

100% certainty) that the assistive technology devices that were implemented as accommodations are working to meet the needs of the student. If the student made progress, keep using what's being used and let the big wheel keep on turnin'.

2. Goals are still not being met.

Prior to the involvement of the assistive technology trainer, the student was having difficulty meeting a goal. Following the implementation of the assistive technology trainer's recommendations, the student has continued to struggle to meet the goal. Rats! Darn it! Pattooey! The IEP team and the assistive technology trainer might read the following while reviewing the progress notes for this student: "The student has demonstrated insufficient progress on goal X, achieving 34% accuracy." Based on this review the IEP team and the assistive technology trainer can extrapolate (not know with 100% certainty, but infer) that the

a shout-out in the progress note

Like a person requesting a song on a radio station, the educator writing the progress note might include a dedication or a "shout-out" to the assistive technology being used to support the student in the achievement of targeted goals. For instance, it would be totally appropriate to see a statement such as "Using her voice output device, Natalie made requests during 75% of the communication opportunities" or "When using a pencil grip, Debbie wrote two complete sentences in four out of five opportunities 75% of the time." It is not necessary to comment on the use of the technology in the progress notes, but including it provides more information about which accommodations continue to be necessary to ensure a free and appropriate public education.

IEP, including the identified accommodations, is not working to meet the needs of the student. However, the IEP team and assistive technology trainer cannot infer that the assistive technology devices that were implemented as accommodations are the reason insufficient progress is being made. There could be many other factors contributing to why a student continues to demonstrate difficulties. In fact, perhaps the assistive technology added as accommodations is the only reason the student achieved to the degree he did. If a student is not making sufficient progress, it indicates that a change needs to be made to the student's IEP.

The change can include alterations and additions to a student's use of assistive technology, but that is only one of a multitude of options set in front of the IEP team. Analysis of the educational situation as a whole, including the student's accommodations of assistive technology devices, should become the focus of the IEP team to ensure that the student begins to meet the goals.

Collecting Data for Progress Reports

Data drives decisions and is essential to substantiating and perpetuating assistive technology services. Data can also be the bane of our existence. For educators, sometimes it might seem as if four arms are necessary to simultaneously conduct a lesson and collect data. We suggest that educators collect data only on IEP goals, just as is mandated. The data on the progress toward goals will indicate whether tools and strategies are successful.

Remember, recommendations outlined in an assistive technology consultation or evaluation are *not* goals; they are teaching practices or accommodations. Educators are not expected to collect data on accommodations, merely to review the accommodations at IEP meetings to ensure that they're necessary for a free and appropriate public education. Educators are not expected to keep empirical data on teaching practices, but to intuitively note and make alterations should that be necessary.

The Data Dragon: Objective Truths

Every once in a while the data dragon emerges from its lair to loom behind educators, breathing hot breath down their necks, reminding them that data, data, data is the only way to know what is really going on with a student. Sometimes that dragon may lie dormant, resting peacefully in solitude in a faraway land, forgotten by all. When the data dragon hibernates, it is easy for educators to lose the objectivity that comes along with data collection. Everyone has experienced the surprising moment when their rose-colored perceptions were smacked in the face with reality once data was collected. (You used the ATM *how* many times this month? Surely someone else devoured that entire one-pound bag of M&Ms in one day? Buying a daily cup of coffee costs *how* much a month?). It's even easier to lose objectivity when working with students because you care about them. These students aren't just ordinary students, either. They are students with disabilities, and everyone wants to see and cheer their success. Unfortunately, when the data dragon slumbers, truth has the potential to be warped into seeing what we want to see that isn't really there. Only the clinical eye of data collection will show the truth for what it really is, and only if the methods of collecting that data are empirical and unbiased.

Here a Datum, There a Datum, Everywhere a Datum Datum

In order for the quality of comparative data to be high, it must be collected in identical conditions over a period of time. Identical conditions? What is the likelihood of that occurring in a classroom? What is the likelihood of that occurring in multiple environments? We might venture to say that the chances of removing or alleviating variables from student performance are slim to none. Educators need to realize that variables are impossible to control and that the variables contribute to and affect the data, leading to data that might not be accurate. Realizing that variables are impossible to control and that those variables contribute to and affect the data can help illuminate the stairway to progress for educators. Or to put it less poetically and more succinctly, educators should: "Look only to what can be seen."

growing before your very eyes

Working with a student on a daily basis makes it harder to recognize the tiny incremental changes taking place. This is why parents don't notice their children growing—it's not until their kid puts on his dress pants from last holiday season and they reach to somewhere shy of flood level that they actually notice his height change. Educators need to collect data to see the significant positive changes in a behavior that have taken place over the course of the quarter or school year.

Collecting the Right Data

Assistive technology is only one of many contributors to student success. So when it comes to documenting student success, assistive technology is not an entity unto itself. It is assistive. It exists as the means to an end and cannot be judged in isolation. Assistive technology in and of itself cannot be considered successful or unsuccessful. Assistive technology does not exist in a vacuum. Too many variables intervene to let us judge an assistive technology device all by its lonesome (Fig. 17.1). Therefore, collecting data on assistive technology is meaningless.

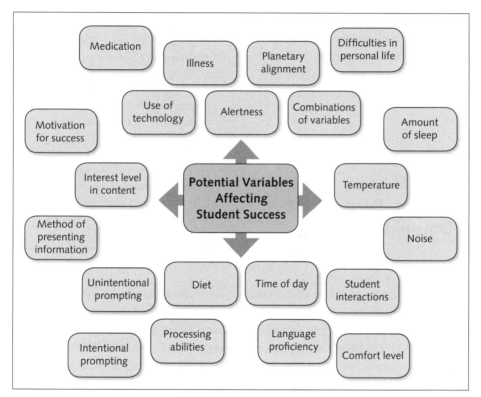

Figure 17.1 Student success may be affected by many variables

It is important to realize that just because the student has begun to make progress on the targeted goal, one cannot conclude that it is due to the assistive technology that was implemented. Likewise, if a student continues to demonstrate difficulty with making progress on targeted goals, it doesn't necessarily mean that the assistive technology implemented was ineffective. The assistive technology that was added as an accommodation might be the reason for the student's success, or it might not be. Without collecting data on the accommodation, the world will never know, and no one is expected to collect data on accommodations. There is no doubt that time could be spent measuring factors pertaining to an assistive technology device, such as how often it is used, in which environments it is used, and who is around when it is being used—but in the end, it is impossible to know with 100% certainty whether or not that piece of technology was the reason for success. There are too many other intervening variables. Therefore, spend the time collecting data that measures student achievement, student behaviors, and student progress toward meeting the goals, because the goals set the expectations of the student's education for the year.

The IEP, the driving force behind services provided to students with disabilities in the schools, is not a plan for how successful assistive technology will be. Answering the question of how successful the assistive technology will be provides irrelevant information. The IEP is a plan for student success. Therefore, the question to ask is, "How successful is the student?" The primary reason for the IEP, some might say the reason for legislation, is to drive student access and success in education. Remember that, by definition, assistive technology is in place "to increase, maintain, or improve functional capabilities of individuals with disabilities." It follows then that what is measurable is the functional capability, the outcome, the improvement. Assistive technology devices are not goals but accommodations. Assistive technology can only be reported in that context, the context of the goal itself. Assistive technology is definitely a means to that end, but it is not the end in itself. Achievement of educational goals is.

Across All Disciplines

If a student has a goal for successful composition of a five-sentence paragraph and uses assistive technology, say a portable word processor, to help reach that goal, the fact that a student has not mastered the five-sentence paragraph essay cannot be attributed solely to the portable word processor. If that were the case, we could blame our laptops for not writing this book more quickly. The principle that all variables cannot be controlled or accounted for holds true across all disciplines.

In speech therapy, the speech-language pathologist can never really be sure that her weekly sessions were the reason the student can now say, "I want more." Perhaps it was the fact that the student's sibling at home is also learning to talk and relishes the ability to repeat "I want more," reaping the rewards that phrase brings. This modeling behavior may have significantly contributed to the student using the phrase "I want more." The speech-language pathologist never really knows which variable or what combination of variables led to the increase in production. The speech-language pathologist can only report that the goal has been met because the desired behavior is now being demonstrated with consistency across all environments.

In another example, after six weeks of using particular software at school to assist with a math goal a student begins to demonstrate success and significant progress toward the goal. During week 7, in a parent conference, the father of the child reveals that the student has been receiving math tutoring after school. Which variable, the software or the tutoring, is producing successful results? Could either the tutor or the software be eliminated as an intervening variable and still chart success? Like the number of licks necessary to reach the center of a Tootsie Pop, the world may never know. Is it worth the risk to the success of the student to eliminate one of those variables? The truth is, you really never know why a student does or doesn't reach some goals—you only know if the goal has been met, if the behavior has been demonstrated. The rest is guesswork.

if i had a hammer

A device is just a device. A tool is just a tool. A hammer is just a hammer. The tool means nothing unless it used to do something. The hammer lies inert in the toolbox until someone comes along with a need to use it. And, whaddya know? Here comes Scotty, who needs to hang that picture of dear ol' Mum on his wall. Awww, look at her there smiling with her nice warm face. How sweet! Scotty is so nice to hang a picture of his sweet, darling mother. The job is simple. Scotty takes the nail, puts it against the wall, and immediately brings the hammer down. Smash! Right onto his thumb. He doesn't scream or swear, not in front of his mum, even if it is just a picture of her. It takes him a few more jolts to the thumb, but Scotty fights through the pain because he has a goal. Scotty wouldn't want to let his mother down. Once the nail is firmly in the wall, Scotty hangs the picture up, smiles, and walks away satisfied. It isn't until a few minutes later when Scotty's on the phone (with his mum) that the picture comes crashing down to shatter on the ground.

Why did the picture fall?

- Was the nail not in far enough?

- Was the picture too heavy?

- Did the drywall give way?

- Did a small, imperceptible tremor shake the picture off the wall?

- Did a ghost pull it off the wall?

Why did Scotty hit his thumb?

- Did he have bad hand-eye coordination?

- Was it too dark in the room?

- Did he have a one-time spasm, making his thumb twitch?

- Was his hand too close to the head of the nail?

- Was his thumb too large?

Was the hammer an effective tool?

- Did the hammer do its job?

- Did the hammer fail to do its job?

- Did the hammer do its job for a while?

- Is it the hammer's fault the picture broke?

- If the hammer had been used differently, would the picture still be on the wall?

- If Scotty had more training on the use of hammers, would the picture still be on the wall?

- Would a screwdriver have been a better tool to use?

The answer to all of these questions is unknown. Collecting data on the hammer would not have changed the outcome that the picture rests shattered on the floor. You never know if a tool is effective or ineffective—you only know if the job was accomplished or not. If the job was accomplished, then you can assume, but not know, that the tool was effective. If the job was not accomplished, then you can assume nothing.

■ ■ ■ ■ ■

The Data Collection Quandary

We invite you now to consider the alternative point of view by challenging yourself with the following set of riddles. The premise is simple. You are a member of an assistive technology team that exists in a parallel universe (where circles have straight lines, fish live on dry land, and evil Spock has a beard). Your assistive technology team has decided that it is going to collect data on every assistive technology device that has been included in an IEP as an accommodation, and it is not considering every accommodation as an AT device. To provide services equally to all students, you must solve each of the following riddles in such a way that you feel you have a satisfactory answer to each:

Riddle 1: Equity. If you are collecting data on one accommodation, should you be collecting data on all accommodations? If you are collecting data on only some of the accommodations, who decides which accommodations are worthy of data collection?

Riddle 2: Cost. One accommodation is to turn lined paper horizontally during mathematical computations to assist the student in aligning numbers into columns. Another accommodation is to use a word prediction program while typing, which requires the purchase and installation of software on multiple computers. Is it acceptable to collect data on just the word prediction accommodation on the sole basis that funds are needed to implement it?

Riddle 3: Extraction. Through the data collected, it is determined that it is likely that a student no longer requires a device as an accommodation. There are two months remaining before the IEP team is scheduled to meet to conduct the annual review. Is it prudent to ask the case manager, administrator, parents, student, general education teachers, and others to schedule a review and revision of the IEP in order to eliminate the accommodation immediately from the

IEP so that the device can be extracted? Repeat this question substituting the following durations in the question: one month, three months, four months, five months, six months, seven months, eight months, nine months, and ten months remaining before annual review?

Riddle 4: Duration. A student with a visual impairment has had an accommodation in his IEP for three years to use screen-reading software for accessing the computer. The student has relied on using the software for access to the computer for three years. When using the software, he has access to the computer. When not using the software, he does not have access to the computer. How long and how often should data be collected on this accommodation?

Riddle 5: Comparison. A student with attention difficulties has an accommodation for preferential seating. Should data be collected about proximity to the teacher, length of time of instruction the student sat in the preferential seating, proximity to the board, proximity to the television, noise level measured from the preferential seat during various times of the day, and so forth? Should data collected on all of these measurements prior to the preferential seating adjustments be used as comparisons?

Riddle 6: Personnel. Who conducts the collection of data on an accommodation and, if it isn't the assistive technology trainer, who tells that person to collect more data above and beyond the goals?

If you found yourself struggling to answer these riddles, well, then, you're not alone. Phase-shift back to this universe, leaving that other assistive technology team to muddle through those questions. Here, in this universe, you don't have to answer all of those questions because here, in this universe (where circles have no straight lines, fish live in water, and Spock is clean shaven) we collect data on goals, not accommodations.

Addendums and the Three-Year Itch

The time to review an assistive technology evaluation is when it is necessary. If a student is struggling and the suggested strategies are ineffective, it's time to dust off the assistive technology evaluation that was completed for the student and have another look at it. There might be some other recommendations in the assistive technology evaluation that are pertinent to the situation. Perhaps the team has not chosen to implement all the original recommended strategies, initially. At this point it would be time to review those other strategies, to see if any of them would be useful in helping the student meet the targeted goals. If it turns out that recommendations and resources outlined in an assistive technology evaluation report are still relevant to the student's situation, then by all means, consider implementing them. The IEP team can always reconvene to discuss changes in accommodations or include additional ones. In this way, the assistive technology evaluation can be reviewed by the IEP team as often as necessary. The customary environment, educators working with the student, and especially the goals the student is working toward will change periodically. As these changes occur, so do the needs of the student. A student might demonstrate difficulty achieving a goal at any point in time. Yet, if a student just received an assistive technology evaluation five or six months ago, a brand-new assistive technology evaluation may not be warranted. In these situations the assistive technology trainer might be called upon to revisit an evaluation, reconduct portions of the evaluation, and then generate an addendum to the current assistive technology evaluation with new recommendations or resources. The addendum to the assistive technology evaluation can then be reviewed by the IEP team just as if it were a complete evaluation.

Like milk in the fridge or your license from the DMV, the assistive technology evaluation should have an expiration date. The assistive technology team should develop a time period for how long evaluations are valid before a new assistive technology evaluation is required. We suggest considering a minimum of one year and a maximum of three years for validity. That means that at any point within that three-year time frame, an assistive technology trainer can revisit any portion of the evaluation and generate an addendum to the current individual assistive technology evaluation. Once the established validation period has expired, the IEP team would be required to reinitiate the process of requesting an evaluation through the IEP. In the new assistive technology evaluation report, the assistive technology trainer might state that an evaluation was completed in the past, referencing the date of the original evaluation for the sake of continuity. The new evaluation should stand alone, with new recommendations addressing the student's current goals and educational environment.

chapter 18

assistive technology
in the
summer

We realize that not every school district has a summer vacation and that some school districts operate using a 12-month cycle, opting for multiple shorter breaks rather than one longer summer break. Although this chapter is written from the perspective of school districts that have a summer vacation, we believe the content within this chapter applies to any extended breaks in the schedule. Summer vacation or no summer vacation, we think you'll still find the information in this chapter useful and applicable to your situation.

June, July, and August

Giving support to students over the summer break is extremely difficult to accomplish when the assistive technology trainer is not working. We're going to climb out on a limb here and guess that most assistive technology trainers don't want to work during the summer unless they're getting paid. We couldn't agree more. Yet, the fact remains that there may be some students who need the support of an assistive technology trainer during those months. Therefore, a pitch has to be made to the administration that having assistive technology support throughout the summer is necessary. It's a pretty simple sell. Something like, "Hey administrator. We need to make sure students get what they need throughout the summer. We need to make sure that teachers receive training to use those devices. We also need someone available to answer questions and do consultations during the summer. The assistive technology team (or some individuals on it) would be the natural candidates for the job. Can you squeeze into the budget funding for assistive technology summer staff? Whaddya say?" How can an administrator turn down that plea?

Payment schedules can be developed in a number of ways, including extending a contract to 11 months or 12 months long. If that doesn't fit nicely into how your school district does things, then maybe the assistive technology trainer can receive an hourly wage. Whatever the scenario, something needs to be worked out so that at least one member of the assistive technology team can remain on active duty during the summer months.

pictorial tutorials for transitions

To assist and help train the summer school teacher or any educator working with an unfamiliar student who uses an assistive technology device, the assistive technology trainer can work with the current educator to create short tutorials using pictures of the student accessing the device. Along with each picture, a brief description can be included of the way the student uses the device, such as optimum switch placement. The student, educator, and assistive technology trainer could work together to create a mini-book about how the student uses the device. The student could then be invited to present the book to the new educator. This strategy assists the student in buying into the use of the device and provides the teacher with the information about how the device has been used in the past. Similarly, short videos can be taken and used to demonstrate how a student uses the device. In some cases the student can assist in the creation of a short video demonstrating how the device has been used in previous educational environments.

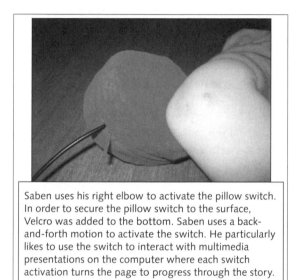

Saben uses his right elbow to activate the pillow switch. In order to secure the pillow switch to the surface, Velcro was added to the bottom. Saben uses a back-and-forth motion to activate the switch. He particularly likes to use the switch to interact with multimedia presentations on the computer where each switch activation turns the page to progress through the story.

Figure 18.1 Example from pictorial tutorial

Summer Scenarios

As the school year winds to a close, students will no doubt begin to daydream about the impending summer. Whether those dreams include playing with neighborhood friends, flirting with the cutie at the summer job, or sitting in a summer school class, students will begin to think about what's going to happen when school's out for summer. Following the students' leads, the educators should also begin thinking about what's going to happen for a student during the summer. While pondering that, the educator should consider which assistive technology devices that student will need throughout the summer as well. Every student will fit into one of the following scenarios:

Summer services and summer school. A student will be receiving summer services or be participating in summer school, or both. The IEP team may decide that the accommodations outlined in the IEP should be continued during summer school and those summer services. In this scenario, the student should continue to have access to assistive technology devices as outlined as accommodations in the IEP. For example, if a student has "calculator with auditory feedback" as an accommodation on the annual IEP and is working on a math goal during the summer services, then it makes sense for the student to continue to have access to that software when those services are provided.

Functional life skill. A student will not be receiving any summer services and will not be participating in summer school, but because the assistive technology device is necessary for the student to participate in a functional life skill, it may be necessary to retain the device throughout the summer. In this scenario, the student should continue to have access to the assistive technology devices that provide the student the ability to participate in the functional life skill. For example, if a student has been using a portable magnifying device because of a visual impairment, the student might need that device to use regardless of participation in extended school-year services or summer school. Determining whether a student needs a device for a functional life skill can be a simple process. In fact, the case manager could simply ponder the question, "Does this student use this device outside of school?" If the answer is "yes," then the student should have the device throughout the summer. If the answer is "no," then the device should be retained by the school district until the student returns to school in the fall.

Summer services/summer school and functional life skill combination. A student not only will be receiving summer services or participating in summer school, or both, but also will need access to an assistive technology device to access a functional life skill. In this scenario, the student might be receiving summer services and/or attending summer school during a portion of the summer. During the portions of the summer when the student is not receiving summer services and/or attending summer school, the student needs the assistive technology device to assist that student with a functional life skill.

No services, no need. A student will not be participating in summer school, will not be receiving summer services, and does not need access to a device for a functional life skill. In this scenario, it is best to retain the device within the school district for safekeeping and return it to the student at the onset of the new school year.

Functional Life Skills Form

Before you go whitewater rafting, bungee jumping, or skydiving, the company requires that you sign a form stating that you understand that you're about to do something

functional life skill list

The following are some possible reasons (functional life skills) a student might need access to a device over the summer:

- Reading
- Writing
- Communicating
- Organizing
- Ambulating
- Seeing
- Hearing

pretty gosh-darn dangerous and that the company has warned you that you're about to do something pretty gosh-darn dangerous. Yeah, as if you didn't know that plummeting from a great height or barreling through class 5s didn't involve a little spot of peril! But signing that piece of paper documents that both parties are aware of the situation.

If a student is going to retain an assistive technology device during the summer, it couldn't hurt to invite the parents or guardians and the student to sign a form stating that you know and they know they have the device for the summer. The form cannot state that the parents are responsible for the device or responsible for the cost of the device, because the law states that assistive technology devices are to be provided at no cost to the family. The purpose of the form is to document where the device is located during the summer in case any discrepancies might occur.

Assistive technology trainers facilitate the process of getting the form signed by parents or guardians by completing all the fields on the form except for parent signature. Keeping the form short, with only fields that are absolutely necessary, helps to streamline the process. The following information, at a minimum, should be included on the form:

- Student name/identification

- Current school

- Assistive technology device (name and tracking number)

- A statement about how and where to contact an assistive technology trainer in case the device malfunctions or is lost. For example, "If the equipment is lost or malfunctioning, or if you have questions regarding the equipment, please contact the Assistive Technology Team at 123-456-7890."

- A statement that the signature indicates an awareness that the device will reside at home and that signing the form does not signify financial responsibility for the device. For example, "In signing this form, it is understood that the equipment listed above is functioning properly. Any repairs or maintenance that may be required for this equipment should be promptly brought to the attention of the Assistive Technology Team. All financial obligations associated with repairs or replacement of this equipment will be the sole responsibility of the school district."

- Parent signature

Collection Conundrum

Keeping track of assistive technology devices from year to year can be a tough task. Educators pack up their classrooms at the end of the school year and devices get shoved in boxes or closets. Some responsible educators might ship equipment to the summer school teacher or to the teacher who will use the equipment during the next school year. Sometimes these devices arrive at the desired destination, and sometimes they get lost in transit. Occasionally devices make it to their desired location but never make the return trek from whence they came. Invariably, some get lost in the shuffle and it is impossible to track them down. Short of slapping a GPS homing device on each, there is little an assistive technology trainer can do when educators have the responsibility of housing and shipping devices.

To maintain inventory, minimize confusion, and relieve educators of a burdensome responsibility, the assistive technology team can collect every assistive technology device at the end of the school year. The assistive technology trainer can also deliver equipment to the summer school teacher or to the next teacher in the upcoming school year. Depending on the geographical area and the number of assistive technology devices distributed throughout your school district, the task of collecting devices at the end of every school year might prove daunting. It will take some time to travel to every location to collect equipment, but it will be worth the time invested. The following is a list of reasons as to why it is best to collect every device at the end of the school year:

Additional face time. By collecting devices at the end of the year, the assistive technology trainer has an additional opportunity to make face-to-face contact with each educator. The educator can provide any additional information pertaining to the use of the device in the final weeks of school as well as strategies for implementing the device during summer school or in the upcoming school year.

Inventory maintenance. Collecting every device helps to maintain inventory by decreasing the number of devices that are lost in transit, swallowed by the monsters that lurk in the back of closets, or dropped into the bottomless pit lurking in the cardboard box underneath other teacher materials when teachers are eager to begin their well-deserved vacations.

Clean-up opportunities. The dirtier a device is, the more it has been used, and nothing fills an assistive technology trainer with more joy than seeing a recommendation turn into something a student uses consistently. Grime may warm a trainer's heart, but when the device returns to AT headquarters, it's time to break out the disinfectant, rubber gloves, and toothbrushes and scrub it down to make it shine again like new. Collecting every device allows the trainer the opportunity to clean every device and give it the tune-up it might need before it makes its way back into the classroom for another school year (or summer school).

Training opportunities. When it's time to deliver the assistive technology device(s) to the summer school teacher or to the teacher in the upcoming school year, the assistive technology trainer will be able to provide some initial training on the device as well as some insight as to how the student incorporated the device to work on the targeted goals. For more complex devices requiring additional trainings, the new teacher and the assistive technology trainer can schedule those appointments upon delivery.

To streamline the task of collecting devices, a reminder e-mail should be sent to each educator working with a student using a device. The e-mail can state that the assistive technology trainer will be coming 'round the mountain to pick up the assistive technology devices when she comes at the end of the school year. A list of the assistive technology devices can be included with the e-mail. If the trainer is really slick, along with the list of devices, pictures of each assistive technology device might be included in the e-mail. This reminder will help educators remember not to pack away the devices but to set them aside for the assistive technology trainer's pickup.

Every Minute Counts

When collecting devices at the end of the school year, remember that if the device is listed as an accommodation in the student's IEP, then the student should have access to that device for the duration outlined in that IEP. This might mean that the student has access to a device right up to the very last second of the last day of school. Therefore, the device should not be collected until after the last minute of the last school day. Of course, devices provided through classroom assistive technology evaluations are most likely not documented as accommodations in an IEP and, therefore, can be collected prior to the last minute of the last day. Most school districts maintain one or two workdays for staff following the final day of school for students. These staff workdays are ideal for collecting devices that have been outlined as accommodations on the IEP. As an added bonus, many schools have huge spreads of food to celebrate the end of the school year, and educators will be insistent that the assistive technology trainer partake in the yumminess. How could anyone turn that down?

part 5

putting the pieces
together

chapter 19

on the
horizon

AT Fight Club

"It is better to debate a question without settling it
than to settle a question without debating it."

—*Joseph Joubert*

As an assistive technology team develops there will be
disagreements, arguments, and, yes, even some fights.
The first rule of AT Fight Club? These scuffles should
never be personal and, of course, they should never be
physical—however, they should exist. In fact, if there are
not disagreements among the members of the assistive technology team, then there is probably something
wrong. If people have disagreements, it means that the

people disagreeing have been thinking about what's the best course of action. If people have been thinking about the best course of action, then this means that they are invested in the results. Although it may be awkward or uncomfortable to be involved in discussions with disagreements, these sorts of discussions have a hidden blessing. When a disagreement erupts, it means that people have passion. People with passion care about what they are doing, and people who care will be sure to make the best decisions possible. I am Jack's assistive technology team.

You Can't Always Get What You Want

Team decisions are made by the team. There may be times when an assistive technology trainer believes the course of action the team is taking is not the most prudent, but if the majority of the team believes in the decision, then maybe it is a time for that trainer to just grin and bear it. The next big decision might support that trainer's beliefs. Knowing when to give in and when to stick to your guns is a skill that develops throughout the course of a lifetime. Recognizing that decisions made by the entire team are usually for the best, coupled with knowing that very few decisions are etched in stone, makes swallowing the pill of relinquishment a bit easier. The notion that decisions can be revisited in time can assist individuals in removing their heels from where they've been dug. Furthermore, working out a compromise is a viable alternative to making a black or white decision, but there will be times when a compromise just won't work. Letting go of a position or stance for the benefit of the team is hard sometimes—but the truth is, you can't always get what you want. Don't be discouraged, though: you just might find, if you try sometimes, you get what you need.

On the Right Track

The members of your assistive technology team are on the right track if:

- You're getting "Thank You" cards from parents and teachers

- You've been complimented by a related service provider

- Someone on the team cried during a team meeting

- Everyone on the team belly-laughed during a team meeting

- The room or closet where the equipment is kept is messier than a baby's face after eating a plate of spaghetti

- You've had at least one outside get-together that involved everyone on the team

- Other people want your job

- You have a box labeled "needs repair" or "broken equipment" filled with devices that have been "loved"

- At least once you lost some sleep over what direction the team is headed

- At least once you've driven down the road and heard a digitized voice from your backseat or trunk say, "I want crackers, please!"

- You're greeted in the school hallway with "I'm so glad you're here! I have a question for you."

- The miles are racking up on your car

- Students are meeting their goals

- You are having a blast

Question Everything

The field of assistive technology as it relates to education is ever-evolving. New ideas about how to practice within the field continually change the face of the profession for the better. It's best to never make an assumption and to question everything you learn, the contents of this book included.

Statements like "But that's the way it has always been done" and "But So-and-So said we should do it this way" should send red flags shooting up the flagpole. Decisions made solely on the basis of tradition show little initiative, resulting in little progress. Decisions made solely upon the experience of others often result in outcomes that would work for those individuals, but may not work for your situation. Your assistive technology team is unique, with its own set of challenges. Your assistive technology team is yours.

a pirate's life

"Avast, me hearties, for I be needin' to call upon yer services once more!" called the pirate captain to his loyal band of scallywags and scoundrels, surveying the weary crew as he paced slowly to let the click of his artificial leg echo for emphasis.

The band of scurvy dogs slowly gathered around the stern of the ship to hear the new orders. Bandanas, eye patches, and leathery skin adorned the veteran cutthroats and fresh scrogs who made up the ragged crew of the pirate ship *Pedagogy*. Docked in a foreign port, the crew was recovering from a long, hard-fought battle at sea. Their enthusiasm for more plundering was at low ebb but they knew better than to ignore their captain when his leg was tapping the deck.

Rumors about that missing leg churned through the crew like rum in the belly of a buccaneer in a hurricane. Some swore they saw a cannon ball taking his right leg below the knee. Others told the tale of him sawing it off himself while tangled in the rigging during a battle with privateers. All they knew truly was he didn't wear an ordinary wooden leg. Mayhap it was carved from the bone of a great sea serpent that the captain caught with his bare hands. Mayhap it was solid iron bleached white, able to bend to match the horizon in either direction, and fire a pistol shot. None got close enough to find out.

One weevily piece of plank-bait shuffled forward and asked, "What be the use of more plundering? We have a fine ship and our fair share of treasure."

To quell the restive mutterings, the captain raised his left arm into the air—the arm that ended not in a hand but instead in a gaff covered in small spikes. Like the legendary leg, the gaff, too, was shrouded in mystery. Some argued that the captain lost his hand by dipping it into a vat of boiling oil to win a wager. Others asserted that the captain had purposefully removed his hand because he preferred the gaff for the sheer ruthless message it conveyed.

"So, is that what yer wantin'?" questioned the captain, scratching his chin with his gaff while squinting a knowing smile. "Do ye want to jump ship? Do ye want to settle down with a fine lass and watch yer bellies grow? Do ye want to put yer feet up and watch the tide wash in and out fer the rest of yer days? Those who want to claim their bit of coin and live the lubber life, it's there fer ya and yer cap'n won't be holdin' a grudge. Thar be the plank to walk to take ye to shore."

The crew stood quiet, eyes down. They didn't want to abandon their ship or their captain.

"A good crew ye' been to me lo these many years," declared the captain, seeing no one moving toward the plank.

"Aye," agreed the tired crew in faint unison. "And yer a fine captain."

"We fought and won many battles."

"Aye!" shouted the crew with a bit more enthusiasm.

"Sea serpents, corsairs, the crews of many a swaggy, and other gentlemen o' fortune who dared cross 'er path be fallen to the hands of the crew of the *Pedagogy*. By the powers, we looted our fine share of booty and taken quite a run at the sweet trade, but ye know it weren't an easy journey. Bullion, doubloons, gems, and other treasures didn't just land in our laps from dirty dogs who've passed to Fiddler's Green. Davy Jones didn't just come up and hand us our good fortune."

Sounds of agreement such as "Hear, hear" and "Aye-aye" erupted from the swashbucklers, accompanied with fervent nods.

"No man in any port can say that he ha'n't heard the legendary tales of the *Pedagogy*. But it didn't happen o'er night. Yer reputation has come o'er time," preached the captain. "Aye, mateys, fer we know that we spent as much time diggin' in the dirt as we have rollin' in the coin! We earned our wealth by breakin' our backs! No lad or lass can claim otherwise!"

An explosion of vehement hoots and hollers erupted from the crew.

"There's still fights to be fought, treasure to loot, and plenty o' wind fer our sails. So, mates, I ask ye … who's in fer some more?"

"Aye! We be with ye, cap'n!" came the cheers from one and all.

"Then let's be settin' off, you lazy bilge rats, fer uncharted waters be ahead and the daylight be a-wastin'!"

Every pirate went about his job, understanding now that the life of a pirate, the life they had chosen, wasn't truly about the riches or rewards but about the time spent at sea, breathing the ocean air, scrapping with mates, singing "Yo ho ho" and doing what pirates do.

What can you learn from our pirate tale? Do not be afraid to sail into uncharted waters. That is the only place where you'll discover new lands upon which to build. As a team you'll find that your accomplishments will grow, along with your reputation, when you take the initiative, work together, and move forward casting away aspersions and doubt. Remember that fortune favors the bold.

■ ■ ■ ■ ■

The Faces

Every assistive technology team is on a road, gathering experience along the way. Each endeavor you take on is a river that you'll have to build a bridge to cross. The river is a challenge, but it is also a useful tool for introspection. So while you're crossing that bridge, stop and look at your reflections. The faces will have scars from battles triumphant and wrinkles from debates long lost. The faces will have knowledge, wisdom, and character. Turn back and take a long look at the road that led to the bridge. Study the past, remember the experiences that came before, because they have shaped the faces peering back from the glistening water. Now gaze down the road ahead and ponder. What will that road bring? Perils? Probably. Risks? Likely. Opportunity? Definitely. Look down that road as far as you can see, because that is where you are headed. The next river crossed will reflect faces with even more knowledge, wisdom, and character. No matter how many bridges are built and crossed there will still be one unwavering trait on the faces shining back from the water's surface—a smile. A wide smile— because the faces reflect team members who know they have helped improve the lives of others.

chapter 20

nursery rhyme
review

It's time to summarize everything we've been saying throughout the book; however, rewriting points we made earlier in the book sounded, well, boring. We didn't think you, faithful reader who has made it this far, would appreciate us just saying the same thing over again ... well ... not unless we made it interesting, anyway. So, we present to you now, the main points presented in this book as told by your favorite nursery rhymes. Enjoy!

One, Two, Access for You

One, two, access for you

Three, four, access the door

Five, six, access the sticks

Seven, eight, you're doing great

Nine, ten, let the access begin!

Assistive technology is all about providing access and has nothing to do with restricting students. Any item can be considered an assistive technology device if it is used to increase, maintain, or improve functional capabilities of a student with a disability. Maximizing accessibility is the responsibility of every educator, and an assistive technology trainer can assist other educators in that role.

Little Boy Blue

Little Boy Blue

Come blow your horn.

The team's in the field,

A logo is worn.

Challenging and tough,

They work off their behinds.

Helping teachers' lessons,

Become Universally Designed.

An assistive technology team can work to promote methods for differentiating instruction and providing universally designed lessons. Those seeking to build or expand an assistive technology team might make a more persuasive case by promoting the team as more than just a resource for special educators. The assistive technology team can also provide resources to any student who might be struggling in school. Becoming a presence in the school district by working hard, along with a "never say can't" attitude, draws attention to the good that is being accomplished.

Little Jack Horner

Little Jack Horner

Sat in the corner

Considering his student's AT.

Checklists are fun,

But the work is not done,

He said, "The one who can do it is me!"

It is the responsibility of the IEP team to consider assistive technology that is necessary for a student to receive a free and appropriate public education. Although mechanisms can be put in place to assist IEP teams in considering a variety of tools, these mechanisms are not all-encompassing. Considering a student's assistive technology needs can be effectively done at the same time as considering a student's accommodations.

This Little Team Member

This little team member was a speech therapist,

This little team member taught some,

This little team member knew O.T.,

This little team member led them,

And this little team member cried,

"Wee-wee-wee don't need to be multidisciplinary!"

Hard workers will get the job done.

The most important factor to consider when developing an assistive technology team or considering individuals who should be added to an existing team should be centered around the candidate's work ethic and not professional discipline. The assistive technology team has the opportunity to work with all of the disciplines in the school district when developing recommendations for students.

Baa, Baa, AT

Baa, Baa, AT,

Don't you have a tool?

Yes, sir, yes, sir,

It's already in your school;

One for the teacher,

And one for the dean,

And one for the little boy

Who we haven't even seen.

Baa, Baa, AT,

Don't you have a tool?

Yes, sir, yes, sir,

It's already in your school.

When developing recommendations for a student, the least restrictive solutions will be those that are already available in the immediate environment. Helping to develop a robust menu of tools that are already available in the school will assist every student and every teacher in their educational endeavors. Furthermore, when a student does begin to demonstrate difficulties, in many cases a simple conversation between the assistive technology trainer and the teacher is all that is necessary to generate appropriate recommendations. Contacting the assistive technology trainer prior to initiating any paperwork and having a friendly conversation can spawn ideas and strategies that the educator didn't even know was already available in the educational environment.

Sing a Song of Experience

Sing a song of experience,

A pocketful of try,

Good and plenty teammates

Go to conferences, here's why;

When the conferences are over

The teammates begin to sing,

Was not that an easy way

To share ideas they bring?

One of the benefits of having an assistive technology team is that collaboration is inherent in the structure of a team. Sharing found knowledge, whether it was found online, at a conference, or from previous experiences, helps to strengthen the team as a whole.

Humpty Dumpty

Humpty Dumpty had an eval,

Humpty Dumpty went with a pal;

All of the team pitched in with a grin

And helped write recommendations that win!

When conducting an assistive technology evaluation, one technique to help gather information and make sure nothing is missed is to complete the evaluation in pairs. Brainstorming solutions with either one member of the assistive technology team or multiple members of the team leads to better recommendations for a student. Using the talents and experiences of one or more people helps to ensure that the most appropriate recommendations are being suggested in the evaluation report.

Hey Diddle Diddle

Hey Diddle Diddle

Your inventory is little,

Don't worry, it doesn't need to be new;

Just find a way

To keep track of it today

We did, and you can too!

Nothing drains administrative confidence (and a budget) faster than misplaced devices. Whether adopting an existing inventory or starting out from scratch, develop a coding system and inventory tracking system for devices. This should also include a software installation and tracking system. Devices can be retrieved from most students at the end of the school year for routine mainte-nance, cleaning, and inventory checking purposes. A basic, shared spreadsheet will do the trick in a pinch, but if it lies within your means to develop a more dynamic system, then go for it.

Create-a-Team

Create-a-team, create-a-team, stay on the track,

Choose who you want and don't look back;

Plan it, promote, and mark it with AT,

Advertise a lot for everyone to see.

Once the policies and procedures have been established by the assistive tech-nology team, promote the team's existence by visiting as much as possible with educators. Providing educators with an easy way to get in contact with the assistive technology trainer is really the only information they need about the policies. Rather than bogging educators down with how to do paperwork to request help from their assistive technology trainer, consider inviting them to just contact their trainer via phone or e-mail whenever a student is demon-strating difficulties. The specifics about paperwork and procedure can come later if that becomes necessary.

Simple Simon

Simple Simon met an IT man

Going to a school.

Says Simple Simon to the IT man,

"Let's install this tool."

Says the IT man to Simple Simon,

"Have you considered this?"

Says Simple Simon to the IT man,

"Working together, we can't miss!"

Instructional technology and assistive technology work hand in hand to implement tools to help students. Making an effort to become involved on committees that make decisions about technology for the entire school district will help to demonstrate the assistive technology team's commitment to work together for the benefit of all.

Hickory, Dickory, Dock

Hickory, Dickory, Dock,

Every student is on the clock;

The clock struck done,

And away they run;

Hickory, Dickory, Dock.

The amount of time a student has in school each school year is finite. Each day that student continues to struggle with meeting a goal is one less day the student could be using a tool to help achieve that goal. Therefore, minimizing the time between conducting the evaluation, delivering the report, reviewing the report at an IEP meeting, and implementing the recommendations is crucial. In some instances trying and assessing multiple devices might delay the implementation of an appropriate device. In most cases, the remaining time before the student's IEP needs to be reconsidered can actually serve as the trial period.

Little Miss Muffet

Little Miss Muffet

Started a consult,

Describing the student's delay;

Along came ideas,

That crept up between them,

And tools were used the next day!

An assistive technology evaluation is required only once it is believed that the student will need to utilize a tool that is not already available in that student's educational environment. Starting the process of acquiring assistive technology by scheduling a time to consult with the assistive technology trainer leads to least restrictive solutions that can be implemented immediately.

Tom, Tom, His Eval is Done

Tom, Tom, his eval is done!

Addressing goals was lots of fun;

The eval was thorough,

The eval was neat,

The recommendations will help him get on his feet.

If a student is not struggling to meet a goal, then there is no need for any additional technology to be put into place. When an assistive technology evaluation is being requested, the IEP team should pinpoint the goal or goals the student is struggling to achieve. Most recent progress notes should also be sent documenting these difficulties. Evaluations should contain a review of the student's file, an observation (or observations) of the student working in the area that has been identified as a target, possibly an interview with the student, and interviews with any staff working to address the targeted goals. The information gathered during each of these phases of the evaluation should be documented on the evaluation. The recommendations written in the report should be related to the information gathered during each phase of the evaluation.

Georgie Porgie

Georgie Porgie, consider why

Recommendations are things to try,

Implement them right away

As accommodations to make them stay.

It is the responsibility of the IEP team to review the assistive technology evaluation and determine which, if any, of the recommendations should be implemented. The IEP team should ask the question, "Is this needed for a free and appropriate public education?" If the answer is "yes," then that recommendation should be rewritten as an accommodation on the student's IEP. If the answer is "no," then the recommendation might still be implemented, but that tool or strategy is not documented as an accommodation. Once an IEP team has documented that a tool is necessary for a free and appropriate public education, that tool should be acquired.

Mary Had a Little Device

Mary had a little device

It was as light as snow;

And no matter where Mary went,

The device was sure to go.

It came with her to school each day,

That was the teacher's rule;

It helped the children talk and play,

With Mary each day at school.

It is the responsibility of every educator working with a student to assist in the implementation of a device. Some devices may be required only at certain times of the day for specific activities, whereas others will need to be used all day long in multiple environments. Assistive technology trainers should work to empower onsite educators by providing strategies for successful implementation.

Teacher Bo-Peep

Teacher Bo-Peep needs help with her sheep

And her outlook is filled with gloom;

Schedule a time, more than once is just fine,

And do an eval for the whole classroom.

Doing an evaluation to determine strategies that would benefit all of the students in a classroom is an easy way to implement additional technology. Classroom evaluations can minimize paperwork while maximizing the benefits to the students in that environment. Furthermore, classroom evaluation reports can be written in a friendly style and sent via e-mail.

Mary, Mary, Quite Contrary

Mary, Mary, quite contrary,

How does your student grow?

With follow-up and training

And data collected on each goal.

Plopping a device in the lap of educators often leads to frustration and a sense of abandonment. Comprehensive follow-up and training is necessary to ensure that the educators working with a student feel comfortable with the tool put in place. Furthermore, prior to the implementation of a tool or strategy, the student was struggling to achieve a goal. Once a tool or strategy is put into place, the most relevant and crucial factor is whether or not the student continues to demonstrate difficulty achieving that goal. Data collection should reflect the student's ability to achieve goals and progress toward achieving those goals.

Jack and Jill

Jack and Jill went up the hill,

With tools all year and all summer;

One fell down, and broke somehow,

Without the team, what a bummer.

Students may require assistance with devices all year long, including over breaks and between school years. When developing an assistive technology team, a school district needs to develop a methodology for handling concerns that arise during these breaks.

There Was an Old Trainer

There was an old trainer who worked in some schools,

She had so many students she didn't know what to do!

She gave them some tools, as best as she could,

Building a team would certainly be good!

Hang in there! Isn't it great to feel needed? If evaluations are piling up, e-mails are backing up, and you're feeling fed up, that's a good thing. It means you're busy and there is a need for the assistance you can give. All you need to do now is work a bit more to show those people who can make change happen that you need help. Showing off the successes helps underline the fact that what you're doing matters—and not only does it matter, but it matters in the right places.

You're a Gem!

Mother Goose might not have liked these rhymes (or this book, for that matter), but we hope you did. We sincerely hope that you found some gold nuggets as you were trekking through this mine. If not gold nuggets, then maybe a diamond or two that you can use to cut through the glass container holding preconceived notions about assistive technology. We hope that you can take this book, dissect it, and extract pearls of wisdom that will be useful in your own endeavors. It is our hope that this book helps you become rich in your own right with methods for successful practice. We urge you to keep in mind that the principles outlined in this book are working for us, which means they can work for you, too! Good luck, intrepid assistive technology person-thingy-gal-guy-whatever you call yourself. Always remember to have fun—because the entire job is about helping students … and what could be more rewarding than that?

references

ASHA. (2006). *ASHA 2006 schools survey: Salary report.* American Speech-Language-Hearing Association. Available at www.asha.org/NR/rdonlyres/35DA498F-677E-4B23-831C-7861BF9D0443/%200/SchoolsSurveySalaries.pdf

Kumin, L., Councill, C., & Goodman, M. (1995). The pacing board: A technique to assist the transition from single word to multiword utterances. *Infant-Toddler Intervention, 5,* 23–29.

Option 1. Complain to a special education supervisor. This option would definitely put a damper on the relationship the assistive technology trainer has been striving to create. Furthermore, the accommodation is still written; therefore, it needs to be provided.

Option 2. Inform the school that because they did not consult with the assistive technology trainer first, it is the school's responsibility to provide the device outlined in the accommodation. This option would also put a damper on the relationship. Furthermore, although possibly these would be separate line items within a budget, the money being spent on the accommodation is still, really, coming from the same pot.

Option 3. Bite the bullet and provide the device outlined in the accommodation. Use the mistake as an opportunity to educate the members of the IEP team on the appropriate way to proceed in the future. Specifically, educate the members of the IEP team in the notion that they should know ahead of time exactly where and how to acquire materials included in an accommodation. This option takes a negative situation and turns it into a positive, forging an even better relationship between the assistive technology trainer and the educators.

The Loophole Solved

First, we need to explain the theatrics. Why not just describe the loophole and be done with it? Why all the hullabaloo? Here's why. Because we don't like to tell people about the loophole. Loopholes are meant to be discovered, not pointed out. We don't go around telling teachers how to circumvent the process that we so lovingly toiled to create. If someone finds the loophole, well, then, okay, good for Mr. Smarty Pants—but we aren't about to put up neon flashing signs that read "Loophole Here" or "The Best Loophole Served Here" or "Come Get Your Loophole!"

Having said all that, here it is: the loophole explained. In the process outlined for conducting an individual evaluation, we state that the way a student receives a device to meet a goal or goals is by describing it as a recommendation in an assistive technology evaluation report. In the process we outline, it is only *after* a device is recommended by an assistive technology trainer that an IEP team can consider it. Here's the loophole: What's to prevent an IEP team, at any initial IEP, annual IEP, or Review/Revision, from writing an accommodation for a device without consulting an assistive technology trainer or without conducting an individual assistive technology evaluation? Besides a tongue-lashing from a special education supervisor, there is nothing to prevent the IEP team, at any time, from writing in any accommodation it thinks the student needs.

Consider the following example. What if, out of the blue, a member of an IEP team says, "I think the student needs word prediction software." The rest of the IEP team members, for whatever reason, decide that they agree or they decide that this is not something they want to disagree about for the sake of amicability. Therefore, the IEP team writes an accommodation, "Access to word prediction software for writing assignments," without ever consulting an assistive technology trainer. A few days later, the assistive technology trainer gets this IEP for an unknown student who has never received an assistive technology evaluation. What happens then? The school district must supply the software, but the assistive technology trainer has not been consulted. The assistive technology trainer doesn't know if word prediction software would be the recommendation that would have been made had an assistive technology evaluation been conducted. In this loophole scenario, the IEP team circumvented the assistive technology trainer. At this point, the assistive technology trainer has only the following three options:

Related Titles from ISTE

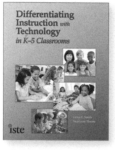

Differentiating Instruction with Technology in K–5 Classrooms
By Grace E. Smith and Stephanie Throne

Differentiating Instruction with Technology in K–5 Classrooms helps educators understand how to immediately use technology as a tool to differentiate instruction. The authors provide a variety of practical instructional strategies to accommodate a broad range of learning styles, abilities, and curriculum content. Creative, ready-to-use lessons mapped to curriculum content standards, activities, and templates allow teachers to kick-start their use of technology in differentiating instruction.

ISTE Member Price $26.55 ■ Nonmember Price $37.95 ■ www.iste.org/diffk5

Differentiating Instruction with Technology in Middle School Classrooms
By Grace E. Smith and Stephanie Throne

This book offers an overview of research on the uniqueness of middle school students and illustrates the importance of using technology to create differentiated lessons, especially with this age group. It lists the fundamental components of DI, student traits that guide DI, and Web 2.0 resources that can help make DI a reality in the middle school classroom. It also includes sample activities for incorporating DI in multiple subjects: math, science, social studies, and language arts.

ISTE Member Price $26.55 ■ Nonmember Price $37.95 ■ www.iste.org/diff68

National Educational Technology Standards Booklet Bundle

The NETS provide the pathway for students to build the global skills they need for the global competition they will face. Widely adopted and recognized in the United States, and increasingly adopted in countries worldwide, the NETS' unique advantage is their integration across all educational curricula. While most educational standards apply to a specific content area, the NETS are not subject-matter specific, but rather a compendium of skills required for students to be competitive and successful in a global and digital world.

And while the NETS are for a technology-rich environment, they are not about the technology. They are standards that address learning and teaching across entire educational systems and at all student levels. The NETS transform how students learn and how teachers teach.

The NETS Booklet Bundle includes all three updated NETS booklets—NETS for teachers, students, and administrators. Also included are student profiles, examples, scenarios, and rubrics.

ISTE Member Price $25.25 ■ Nonmember Price $34.95
■ www.iste.org/ntsbun

www.iste.org/bookstore

117.10